Armchair Theatre

Armchair Theatre

The Lost Years

Leonard White

KELLY PUBLICATIONS
2003

Photographs copyright ABC Television

First published by
KELLY PUBLICATIONS
6 Redlands, Tiverton, Devon EX16 4DH UK
2003

ISBN 1 903053 18 8

CONTENTS

Forewords

Teddington Studios in the 60's was a hotbed of new Television Drama. It opened up opportunities and creative chances galore for new writing and performance, unknown today, a great deal of which was driven by Leonard White, my Producer in *The Avengers*. It proved a very welcome watershed in my career. And hundreds of others were able to contribute to that unique period of TV Drama.

I'm thankful to have been a part of it.

Honor Blackman (2003)

A unique series – that was *Armchair Theatre*.

A Sunday night event; most television writers wanted to get on it!

The most-watched dramatic items of the week. Now I know no play series that could come up to it. They are all soaps.

I wrote my first in 1956 (*The Common Man*, a comedy) and almost ten years later, *The One-eyed Monster*, a dramatic piece about television; and *They Throw it at You*, *The Girl in the Picture*, and *I've Got a System* – three plays in a Blackpool Trilogy.

A word to the Producer, Leonard White: a page of paper and an hour was yours, speaking virtually to the nation!

That was Armchair Theatre.

Allan Prior (2003)

Preface

Armchair Theatre provided over 400 single drama productions for the ITV Network, variously described as—

> "A landmark in TV Theatre"
>
> (James Thomas, *Daily Express*)
>
> "ITV's most distinguished television 'playhouse' … this crusading drama series"
>
> (Stanley Reynolds, *The Guardian*)

I have put together this chronicle to fill the gap in the records of this anthology covering the 1963-69 period during which I was the producer. To put that into perspective I have drawn on the earlier work from 1956, which includes my background with *Police Surgeon*, *The Avengers*, *Out of this World* and *Armchair Mystery Theatre*, etc.

But essentially this book is to give due credit to the stunning list of writers, actors, directors, technicians and all who came together to create this important period of television drama.

Many colleagues have urged me to provide this record—

> "Both the subject and the content of your book are a valuable addition to the history of television and definitely worth publishing"
>
> (The Archive Group, Royal Television Society).

I hope that it will be of archival value.

And I do thank my wife, Margaret, very much, for putting up with me during the very long time of research – much of it in the loft!

LW

Prologue
Stranger than Fiction

The headline screamed—

MARTIN LUTHER KING ASSASSINATED

In the departure lounge at Heathrow I had picked up the midday edition of the *Evening Standard*. Later that same day, in my room at the Waldorf Astoria in New York City, I switched on the TV for an update. It was a grim story from Memphis but I was bound for Washington DC next day and nothing would, seemingly, staunch the excitement of receiving an EMMY Award in the capital city of the USA. A rare honour for British television drama at that time, an *Armchair Theatre* production had won an International Award.

Late though it was I switched off the TV and walked-off my jet-lag around the streets of Broadway. A habit of mine of old. I never feel that I have 'arrived' anywhere until I have walked the streets. Mad dogs and Englishmen walk the streets of Manhattan alone in the early hours but the stimulation of that city at night was unique. Not so relaxed and enjoyable as my first stay in NYC in the early Fifties, when nightly after performing in the American premiere of Christopher Fry's fine play, *A Sleep of Prisoners*, Stanley Baker and I would walk the twenty blocks from Madison and 7lst to our hotel long after midnight, taking in a bar or two and an automat en-route without any qualms. Never any question of early to bed in Manhattan. Sleep was an unnecessary interruption.

But now it was April 1968.

The morning of the 6th broke a beautiful day with that bright dry sunshine so typical of New York spring, and I presented myself at American Airlines check-in at La Guardia for my onward flight to Washington DC. No problem, seemingly: "Have a nice day, sir."

A full plane, a comfortable flight and only a short time at altitude before the approach to land started.

"If those of you on the starboard side, the right hand side of the aircraft, look out of the windows – you'll see the fires are still burning in the city." The pilot's voice over the intercom was as matter-of-fact as if he'd been telling us that we had a good view of the Capitol. *Still burning!* What was this? There was a marked lurch as passengers moved to get a view.

What was going on?

There was no warning of trouble when I booked in at La Guardia. No questioning of the necessity of my journey. Not a word of anticipation of this at the hotel in New York the night before. But, now, here approaching to land in Washington: *The fires are still burning.* Blue-black smoke shot with vicious flames licking and billowing upwards in mushrooming clouds – upwards to us, losing height, as the plane approached the runway.

Only a few passengers left the plane here. Most stayed on for Atlanta. They knew something I didn't. Out of the bright hard sunlight into the terminal building I couldn't believe my eyes. I wasn't seeing very well! I could feel that the place was packed with people but the scene was a dim-out. After a few minutes adjusting I realised that the whole place was lit only by a few emergency lamps. Here and there the only bright pin-points of light were over the cash tills. Prohibition again? My memory flashed back to earlier days in Chicago. I tried to push through to find an exit, but I was moving against the crowd. Everyone else was going the other way: leaving the city.

The scene changed completely as I moved from the black hole with its crush of bodies trying to fly out, and emerged into the sunshine and fresh air. It was uncanny. The wide side-walks outside the terminal buildings were almost empty of people.

All was strangely silent.

No bustling traffic. Just a few people lined-up at one taxi stand; but no taxis. The twentieth-century clamour of the big city reduced to a high-noon quiet. I went back to ask a Redcap if this was the right place to get a taxi for my hotel. "Yeh. If one comes." I was now feeling less elated. *If one comes?* And this the city of the seat of Government of the US of A? I joined the small group at the taxi-stand. No one spoke.

Eventually, one taxi did arrive – and filled with those ahead of me in the line. There was no room for me. Then it moved off. I was the only one remaining. Left on a side-walk, wide white-heat baked, of this foreign city. Alone.

Unbelievable. In some sort of limbo-land. Perhaps I'd fallen asleep on the plane. Like Churchill I can fall asleep at any time. But, no, this was real. As I watched, the lone taxi circled the large forecourt and stopped briefly on the far side. Then, completing a circle, surprisingly, it returned to me.

"Where d'yer wanna go bud?"

Travel instructions in a sweaty hand, I told him.

The driver's look said it all – "Another Limey."

On these occasions the English always use too many words. My mind flashed back to my first visit to New York, when actor Stanley Baker and I had gone into a drugstore for the first time. We wanted tooth-paste, nothing special, but our request met with little response from the girl behind the counter. She called several other salesgirls to join her so that they also could hear us speak. We had to order again. Two nations separated by a common language! I repeated the name of the hotel to the cabbie, cutting out all the superfluous verbiage.

"Better pile in then. Might not be another."

This news was quite startling. *Might not be another?* I squeezed into the already packed cab, uttering all too flowery English thanks and apologies. I was twisted half on someone's knees and half crouched on the floor. The cab moved away again.

We turned into the main multi-laned highway and along that Appian Way-like thoroughfare into the city. A ghost city. Only one car passed us. The scene resembled a massive Cecil B De Mille film set waiting for the 'supers' to be called. Everyone in the cab was concentrating on the radio as it was switched around the local stations.

"Just checking the best route to avoid the fires," the driver explained.

The eerie journey continued.

"Look right at the next inter-section – you'll see the fires downtown."

And, sure enough, there were blocks blazing furiously as I stared in amazement. Heat upon heat. I didn't see any fire-fighting – just the empty streets and the fires.

The driver tried yet another radio station. A young woman passenger, pale and very nervy said, "I thought it was all over – it was okay to come back."

"No way!" he told her. "The curfew is on again at four o'clock."

A curfew! What was this?

We slowed to cross another inter-section. A soldier came out of the shadows on the side-walk, his gun poised. Our driver lifted his hand in salutation.

The GI looked hard at us, then waved us on with the muzzle of his gun.

I saw more soldiers and a massive tank, bristling alert, around the corner.

The driver continued what was obviously a roundabout route to each dropping point, avoiding the troubles. I was the last to be dropped.

My first view of the hotel was with all the lower windows boarded-up. Briefly, I stood outside to survey this macabre sight of the wide Washington street in the bright daylight, totally devoid of people, but me; and no traffic except the one taxi moving away. No film director could have achieved *this* set-up.

I moved into the lobby, dimly lit, the windows boarded up. A small hobble of geriatric permanent residents stood around aimlessly in the grey coldness with just one emergency lamp at Reception. I went to the desk. I felt a perfect idiot yet compelled to proceed as though all was normal. To the Southern black behind the desk I announced my name, 'White'. No sooner had I said it, I wished I hadn't.

He gave the slightest, the very slightest, smile, but went through the motions and handed me a key. "The elevator's not working. No power."

I climbed the stairs, found my room and threw my bag on the bed. What now? Washington under curfew; the military policing the city; and downtown on fire. And here was I expecting to attend a highly sophisticated Emmy Award ceremony and celebration. Bizarre.

I found my travel instructions and dialled a number. Fortunately the phone was still working. A long wait, but eventually a woman's voice. I explained my mission. Some surprise at the other end.

"Oh, there's no one here. They've all left. It's all cancelled."

"Well, what do I do...?"

A pause, then, "There's no one here to ask. I'm only the operator."

"Thank you!" My emphasis had a tinge of despair.

"You're welcome."

I couldn't have felt less welcome. Everyone who could leave the city had fled. And I had just arrived.

I didn't unpack. The prospect of spending a week-end in a hotel with only an emergency power supply; inhabited, seemingly, by just a few geriatrics who couldn't move; in a city under curfew, with the fires still burning downtown; was bleak, if not frightening.

Within minutes I was back, bag in hand, in the lobby. "I want to check out." I wanted to sound as though I knew what I was doing, but desperation in my voice was probably the only note I communicated.

Again, the subtle smile from the elegant black as I gave my name. He had not forgotten. I must have been the only one to book-in that day and here I was booking-out all of fifteen minutes later. I had to get out, but how, I didn't know.

I found the doorman. He was avoiding the door. I wanted to call a taxi.

"Curfew sir. They won't come out."

It was a sweltering day but I, suddenly, was cold. I'd never felt so foreign or alone. "I have to get to the airport." I tried to sound important. A stupid English ploy I really deplored. The Emmy Award now had dwindled to insignificance and my only thought was to get out of Washington – anywhere – but hopefully to get back to New York and thence to friends in Hartsdale.

The doorman shrugged his shoulders. "We're supposed to stay in. Except for emergencies. The Civil Guard don't want people on the streets."

I ventured just outside. My chill turned to a hot sweat. Not a sign of anything. All so unbelievably quiet and deserted. Then an engine, distant – but it was only the chugging of an Army chopper. As it passed low overhead I instinctively edged back under cover. Then a gentler engine and, glory be, a taxi was coming. My prayers were answered. I ran out, waving like a drowning man.

The driver was cautious, very cautious, as he eased up, still moving slowly. I kept up with him.

"I want to get to the airport." I tried to be calm, controlled, in the true English tradition, but I couldn't conceal desperation.

"Can't go through the city center. Have to go round – the long way."

I didn't care which way he went. Within seconds I'd grabbed my bag and I was in that taxi and on my way to escape. Relief! I was in a lone taxi on a multi-lane highway skirting this city with the fires still burning downtown.

I mused. I thought of a nuclear accident, but it wasn't like that. It was as though I was in limbo. No time for time to pass. A button in the Great Power House is labelled 'TIME STOP' and someone had pushed it. And, of course, the finger had stopped too – with the button depressed.

The broadcast voice on the taxi radio cut in— "Emergency announcement. If you need medicine, baby food or any urgent supplies call this number. They will be brought to you. *Keep off the streets*."

We drove on deep into a concrete under-pass. The driver slowed as he approached a high bridge crossing above. Up there a lone GI looked down, his gun covering us. The driver looked out and waved acknowledgement. The soldier accepted this recognition of his authority. We were waved on and passed under the bridge; slowly at first and then away, faster.

The airport was as I'd left it: lifeless outside yet packed with 'refugees' inside. Uncanny lighting. The foyer of hell? Could I get a plane out? I had no booking. I'd have to try to re-route my ticket.

I scraped together enough nickels and quarters to make a call to my good friends in Hartsdale, New York. I only had time to ask if I could come to them that night.

"No problem. But why? What's gone wrong?"

They didn't know? I had no more coins to feed the pay-phone.

I went from check-in to check-in trying to find an airline that would accept my ticket and re-route it, and get me a flight to New York.

Several line-ups later – success. What relief. I felt very tired.

The aircraft climbed away in the twilight, skirting the black smoke clouds of the fires below. Martin Luther King was dead in Memphis. There was rioting in the streets of Washington DC.

And so, via the flight back to La Guardia and the train from Grand Central, I put that quite extraordinary day in the capital of the USA further and further behind me.

Late that night I relaxed in the comfort of my very good friends in Hartsdale: an American measure of whisky in my glass, and I was telling my story.

"We didn't know about any trouble like that in Washington," they were saying.

I truly believe that my hosts Martha and Walter Diehl thought that I was making it all up or, at least, decorating it for effect. A scenario, maybe, for another drama? I couldn't understand that they, in New York, did not know what was really going on in Washington that day: in this age of free instant communication, and in this high-tech country. Was someone denying communication? Was the reality too frightening? Was news management that possible in the 'free society' of the USA?

The week-end over I tried to pick up the pieces of the reason for my journey. I called the New York offices of The National Academy of TV Arts. They were trying to arrange another ceremony for the Awards. But it proved impossible.

April 1968
Sonny Fox (Senior Vice President, the National Academy of Television Art and Sciences) and Leonard White [right] receiving the Emmy award for *Call Me Daddy*

Eventually, a couple of days later, the Emmy Award was handed over to me unceremoniously by Sonny Fox (Senior Vice President of the National Academy of TV Arts & Sciences) in an office of the International Press Club in New York City. Just a few people were present, including a representative of the French Broadcasting System who was receiving the News-Documentary Award. Quite an anti-climax.

Normal time was resumed when a few days later I arrived back at Heathrow with the Emmy statuette as part of my luggage. I had to unpack it for Customs to convince them. I don't think they had seen one before.

At home, eventually, I was surprised to find that I'd made headlines in the local Brighton papers—

SUSSEX TV MAN IN RACE-HATE CITY

TV MAN IN REAL-LIFE DRAMA

Sussex had never seemed more peaceful.

A coda to this adventure occurred a few weeks later, when I was in Edinburgh visiting writers Ronald Mavor and Gert Hofman. Mavor was then with The Scottish Arts Council and we talked in his office. I told him the full story of my recent experience in Washington. He let me go on right to the end, then asked me which hotel I was in? I told him and he calmly announced that he too had been in that very same hotel; holed-up with nowhere to go, at the very same time. He had been on a lecture tour which, like the Emmy ceremony, had been cancelled because of the riots. A small world.

So, the accolade and international acclaim awarded during the twelfth season of *Armchair Theatre*, and the last for ABC Television was something of a non-event. In keeping with the entirely ephemeral nature of television at that time, alas.

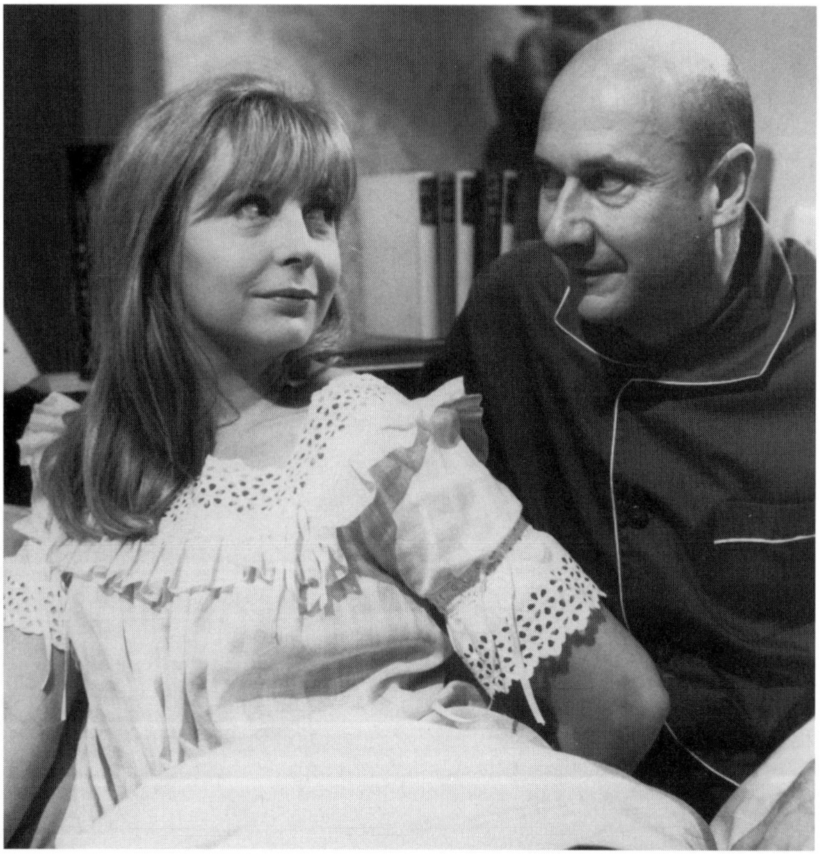

Call Me Daddy
Judy Cornwell and Donald Pleasance

The achievement of that excellent comedy-drama, *Call Me Daddy* – specially written for *Armchair Theatre* by Ernie Gebler, starring Donald Pleasance and Judy Cornwell, and directed splendidly by Alvin Rakoff, with Terence Feely as story editor, and designed by David Marshall – was muted.

Rakoff was rightly angry at not being invited to accompany me to Washington to collect the Award, but I could do nothing about that. And, as it happened, he missed nothing – the event being overtaken, on the one hand, by the drama of history in the making in the USA, and, nearer home, by the demise of ABC Television when that company was about to disappear in the shot-gun wedding with Associated Rediffusion to become the new Thames Television. Off with the old and on with the new.

Whereas ABC, week-end contractor for the Midlands and the North, had made drama production for the ITV Network it's major concern (*Armchair Theatre* alone providing some thirty-nine hours of single dramas a year) Thames Television had a new brief and had to look at broader programming for the week-day franchise.

Now drama (and in particular the single teleplay) had to fight for its corner. A very different climate. The past successes were irrelevant. Not even so much as a drink of celebration for all those talents who had contributed to winning the Emmy Award.

Off with the old.

PART ONE

1960-62

Early *Armchair Theatre*

Inside Story

Armchair Mystery Theatre

Police Surgeon

The Avengers

Out of this World

CHAPTER 1

1960

"A Producer—Why Me?"

Camera card

It all began when *Armchair Theatre* was launched for its first season in 1956 – pioneered by Producer-Director Dennis Vance, with Howard Thomas, Managing Director of ABC Television.

The first production – transmitted live – was a medical drama, adapted for television by George Kerr (who years later became Head of Drama at ABC).

The Outsider	July 8, 1956
Written by	Dorothy Brandon
Teleplay by	George Kerr
Cast included	Adrienne Corri, David Kossoff and Raymond Huntley
Director	Dennis Vance
Designer	Bertram Tyrer

The Outsider played to an audience of 390,000 homes (51% of homes equipped to receive ITV at that time). Not to be compared with later top-rated figures but a healthy percentage upon which to build.

Eight years later, this audience had risen to over eight million *homes*. In December 1964, at the end of my second year as producer of the series, the record viewing figure of *Armchair Theatre's* first ten years was achieved by Donald Churchill's comedy, *The Hothouse*. It was seen in 8,260,000 homes, and headed TAM's Top Twenty TV Plays of the Year, of which *Armchair Theatre* took 13 places including the first three. The 'average viewers' at that time was regarded as 2.4 per home, which adds up to a staggering nearly 20 million viewers watching *Armchair Theatre.*

The Hothouse
Sharp At Four
The Pretty English Girls
They Throw It At You

The Girl In The Picture
Always Ask For The Best
You Must Be Virginia
Old Soldiers

Something To Declare
The Cherry On The Top
Admirer At Number Eight
Last Word On Julie
A Nice Little Business

Television Audience Measurement (TAM)

The second presentation in the first season of *Armchair Theatre* in 1956, started to establish the programme's mainstream commitment to commissioning original TV drama scripts. A double-bill of new works:

The Handshake

Teleplay by	Peter Key
Director	Stuart Latham
Cast included	Rosalie Crutchley, Anton Diffring, Robert Brown and Billie Whitelaw

Bid For Fame

Teleplay by	Duncan Greenwood
Director	Janice Willett
Cast	as for *The Handshake*

That first season, 1956-57 – presenting 41 single-play productions – included much new writing. Star actors headed the casts – all under the superb guidance of Casting Director Dodo Watts who remained a strong member of the *Armchair Theatre* team longer than anyone. Her judgment in casting and her eye for a new talent stimulated us all. Bertram Tyrer designed most of the shows. Later, Tim O'Brien took over as the head of our first-rate design team for a number of years.

ARMCHAIR THEATRE
FIRST SEASON

Casting Director
Dodo Watts
Writers
Elliott Baker
Joseph Carole
Sidney Carroll
Maurice Edelman
Steve Ellers
Miles Fleetwood
Duncan Greenwood
H.V. Kershaw
Peter Key
John Kruse
Iain MacCormick
Sidney Nelson
& Maurice Harrison
James Parish
Allan Prior
L.A. Reece
Lister Sinclair
Hugh Stewart
& Michael Nightingale
Irving Werstein
Actors
Terence Alexander
Dorothy Alison
Avril Angers
George Baker
Ian Bannen
Patrick Barr
Jill Bennett
Lyndon Brook
Robert Brown
Hugh Burden
Peter Butterworth
Paul Carpenter
Sarah Churchill
Patience Collier
Fay Compton
Adrienne Corri
Andrew Cruickshank
Rosalie Crutchley
Paul Daneman
Isabel Dean
Derrick de Marney
William Devlin
Anton Diffring
Sonia Dresdel
Gracie Fields
William Franklyn
Wyndham Goldie
Michael Gough
Harry Green
Joan Greenwood
James Hayter
Joan Haythorne
Hy Hazell
Charles Heslop
Thora Hird
Michael Hordern
Donald Houston
Ronald Howard
Raymond Huntley
Peter Illing
Pauline Jameson
Katherine Kath
Geoffrey Keen
Barbara Kelly
David Kossoff
Avice Landon
Ronald Lewis
Moira Lister
Ralph Michael
Yvonne Mitchell
Andre Morell
Barbara Mullen
Lionel Murton
Henry Oscar
Mary Peach
Tyrone Power
George Pravda
Cyril Raymond
John Robinson
Flora Robson
Frances Rowe
Margaretta Scott
Michael Shepley
William Sylvester
Robert Urquhart
Adelaide Vandermost
Sam Wanamaker
Billie Whitelaw
Noel Willman
Mai Zetterling
Directors
John Nelson Burton
Philip Dale
Wilfred Eades
John Knight
Stuart Latham
George More O'Ferrall
David Paltenghi
Peter Potter
Philip Saville
Dennis Vance
Janice Willett
Designers
Timothy O'Brien
Reece Pemberton
Bertram Tyrer

Altogether an impressive start for *Armchair Theatre*, giving ABC Television a strong share of ITV network programming in direct competition with Lew Grade's ATV for the weekend schedules.

This first season was also my own introduction to *Armchair Theatre*, but not in the role that I came to play later. I was still mixing acting and directing at this time and I was cast in a small role in the sixth production of the series, an original screen-play:

The Hollow Crown		October 7, 1956 (9.00pm—live)
Teleplay by	H.V. Kershaw	
Cast included	Margaretta Scott, Ronald Lewis and Peter Illing – and Leonard White	
Director	John Knight	

The Hollow Crown was transmitted live from a converted cinema in Didsbury. Although ABC Television was the ITV contractor for the Midlands and the North (week-end programming) the Drama department was based at this time in London's Soho, under the auspices of the parent company, Associated British Picture Corporation (ABC Cinemas): at first in Wardour Street and then at Pathé House in Oxford Street.

Rehearsals were held in London and then the whole team was transferred to Manchester, Studio 1 (actually the converted cinema in Didsbury) for camera rehearsals and the live transmission. On the occasion of *The Hollow Crown*, which was only a half-hour drama, it was a one-day schedule starting at 9.30am for make-up and wardrobe, and with cameras at 10.30. Thence through the day until On-Air at 21.00hrs.

My only distinct memory of that occasion was when, after one of the run-through rehearsals, I happened to look up at the old cinema balcony at the end of the studio floor to be surprised to see Canadian Silvio Narrizano looking down at the scene. Silvio was one of the top directors of CBC whom I had known in Toronto during my work there. Indeed, I had shared the same rooming house with him. No.9 Prince Arthur Avenue also housed Patrick Macnee (later *The Avenger*) and Herbert Whittaker (doyen of the Theatre critics in Canada, with the *Globe & Mail*). Quite a house of drama. However, Silvio had just left the CBC in Toronto and joined Granada TV in Manchester. He was taking a look at ABC's facilities. Looking down on this converted cinema I fancy he must have wondered why he had left Canada.

Later that night, after the transmission, Silvio observed that he thought the run through he had seen earlier was better than the on-air performance. This was a continuing problem with live TV drama performances. Throughout the hours of camera rehearsal, the performances would be low-key, thoughtful word-rehearsals, with considerable awareness of the mechanics going on around; but, as the critical moment of on-air approached the adrenalin started to pump with the focus settling on the actor. This so often caused a heightening of the performance with over-projection, and the camera lens would see superficiality rather than the desired spontaneity.

Of course the required new acting technique was soon to be learned by experience (it took a long while before this was thought important enough to be taught in the drama schools).

Nowadays, the very reverse is all too often the case in theatre, where many performances hardly seem to be projected beyond the noses of the actors. That old intuition, whereby the actor would instinctively be aware of the space in which the performance had to be delivered (week by week in the old Repertory and touring system) and gear it accordingly has, alas, died. Silvio Narrizano's comment, over forty years ago – that he enjoyed the rehearsal more than the performance – was a rare pertinent assessment at that time.

Silvio was part of that important Canadian influence upon British television drama.

The second season of *Armchair Theatre* consisted of 44 productions running almost continuously from September 1957 until August 1958. Many writers contributed drama scripts specially for television to this season. Actors coming to terms, in the late fifties, with the immediacy of the vast audience, were attracted to and enhanced *Armchair Theatre* in those early days.

ARMCHAIR THEATRE
SECOND SEASON

Writers (of teleplays)
Patrick Alexander
Horton Foote
John Kruse
Coral Lansbury
John Manchip-White
Tad Mosel
Michael Pertwee
J.B. Priestley
Mordecai Richler
Reginald Rose
Rod Serling
Morris West

Actors
Maxine Audley
Alan Badel
Reginald Beckwith
Harry H. Corbett
Findlay Currie
Marpessa Dawn
Hilton Edwards
Denholm Elliott
Joan Greenwood
Hugh Griffith
Kenneth Griffith
Michael Gwynn
James Hayter
Freda Jackson
Mervyn Johns
Edward Judd
David Knight
John Laurie
Sarah Lawson
Ronald Lewis
Jack MacGowran
Raymond Massey
Neil McCallum
Andree Melly
Al Mulock
Marie Ney
Henry Oscar
Natasha Parry
Donald Pleasance
Maureen Pryor
Brian Reece
Paul Rogers
George Rose
Leonard Sachs
Janette Scott
Elizabeth Sellers
Athene Seyler
Maggie Smith
Kim Stanley
Paul Stassino
Joan Sterndale-Bennett
Jon Sullivan
Basil Sydney
June Thorburn
Ann Todd
Margaret Tyzack
Kenneth Warren
Thorley Waters
Hugh Williams
Peter Wyngarde

Directors
Leonard Brett
Stephen Clarkson
Desmond Davis
Jack Dixon (from Holland)
Wilfred Eades
Rosemary Hill
William 'Ted' Kotcheff (from Canada)
Vivian Milroy
Alvin Rakoff (from Canada)
Wolf Rilla
Peter Zadek

This second season opened with an original television script.

Now Let Him Go September 15, 1957 (live)

Teleplay by J.B. Priestley
Cast included Hugh Griffith and June Thorburn
Director Dennis Vance

Ted Kotcheff, newly arrived from CBC, Toronto, began ABC Television Drama Department's strong Canadian links which followed. He was a prime example of the unique style of a television drama director who had learned by doing the job at the Jarvis Street studios of CBC. One of the group who came to television unfettered by preconceptions.

They regarded television as a completely new medium, special and unlike any other. Whereas in the UK the general influence on television drama in the early years was from theatre, and in the USA from cinema, in Canada there was no such strong single preconditioning. There, the small band of television drama directors at the start of CBC's operation used the television camera uniquely.

This was highlighted in the particular use of the pedestal mount of the camera by the Toronto group. In my earlier days as an actor I had many opportunities to observe the use of this standard camera mount both in BBC Television and early ITV productions. The norm was to use the camera mounted, and fixed, on a pedestal. Often there was a stool placed behind the camera for the cameraman to sit down – he wasn't going anywhere. If any movement was necessary the heavy, larger, cumbersome and limited crane mounts (shades of film) would be used.

Not so with the Toronto group. They used the pedestal camera as a hand-held, entirely mobile unit. It rarely stood still for long. This demand created a new type of cameraman – strong and agile. Not to mention the cable-bashers who had to lift and run with the, then, heavy cables. This change in the use of a basic tool changed the style of television drama in the UK. No longer the stand-off and photograph, theatre-wise, but to get in close and move with the action.

Other directors at ABC were quick to learn. None more so than Philip Saville, now into his second season of *Armchair Theatre* and destined to become one of the finest television drama directors in the business – if not *the* finest.

Looking back over credits at this time it is interesting to note that the 'director' (who was responsible for budget control) was given the 'producer' credit. No one was called 'Director'. Dennis Vance – who by today's terms would be called 'Producer' or perhaps 'Executive Producer' – was titled as 'Supervisor of Drama'. All that was to change with the next season.

The third season started on-air on September 14, 1958 with a new Supervisor of Drama and Producer of *Armchair Theatre*. Dennis Vance had decided to go free-lance, and he and Howard Thomas (doubtless with strong back-up from director Ted Kotcheff) had lured Sydney Newman from CBC Toronto to take the hot-seat at ABC Television

Sydney had already built a strong reputation in Canada and the USA for producing spunky single-play drama series which had to satisfy both the public service and the commercial (sponsored) elements of CBC: in direct competition with the USA networks available to Canadian viewers from across the border. This was not unlike the needs of an ITV franchise holder here in the UK in those early days.

British television drama was in for some shock treatment with Newman, the non-conformist outsider at the helm at ABC Television – and several years later, too, when he was to deliver the same treatment to the BBC drama hierarchy. A kind of leadership, many say, much missed in the stormy and upsetting days of the 1990's, and after.

He started conventionally at ABC with a few thrillers, a mystery and a medical drama, but soon the tag 'domestic drama' became a running theme – and with Ray Rigby's *Boy with the Meat Axe* in November 1958, *Armchair Theatre* began to be dubbed 'kitchen-sink drama'. I preferred to call it 'sweat-shirt drama' because it focussed more on a different social strata rather than just a move from the 'drawing-room' setting. As television was becoming the popular form of communication (a TV set would be bought by many before a telephone) so Sydney Newman set about getting the weekly drama diet to reflect day to day life of the populace and social issues of that time.

But 'kitchen-sink drama' it was called, and the name stuck. Certainly Sydney homed on naturalistic dialogue. Not for him the oh-so-English Shakespearean delivery by actors competing to out-play Gielgud or Olivier; the 'London style' as it was known in the USA.

I well remember a couple of years later, Sydney quizzing me about a new Harold Pinter play as we drove along the the new M1 motorway en-route for Alpha Studios in Aston, Birmingham. Did I think that Pinter was using 'natural' dialogue? Sydney, through and through Canadian, found English speech fascinating and he could never be quite sure of the many variations. So, he wanted confirmation that Pinter's was natural.

I ventured a suggestion that I thought Pinter was cleverly giving the impression of being natural but actually was using a theatrical orchestration of the language.

Sydney was not convinced. He wanted yes-or-no answers. He was very impressed by Pinter and later regarded him as one of the highlights of his time at ABC when he commissioned him to write a new work for *Armchair Theatre*: the very successful *A Night Out* (1960) directed by Philip Saville and starring Vivien Merchant, Madge Ryan, Tom Bell and Arthur Lowe.

'Kitchen-sink' was, of course, only a convenient generalisation. Actually, during the four and a half seasons that Sydney Newman was in charge of *Armchair Theatre* (September 1958 until December 1962) there was considerable variety in the writing. Stories and settings as far from 'kitchen-sink' included—

> *The Fabulous Moneymaker* – Norman Ginsbury
> *Strange Meeting* – Paolo Levi (adapted by Robert Rietty)
> *The Big Client* – Malcolm Hulke & Eric Paice
> *Girl On The Beach* – Enid Hollins
> *Light From a Star* – Ian Dallas
> *The Golden Horn* – Donal Giltinan
> *The Last Tycoon* – F. Scott Fitzgerald
> *Lord Arthur Saville's Crime* – Oscar Wilde
> *Come In Razor Red* – Rod Serling
> *Pink String and Sealing Wax* – Roland Pertwee
> *Roman Gesture* – Ira Avery
> *On The Spot* – Edgar Wallace

But notably this variety in style was seen in *His Polyvinyl Girl* by Stephen Vinaver and Carl Davis, 1961; described as a 'Musical Satire'. A far cry from 'kitchen-sink'.

Nevertheless, despite these variations, the main theme for Sydney Newman was his concentration on new writing and new writers, dealing with contemporary subjects.

Earlier influences from Grierson and the National Film Board of Canada, and his political leanings when younger, together with his dislike of Hollywood, all provided a driving force for him to stir-up British television drama. And it was most welcome and successful.

By his third season as Producer in charge of *Armchair Theatre* no less than thirty of the thirty-nine productions transmitted were original television scripts. And this high proportion was maintained, highlighted by works such as—

> *No Tram to Lime Street* and *After the Funeral* – Alun Owen
> *Afternoon of a Nymph* and *Night Conspirators* – Robert Muller
> *The Irish Boys* – Hugh Leonard (nom-de-guerre of John Keyes)
> *Clip Joint People* – Alexander Baron

The Stranger and *After the Show* – Angus Wilson
I'll Have You to Remember and *Hold My Hand Soldier* – Clive Exton
Seige at Killyfaddy – Denis Johnston
The Scent of Fear – Ted Willis
and others.

However nothing could have been a better example of the immediacy of this drama series than when Donal Giltinan's *The Man Out There* – a Space Drama – was transmitted just a few weeks before Yuri Gagarin made his space flight in 1961. Timely indeed.

Altogether, Sydney Newman produced 152 *Armchair Theatre* dramas at ABC Television for the ITV Network.

My early experience as an actor in an *Armchair Theatre* production during its first year (1956, while Dennis Vance was in charge) was followed by another during Sydney Newman's first season. That was in *The Big Client* (Malcolm Hulke and Eric Paice) directed by William 'Ted' Kotcheff, 1959. A small part, and it was almost at the end of the period when I mixed acting and directing – but it enabled me to make contact again with Newman and Kotcheff who had both been at CBC in Toronto at the time when I had the great good fortune to be in Canada.

Before then I had made several attempts to get trained in TV production at the BBC (I had been acting on BBC Television since the early 'Ally Pally' days) but I was never able to get beyond filling in (or 'out', according to which side of the Atlantic this is being read) the application forms. I had no university qualifications, and at that time it was an automatic disqualification without them. It is ironic that many years later, *after* my work at ABC, I had two invitations to join BBC Television, and without any form-filling! At those times I was unable to accept either. I often wonder just how my career might have changed if I had taken up one of those offers? A pension probably.

Sufficient to say, however, that on one of my happy visits to Toronto in 1957 (I first went there to direct in theatre in 1953) I was given the opportunity to join CBC on their first training course for producer/directors, under the expert guidance of Robert Allen and John Barnes.

There was another Englishman I met on that course, an actor, Charles Jarrott, who was in Canada touring with the London Theatre Company. Jarrott was an appointee to the course by Sydney Newman for the Drama Department. I was under the auspices of Robert Allen who was responsible for Special Programmes (mainly the big Arts shows. My previous experience with Christopher Fry and Shakespeare plays rated me , I believe, as too 'arty' for the commercial-fare of the TV drama department that Newman was running!). Jarrott and myself were the only two drama people attending that course. Afterwards Jarrott followed Sydney Newman to England and worked with him, and later with me, at ABC. Then the call of the big screen came and Jarrott steered his career to Hollywood, to join many of the ex-CBC crowd on the West Coast.

As it turned out, this CBC course was the best training I could have found anywhere at that time. Not only because it was not specialist-based and therefore covered all types of programming (no special treatment for *drama* people) but also because CBC was both a public-service *and* commercial programme maker. This proved to be a great help when later I joined an ITV company in Britain.

It was never my intention to leave Canada after my CBC training, but unexpected family events brought me back to England. It was the time of the early days of ITV and immediately, as a free-lance programme director, I joined TWW (Television Wales and West) at their Cardiff studios. No drama there (at least not drama programmes) but welcome experience in programmes of all sorts, and all live of course – and also some film. A very welcome perk at that time was to be able to get away from the normal day-to-day confinement of the control room multi-camera set-ups and get out and about with a 16mm film camera shooting pony-trekking on the Welsh mountains.

As the Relief Director, I found myself doing programmes I had never expected such as *Double Chance*, described as "a new show for young entertainers". Bryan Michie was host and compere; and on the bill at that time were singers Jackie Dee and Maureen Jones.

I was also thrown-in to do advertising magazines (*Friday Shopping List*), *Sports Preview* (Bruce Lewis), and then my first (and last) brush with a quiz programme. I directed a run of episodes of *Abracadabra* (a sort-of early version of *Countdown*) devised and produced by Canadians, Roy Ward Dickson and Shirley Dickson. This programme provided me with my first experience of recording programmes. They were still done 'as live', of course: there was no thought of editing. TWW had no recording facility of their own and so we booked lines all the way to ATV's Foley Street Ampex operation in London. I would do four programmes in one session. One hour rehearsal, then three hours in which to do and record the four programmes. Those were the days when the director relied enormously on an expert vision-mixer ('switcher') and I was very lucky to have Terry DeLacey 'on the board'. Terry went on to be a fine writer and director years later.

The biggest surprise during that short period at TWW, Cardiff, was when I was asked to direct Welsh language programmes without knowing more than a few words of Welsh: *Orig Yr Ifanc* (*Accent on Youth*); *Pnawn Da Blant* (*Good Afternoon Children*); *Amser Te* (*Tea-Time*); *Cipdrem Ar Fywyd* (*Glimpse of Life*) all produced by Wyn Roberts (who later graced the House of Lords). And all with the help of a first-rate Welsh-speaking Production

Assistant Jean Parry Jones, who really did all the work. *That* wouldn't happen now of course. Hardly likely nowadays that anyone not Welsh and fluent Welsh-speaking would get within a million miles of a Welsh-language programme.

But, although I wasn't doing drama – the only programming I thought I knew anything about – it proved to be stimulating times. With every programme, on entering the control room for transmission on-air, one's reputation was at stake. No hiding anything. Mistakes and all were there for everyone to see. Stage-fright I had known, but this was nervous tension *plus.*

The past caught up with the present again while I was with TWW. Some seven years before in London I had been acting in Christopher Fry's play *A Sleep of Prisoners,* and most nights after the performance the cast (Denholm Elliott, Stanley Baker, Hugh Pryse and myself) and friends would meet for a drink and chat at the Cumberland Arms in Kingly Street in the West End. Frequently, on those occasions during the run, I was aware of a small group of students who turned up and joined in the conversation. They were regulars at the play. I discovered that they were planning to put on the play themselves at college, and attended time and time again to take notes!

One of those students who introduced himself was named Don Leaver. That was in 1951, Festival of Britain year. Then, years later as I turned up at the Pontcanna Studios of TWW in Cardiff, there, now directing television programmes, was the same Don Leaver. A world away from the marvellous language of Christopher Fry's theatre for both of us.

A few more years after that Don Leaver was (with Peter Hammond, a unique duo) working with me at ABC on setting the style for *The Avengers*, which I was producing.

After the short spell with TWW, I had an even shorter spell with Southern Television at Southampton, attached to a sub-contractor (Yes! Contracted-out programmes even in those days). I was doing 'Advertising Features' for Ad-mags: *Counterwise* (with Frances Bennett and Tom Mullis) and *Shop in the South* presented by that lovely television personality, Mary Malcolm.

Thence, and again as a Relief Director as I had been at TWW, I joined Tyne-Tees television in Newcastle, covering all types of programmes, allowing the staff directors to go on holiday one by one. Little chance of stock-piling programmes in those days. Recording was still a rarity.

It was one Friday afternoon (January 1960) in my office at City Road – I'd just done the transmission of the *One O'Clock Show* and I was about to leave to catch the train to take me home for the week-end – when the telephone rang.

That phone call was to change my life considerably.

It was Sydney Newman calling from his office at ABC Television's Teddington Studios. He didn't know that I hadn't returned to Toronto. Direct as ever, "What the hell are you doing in Newcastle?" I didn't have time to tell him as I was rushing to catch a train. "Come and have lunch on Monday," he said.

I did.

He wanted me to join him at ABC and asked me to be a producer. "No, not to direct – I've got plenty of directors – to *produce*." To say this was surprising is an understatement. Sydney was the only one in ABC's Drama Department to take the producer credit and he used it in the American sense. He was the boss.

In that regard, and at that time, I hardly saw myself as being a Sam Goldwyn or J. Arthur Rank. After a long time as actor, and then a theatre director, I was only recently establishing myself as a television director, and now to be asked to take on the producer role was totally surprising: indeed, quite unlooked-for by me. I demurred, making all sorts of excuses concerning my suitability. But Sydney was very persuasive.

The lunch went on long enough for me to consider the advantages – and there were many. First: I'd be working as 'Associate' with Sydney Newman whose talent, producing the single-play series for CBC in Toronto, I'd long admired. The work would be entirely in drama, which I wanted. And it would be in the Drama Department of ABC Television, which had become the focus of attention in television in the UK, attracting top talents in the profession. Also, I was intrigued by the fact that it was the first time in my career that a job had come to me quite out of the blue, entirely without my going after it. As an actor I'd been used to the usual conduct of chasing casting; making sure if possible that the next role was a progression from the last. Or looking for plays that I might direct. But never before had a job been offered me that was not in my track-record – and a very responsible position at that.

The proposition did not seem anything out of the ordinary to Sydney. My misgivings were hardly more than inconsequential to him. I've long since thought that the CBC training probably supported the premise that the director should be essentially a producer first; whereas directing in the UK had become a quite separate endeavour enshrined as the creative element.

Nevertheless, before the coffee was served, I was delighted and honoured to accept Sydney Newman's offer. The challenge, and Sydney's confidence, were compelling.

Soon, I was whisked off to meet Howard Thomas (Managing Director) and Bernard Greenhead (Head of Engineering). I'd never met a managing director before. The world of commerce and big business seemed to me so far away from the world of acting or even directing a play. I've met a quite a few since then (and even been approached to be one myself – Stanley Baker, later *Sir* Stanley, wanted me to be Managing Director of HTV when that company started... but that's another story). Certainly, the closer one gets to the man of power, the more the god-figure diminishes and the human being is revealed. Warts and all with some. But I found Howard Thomas to be a man of considerable understanding and warmth. Even so, I was nervous.

It was perhaps a formality, but Howard Thomas, perceptive as ever, simply put the question: "Why do you, a director, want to get involved in all the administration of producing?"

That was a problem. I certainly didn't want to give any impression that I'd given up directing, or that I'd forego any of the creative drive and just be tied to a desk job. I came out with a reply to Howard Thomas's question – the most inept response, which has been trapped in my memory ever since. It remains there, refusing to be forgotten. "I don't want to be that sort of producer. I want to be an *artistic* producer."

Such a naive pronouncement was worthy of a guffaw, or a chuckle at least. It got both. However, Howard Thomas, with a slight smile crossing his face, took my blind confidence as an expression of enthusiasm, which was to be welcomed. And welcome me he did.

In spite of my seeming naivety, there was a desire – albeit unformulated – to make my role as Producer something other than an administrator. Most of those elements were better taken care of by production managers, accountants and secretaries, and even line producers (what an awful title) as we have today.

If I couldn't stimulate the production team in all its creative elements, fusing them all, so that the machine delivers more than the machine, then I would have no inspiration. Indeed, had I not done this, I would never have been able to remain at Teddington Studios for the ten years that I did.

I returned to Newcastle to work out the remaining weeks of my contract at TTTV, full of the joys of anticipation. I continued with live commercials: advertising magazines – *Come Shopping With Daphne Padell* (and with Barry Gosney), and *Trader Horne* (with Kenneth Horne, Ann Croft and Stallibrass). Advertising magazines were much maligned, but they were undeniably popular, having high-calibre personality presenters. Remember *Jim's Inn*? In their time they were a much more honest amalgam of the commercial and programme interests than spot commercials interrupting the flow of programme content, as now they do.

This temporary aberration in my career in drama, although very instructive (and I was glad to have it – after all, isn't all life a drama?) ended on February 27 1960.

On February 29, 1960, I joined ABC Television as a producer in the Drama Department.

A special day: Leap Year Day.

CHAPTER 2

Inside Story – 1960

Thrown In—The New Adventure

Early this year saw my transition from directing an advertising magazine (*Trader Horne*) in the studios of Tyne-Tees TV in Newcastle on Friday February 26 (my diary records the stark note "Ampex 9.30pm" – Ampex, the tape-recording method) to starting a contract as a drama producer on the following Monday with ABC Television at their Teddington studios. Or so the gods decreed! I hadn't planned it.

Another note in my diary records that my weekly rail season ticket from my home on the Sussex coast to Teddington cost me three pounds, two shillings and sevenpence. I wasn't sufficiently assured to invest in a ticket for any longer than one week. My first contract at ABC (Iris Productions) paid me about £40 a week, and was for three months. I thought Heaven had come. I stayed ten years.

I was not alone in joining ABC Television at that time. On the same day I arrived, I was introduced to Irene Shubik, who was joining Sydney Newman's story-editing team. She was also later to work with me on several different projects; and much later still she became a producer, and has a list of fine credits, notably launching the famous *Rumpole* series.

Story editors (NB not *script* editors) were of massive importance in our Drama Department. Highly respected and experienced motivators and searchers – the writers' friends. Their job was inspirational but often very difficult. Irene Shubik in her early days received a letter from writer Ted Allen concerning one of his play scripts—

> I wrote in a completely new speech for the character in which he repeats, as a chant, words like crap, shit, damn, goddam, hell, crissaake, fuck. In this speech the repetition of these words is vital for an understanding of his character. They reveal his fantasies and the basic problems he faces as a man. These words are key words later used in act three to indicate how he associates them with other, apparently meaningless symbols. Without this particular chant the character will never be understood and the whole play stands or falls on an understanding of his character.
> What are we to do about this?

While I believe that Ted Allen was teasing in this, Irene Shubik copied the letter to Sydney Newman and me with the comment, "I thought this might show a few of the story editors' problems!"

A very talented young woman, sensitive to writers and their craft, but perhaps over-sensitive. I remember my embarrassment when, years later, she reacted to one of my decisions by dissolving into tears. For some inexplicable reason, I seem to have suffered that same embarrassment several times. Particularly when directing theatre productions, I have been entirely surprised by one actress or another bursting into tears during rehearsals. I never thought I was a hard man. And I'm not.

Arthur Johnston, Newman's 'left hand', gave Irene and me the 'greeting' lunch on our first day at ABC Television. Arthur looked after the admin of the department. He was an 'old-school-tie' gentleman, a prize example of the Englishman: remote, cool and entirely reliable. And probably Sydney's entré into British society, which fascinated him at that time.

We lunched at a pub in the High Street in Teddington on that first day. A frugal affair. Later on, the lunches that Sydney Newman hosted were more in keeping with a successful commercial television company and his own flamboyant nature. He introduced me to 'whisky sour'.

I had the great good fortune to be introduced into a very successful and well-run department. It was large enough to be the supplier of a major part of ITV's drama output, and yet small enough to be a 'family affair': a team all pulling together yet challenging each other. Arguments galore, yet always stimulating and constructive.

The offices, overlooking the Thames, were not 'open plan' I'm glad to say. The closed door of an office was always respected – but generally, we were happy to keep them open, encouraging and expecting discussion on any level and subject. Successes and problems were shared. A very free atmosphere. Not even the flamboyant histrionics of a Ted Kotcheff, a Philip Saville or a Dennis Vance, against the quieter Charles Jarrott, Basil Coleman or Jonathan Alwyn and suchlike directors, ever rocked the wagon.

With Sydney Newman running the ranch, it never came to a shoot out – unless Sydney was holding the only gun! Even then, he'd only use it to defend his 'family' against all predators.

Prior to my arrival, ABC had seen the need to enlarge their drama output by moving into other formats, and was making a series called *Inside Story*. Set in a modern block of flats, each episode dealt with a 'how the other people live' story.

Ted Willis (long before he was elevated to the House of Lords) wrote some of the episodes and was the overall story editor.

The series never had an accredited producer. Sydney Newman had more than enough to do with running the department and in producing *Armchair Theatre*: and he had persuaded his fellow-countryman, Ted Kotcheff, to "look after it". That didn't last for long. Kotcheff was

ABC Drama chief Sydney Newman, during rehearsals of *Inside Story*, chats to Mary Peach who plays the secretary to the superintendent of a block of flats

Inside Story

13 episodes – 9 produced by Leonard White

Writers
Larry Forrester
Peter Myers
Ted Willis

Running characters
Mary Peach
Robert Brown
Brian Phelan

Casts included
Harold Berens
Margaret Courtenay
Lois Dane
Reg Dixon
Joseph Furst
Betty Huntley-Wright
Hanna Pravda
John Salew
Sophie Stewart
John Warner
Edward Woodward

Directors
Wilfred Eades
John Knight
Royston Morley
Dennis Vance
Guy Verney

Designer
Alpho O'Reilly

Overall story editor
Ted Willis

much more interested in continuing his successful career as director working with writers like Alun Owen and Clive Exton – and he wasn't going to be sidetracked.

Thus, it fell to me as my first assignment at ABC to take over the 'producer' role for the nine remaining episodes of *Inside Story*.

The pattern was to rehearse in various rehearsal rooms in London. I would attend a producer's run-through on the Saturday of each week – and on the following Wednesday we would go to the Manchester Didsbury studios to record the show 'as live'.

Inside Story didn't last beyond its thirteen episodes, and it was all over within some ten weeks of my joining. However, even as I worked myself into the new environment and job, I was assigned to put together a thirteen episode series of *Armchair Theatre* for the summer season. The summer season with lower ratings rarely attracted the big time. It was the unfashionable season.

CHAPTER 3

Armchair Mystery Theatre – 1960

Sydney Newman jealously guarded the title of Producer of *Armchair Theatre* for himself, and rightly so. However, he wanted to go on a summer holiday, and ABC was not in the mood to give up its precious on-air time at the weekends. So, I was charged to provide the summer schedule of dramas – with the hope of attracting a more end-of-the-pier summer show audience. Those dramas would be called *Armchair Mystery Theatre*, not to be confused with *Armchair Theatre* 'proper' (Sydney's domain).

I saw no reason for going down-market while attempting a good season of mystery teleplays. To give the anthology an overall personal identity we engaged Donald Pleasance to introduce each story. In his unique way, he created an atmosphere that was both macabre and comic, nicely poised in anticipation.

We opened on the start of the holiday season, Whit-Sunday (second only to August Bank holiday for low viewing figures) with a specially written teleplay:

Eye Witness	June 5, 1960 (10.00pm)
Teleplay by	Leslie Sands
Intros by	Donald Pleasance
Cast included	Diana Wynyard, Paul Daneman, Jean Anderson, Patience Collier, Margery Withers
Director	Charles Jarrott
Designer	Assheton Gorton

The introductions by Donald Pleasance were not entirely successful with the TV critics.

Peter Black of the *Daily Mail* found the teleplay—

> altogether superior to the rather fatuous introduction made by Donald Pleasance ... which sought to catch a Hitchcockian note of the menacing and facetious

To compare Hitchcock and Pleasance ("Mine Ghost" of the series, as Philip Purser described) was hardly comparing like with like; and I know who was the better actor. In that respect, Donald was top billing.

K.Y. in *The Daily Telegraph* described this introduction as—

> jocosely sinister urbanity

The Times review found it—

> most suavely sinister

As for the show itself, Richard Sear in the *Daily Mirror* found it—

> more misery than mystery

Philip Purser (*News Chronicle*) was most vitriolic—

> sad to see so much talent deployed in the interests of so worthless a subject ... discerning viewers would have switched off.

However, *The Times*, both in headline and in their review described it as—

> the most gripping and polished thriller television has yet offered us.

And, more importantly, the audience liked it. Although it was a Whit-holiday-Sunday and a later transmission time in every region (except East Anglia) the programme built on its inherited audience. It was highest or equal highest rated programme for that Sunday evening in six of the nine regions covered by TAM (Television Audience Measurement).

Not a bad debut.

Supplement to Television Mail, December 16, 1960.

TAM'S TOP TEN PROGRAMMES

	Programme	Anglia	Ulster	London	Mdlnds.	North	Sthern.	Wales & West	N.East	Sctlnd.	Network (Homes)
1	**The Cupboard**	66	70	66	76	83	65	71	78	80	7,703,000
2	**Sunday Palladium Show**	66	66	68	73	76	68	65	79	77	7,497,000
3	**Take Your Pick**	74	72	66	70	73	72	69	73	66	7,292,000
4	**The Accomplices**	—	70	56	64	70	—	62	69	73	6,573,000
5	**Bootsie and Snudge**	—	—	—	66	63	71	64	—	—	6,367,000
5	**The Army Game**	—	70	56	66	63	—	65	—	—	6,367,000
7	**Emergency—Ward 10 (Tue)**	70	—	57	62	63	68	—	—	—	6,262,000
8	**The Arthur Haynes Show**	64	68	—	—	—	—	60	68	65	6,162,000
9	**Emergency—Ward 10 (Fri)**	67	—	57	—	—	68	59	—	—	5,957,000
10	**Dickie Henderson Show**	63	—	—	—	—	57	—	—	68	5,854,000

REGIONAL TOP TEN (Week Ending December 11)

***Top BBC Programmes**

LONDON

1	Sunday Palladium	68
2	The Cupboard	66
	Take Your Pick	66
*4	Charlie Drake	58
5	Emergency—Ward 10 (Fri)	57
	Emergency—Ward 10 (Tues)	57
7	Candid Camera	56
	The Accomplices	56
	The Army Game	56
10	77 Sunset Strip	55

SOUTHERN

1	Take Your Pick	72
2	Bootsie and Snudge	71
3	Emergency—Ward 10 (Fri)	68
	Sunday Palladium	68
	Emergency—Ward 10 (Tues)	68
6	The Cupboard	65
7	Riverboat	64
8	The Variety Show	58
	The Verger	58
10	The Dickie Henderson Show	57
*	Charlie Drake	46

NORTH EAST

1	Sunday Palladium	79
2	The Cupboard	78
3	Take Your Pick	73
4	Riverboat	71
5	Huckleberry Hound	69
	77 Sunset Strip	69
	The Accomplices	69
8	The Arthur Haynes Show	68
9	The Variety Show	67
10	Bonanza	66
	Probation Officer	66
*	Charlie Drake	49

S. WALES/WEST

1	The Cupboard	71
2	Take Your Pick	69
	Wagon Train	69
4	The Army Game	65
	Sunday Palladium	65
6	Bootsie and Snudge	64
7	The Accomplices	62
8	Cheyenne	61
9	The Arthur Haynes Show	60
10	Emergency—Ward 10 (Fri)	59
	Probation Officer	59
*	Charlie Drake	58
*	Juke Box Jury	58

EAST ANGLIA

1	Take Your Pick	74
2	Emergency—Ward 10 (Tues)	70
3	Bonanza	68
4	Emergency—Ward 10 (Fri)	67
*5	Dixon of Dock Green	66
	Sunday Palladium	66
	The Cupboard	66
8	The Arthur Haynes Show	64
9	The Dickie Henderson Show	63
10	Double Your Money	62

MIDLANDS

1	The Cupboard	76
2	Sunday Palladium	73
3	Take Your Pick	70
4	The Army Game	66
	Bootsie and Snudge	66
6	The Accomplices	64
	Hawaiian Eye	64
8	Riverboat	63
9	Emergency—Ward 10 (Tues)	62
10	Sing Along with Joe	60
*	Juke Box Jury	46

NORTHERN

1	The Cupboard	83
2	Sunday Palladium	76
3	Take Your Pick	73
4	The Accomplices	70
5	Wagon Train	67
	Hawaiian Eye	67
7	Emergency—Ward 10 (Tues)	63
	The Army Game	63
	Bonanza	63
	Bootsie and Snudge	63
*	Charlie Drake	46

SCOTTISH

1	The Cupboard	80
2	Sunday Palladium	77
3	The Accomplices	73
4	Bonanza	72
5	Cheyenne	71
6	Riverboat	69
7	The Dickie Henderson Show	68
8	Take Your Pick	66
9	The Arthur Haynes Show	65
10	Panic	62
*	This Is Your Life	49

ULSTER

1	Maverick	75
2	Rawhide	73
3	Take Your Pick	72
4	Highway Patrol	71
5	The Army Game	70
	Double Your Money	70
	The Accomplices	70
	The Cupboard	70
9	The Arthur Haynes Show	68
10	Sunday Palladium	66
	Cheyenne	66
*	Charlie Drake	53

The Cupboard* – produced for *Armchair Mystery Theatre* – screened on *Armchair Theatre
Television Audience Measurement (TAM) – Supplement to *Television Mail*, December 16, 1960

However, I soon ran into problems, with my second production of that series, another specially written teleplay, *The Cupboard,* written by Ray Rigby, and starring Donald Pleasance and Elizabeth Begley – directed by David Greene and designed by Roy Stannard. This play had to be withdrawn from transmission at the last minute because of similarity with a real-life murder investigation in the headlines at that time.

My production of *The Cupboard*, although withdrawn, was not lost. It was too good for that, and Sydney Newman took advantage, rightly. It was transmitted a few months later on December 11, 1960 in the *Armchair Theatre* ('proper') season, with my own credit removed, and Sydney Newman's producer credit in its place. It attained that very rare accolade of being No.1 in the Top Ten of all programmes for that week, beating the usual leader, *Sunday Night at the London Palladium*, into second place. It had 7,703,000 homes viewing (something like an audience of 18-plus million!). Only in retrospect do I regret that my credit was not on it when transmitted.

Fortunately, and in keeping with work patterns of that time, I had more than one production being made at the same time – often two and sometimes three at once, overlapping.

My second production on-air was transmitted live.

The Big Wheel June 12, 1960 (live)
Written by John Glennon
Cast included Sam Wanamaker and Gary Cockrell
Director Philip Saville

Declared *The Times*—

> A virtuoso production … nearer to Kafka than to Agatha Christie

Since then, Philip has duly been honoured for his work in television. He set a high and very special standard for others to emulate. I thank my lucky stars that I was able to work with him at that time (and later). Always a challenge: not without problems, but nevertheless stimulating to achieve such standards.

Armchair Mystery Theatre continued through the summer:

The Case of Paul Danek June 19, 1960
Written by Morten Wishengrad and Virginia Mazer
Cast included Billie Whitelaw, Robert Urquhart, Gene Anderson and Edward Woodward
Director David Greene
Designer George Haslam

Next an Australian story, directed by the author. Again, this, and the next production had to be transmitted live from our Manchester studios.

Flag Fall		June 26, 1960 (live)
Written by	Royston Morley	
Cast included	Madge Ryan, Millicent Martin and Patrick Barr – and also Michael Blakemore	
Director	Royston Morley	
Designer	Roy Stannard	

Michael Blakemore, playing a newscaster, later to become a top theatre director.

And on a lighter note:

Toff and Fingers		July 3, 1960 (live)
Written by	Robert Kemp	
Cast included	Roger Livesey, Sophie Stewart and Harold Goodwin	
Director	Robert Tronson	
Designer	Reece Pemberton	

A week later, we presented a play by James Mitchell.

Flight From Treason
Ian Hendry and Avril Elgar

Flight from Treason
Avril Elgar and John Gregson

Flight from Treason July 10, 1960

Written by	James Mitchell
Cast included	Ian Hendry, John Gregson and Robert Brown – with Maxwell Shaw, Avril Elgar and Donald Churchill
Director	Dennis Vance
Designer	James Goddard

Flight from Treason brought together several good portents. James Mitchell later wrote *A Magnum For Schneider* (while I was in charge of *Armchair Theatre*), which developed into the *Callan* series. Ian Hendry was soon to play the lead in the original *Avengers* series, and actor Donald Churchill became a most successful writer for my *Armchair Theatre* seasons. The design team at ABC spawned a number of subsequent successful directors, one of which was the designer of this production, James Goddard.

Adrienne Corri playing the lead in *Madeleine* with Maurice Denham

Described as a comedy thriller:

Madeleine	July 17, 1960
Written by	Alan Caillou
Cast included	Adrienne Corri – with Maurice Denham and Michael Gwynn
Director	Jack Dixon
Designer	Reece Pemberton

The beautiful and fiery Adrienne Corri played Madeleine. Jack Dixon was a Head of Drama for one of the TV organisations in Holland, and we were glad to add a little continental spice to our team, when he was available. There was never a dull moment with the mixture of Dixon and Corri – certainly not during production!

Web of Deceit July 24, 1960

Written by	J.D. Barton
Cast included	Jack Hedley and Margaret Whiting – with Paul Whitsun-Jones, Alex Scott, Kenneth Macintosh and Catherine Woodville
Director	Alan Cooke
Designer	Peter Mullins

Catherine Woodville was the first 'victim' in the launch episode of *The Avengers*. It might also have been the start of something else, because after that, in the USA on the West coast, she and Patrick Macnee got together – for a while at least.

Canadian connections continued with the next production.

False Witness
Sylvia Kay and Neil McCallum

False Witness August 7, 1960

Written by	Philip Levene
Cast included	Neil McCallum and Sylvia Kay – with Frank Gatliff, Mairhi Russell, Stanley Meadows and Michael Hitchman
Director	Ron Weyman
Designer	Paul Bernard

The young and beautiful co-star, Sylvia Kay, was the centre of attraction when a group of drama students from RADA visited the studio during rehearsal to learn the tricks of the trade. Sylvia was then not much older than the students. Indeed, I well remember her as a student at the London Academy (LAMDA) on an occasion when I was a guest teacher there. She fell asleep during my classes, which now I think about it, may well have been the most appropriate reaction! Sylvia later married Canadian director Ted Kotcheff.

Ron Weyman, the director, was on a visit from CBC in Toronto. Ron later headed the film-drama department at CBC and broke the mould for the general acceptance of 16mm film as a medium for television drama. Some ten years later, after leaving Teddington studios, I learned a lot from him when I returned to Toronto and joined his film team at CBC.

Paul Bernard was another designer who went on to become a director.

An American play followed:

Machinal August 14, 1960

Written by	Sophie Treadwell
Cast included	Donald Pleasance, Joanna Dunham and Gary Cockrell – with Sean Sullivan, Dennis King, Libby Morris – and Peter Boretski and James Dyrenforth
Director	Philip Saville
Designer	Assheton Gorton

Machinal was perfectly cast by Dodo Watts and Philip Saville (directing his second for me).

Again, specially for *Armchair Theatre*:

The Man with a Feather in his Hat August 21, 1960

Written by	Peter Barnes
Cast included	Clifford Evans, Allan Cuthbertson, Kevin Stoney and Wensley Pithey – with Thomas Heathcote, Allan McClelland, Delana Kidd, Ronald Adam, Tenniel Evans, Harry Walker, Keith Pyott and Catherine Woodville
Director	Robert Tronson
Designer	Paul Bernard

British film star Clifford Evans had been instrumental in getting me my first film role (*The Silver Darlings*) in my acting days. We had been together in the Army. He was a private and I was his sergeant. After Victory in Europe Day, I organised his early de-mob so that he could get out and make a film to cheer us up after the war effort.

The next was by a well-known actor.

Cul-de-Sac
Left: Irene French and Tom Bell
Below: Martin Matthews and Tom Bell

Cul de Sac		August 28, 1960
Written by	Sebastian Shaw	
Cast included	Gillian Lind and Tom Bell – with Martin Matthews, John Sharplin and Irene French	
Director	Ron Weyman	
Designer	Assheton Gorton	

The summer season of *Armchair Mystery Theatre* ended on a high note with a play in which Cyril Cusack made his British television debut.

The Dummy		September 4, 1960
Written by	Ray Rigby	
Cast included	Cyril Cusack, Alison Leggatt, Diana King, Basil Lord – with Anthony Bate, Gerald Flood, Harold Berens, Norman Mitchell and Ernest Hare	
Director	Alan Cooke	
Designer	Mark James	

This play was Ray Rigby's second for the series and was the top-rated Sunday show throughout the Network, beating Delfont's popular *Sunday Palladium* show in the Top Ten.

CHAPTER 4

Police Surgeon – 1960

The 'Avenging' Surgeon?

Twenty-three productions had taken up my first six months at ABC Television. During that time, Sydney Newman had begun to put together a new half-hour series to capitalise on the fine acting talent of Ian Hendry, and to get the first-rate writer, Julian Bond, into the department. Initially set for thirteen episodes, Julian was to write seven of them in collaboration with J.J. Bernard, the pseudonym of a real-life police surgeon.

Police Surgeon **camera card: Ian Hendry as Dr Geoffrey Brent**

Julian had also been attracted to produce the series, but not for long, because it became clear that he was not enjoying the producing part of the package. Therefore, while still making *Armchair Mystery Theatre*, I was also given the role of Producer of *Police Surgeon*. By that time, four episodes had been made, and I took over for a further nine.

Police Surgeon

13 episodes – first 4 produced by Julian Bond, then 9 by Leonard White

Writers
Julian Bond
Richard Harris
Bill MacIllwraith
F. Woodlands
Peter Yeldham

Running Characters
Ian Hendry
John Warwick

Actors
Pamela Allen
Jean Anderson
Elizabeth Begley
Donald Churchill
Patience Collier
Jane Eccles
Charles Farrell
Dudley Foster
Percy Herbert
Joyce Heron
Arthur Hewlett
Charles Houston
Hazel Hughes
Barry Keegan
Terence Knapp
Rosemary Leach
Donald Morley
Patricia Mort
Maureen O'Reilly
Geoffrey Palmer
Katherine Parr
Edna Petrie
Ivor Salter
John Scott
Nigel Stock
Neil Wilson
James Culliford

Directors
R. Hartford-Davis
John Knight
Don Leaver (8 episodes)
James Ormerod
Guy Verney

Designer
Alpho O'Reilly

Ian Hendry, as Dr Geoffrey Brent took single star billing with John Warwick playing the only other running character. The reputation of the writing attracted the excellent casts.

29 year-old Ian Hendry had come a long way since he started stooging for the famous clown Coco (when he might have taken up a career in the circus), and his later work on *Emergency-Ward Ten*. In *Police Surgeon* he was very impressive and looked set for a long run.

By the first week of November 1960, all thirteen episodes had been made, and the last episode was transmitted on December 3.

Then suddenly it all stopped. Sydney Newman had a problem – a problem never explained – which meant he couldn't go on with *Police Surgeon*. I believe it was some contractual hiatus.

However, Sydney was telling us that a new series must be found for Ian Hendry. It had to be on-air in a matter of weeks, and I was responsible for it. Indeed, only a few weeks later, a new series had been created.

CHAPTER 5

Something Called *The Avengers* – 1961

No one person can claim to have created *The Avengers*: not the head of department, not the producer, not one director, not one writer, not one story editor. It was very much a team effort. All, however, worked like mad and contributed with infectious enthusiasm in all departments. It was indeed 'mad' but always upbeat. There was no more than about eight or nine weeks between Sydney Newman's 'charge' to provide a new continuing series and the first transmission. Urgency and the pressures of publication in respect of all programming at that time did provide an excitement, warts and all! The bland easy-going process of today's concept-to-screen schedule may provide the means of a superficial polish, but more often than not lacks the fire of the need to publish and to publish quickly – the 'live' quality which is the unique essence of television.

Patrick Macnee and Ian Hendry

Ian Hendry's role of the Police Surgeon Dr Geoffrey Brent had to be dropped, which allowed more freedom and scope in the stories when the conventional police element, fortunately, disappeared. But in the new format, Hendry would remain as a doctor: the 'healer', the man of principle. The new character was Dr David Keel (steady as she goes!) who would take up the cudgels as a vigilante, albeit by accident.

A completely new character had to be created to provide a contrast and a link with the underworld, motivated by some conveniently unexplained 'department'. This character had to be 'undercover'. Here, again, we had the actor before we had the role; or at least we wanted to involve Patrick Macnee.

I had first met Patrick when, several years before, we were both acting in the West End in London, in a fine company – Four Seasons Ltd – at the Duchess Theatre. It was put together by Michael Benthall and Tony Guthrie, led by Margaret Rawlings, Robert Helpmann, Martita Hunt, Andrew Cruickshank, Hugh Griffith, Roderick Lovell, Ernest Milton, Audrey Fildes, Erich Pohlmann, Basil Coleman, Margaret Diamond, Arnold Marle, Gordon Davies and with Heather Stannard, and Claire Bloom in bit-parts!

One of the plays performed in that season was Webster's *The White Devil* – and in it, Patrick Macnee had a small role in which he had but one line to utter. But that one line extraordinarily became the lift-off for Patrick's subsequent successful career in theatre, television and cinema. Harold Hobson, reviewing the play in *The Sunday Times* (9/3/1947), picked out that one line, writing—

> ...a Page whom I had not noticed before, and was not to notice again, quietly says these five words, 'This is not true Madam'. That is all ... As this play counts noise, it is hardly more than a whisper. Yet for me it was the most striking moment...

Patrick never looked back. I found him next in Toronto, in 1953, now a 'leading man', and I cast him to play Corporal Adam in the Canadian premiere of Christopher Fry's beautiful play *A Sleep of Prisoners*. (I had acted in the original production in the Festival of Britain year in London and New York.)

Subsequently, Patrick and I acted together several times on Canadian television, where I first met Sydney Newman – then Producer of Drama at CBC. Little did I realise then that some seven years later I would be back in England working with Newman and Macnee!

Patrick commuted between Toronto, New York, Hollywood and London, and he was back in London when we were constructing what was to become *The Avengers*. We fancied that Macnee would make an ideal foil for Hendry in this, as yet, un-named series. We then started on the creation of this new character, knowing that Patrick Macnee would play it. The role was named John Steed (Patrick came from a horsy background: his father had been a racehorse trainer) and although it wasn't casting to type, we unashamedly took advantage of Patrick's natural talents when composing John Steed, the devil-may-care undercover man of the sixties. Macnee described the character of Steed as "a wolf with the women and revels in trouble". Patrick's old Etonian background helped to establish the social context of the character and, sartorially kitted out with smart suits, bowler hat and umbrella, made for a sophistication that avoided the ugly and downbeat side of a crime adventure series. Something of a playboy as the undercover man.

Police Surgeon spawned another character for the new series in that the lovely actress Ingrid Hafner, who played a nurse to Ian Hendry's Dr Brent in several episodes, became the nurse-receptionist (Carol Wilson) to Hendry's Dr Keel. Thus, putting together this series did not start with a story submitted by a writer, nicely packaged, complete with characters. In this case, the actor came first – Ian Hendry – for whom we had to manufacture a series.

Patrick Macnee with Producer Leonard White
"Making a point"

The concept was for a one-hour continuing weekly drama series, produced 'as live', and for which the first transmission was only a matter of weeks away. I have no recollections of this being a daunting challenge. Exciting, yes; frightening, no. It was all part of the pace and thrust of working in television at that time. And the team at ABC Television were first class; the environment progressive.

So, it was to be an undercover crime-busting series. The running characters were in place, but no stories. In order to sustain the continuing series week by week (there was never any thought that this would not be continuing) it would be piloted in ABC's own franchise areas, the Midlands and the North, and paid for locally (something, again unheard of in the present day). This made it very necessary to cast the net wide to involve many writers. We needed a lot of good stories and the opportunity to open the door for new styles and, indeed, to write-off as necessary.

I am quoted in the organs of that time as needing stories—

> Vigorous, fast-moving ... stories described in terms of action ... set in the most original places ... avoiding clichés ... something better than the formula.

Perhaps there was nothing new in that in cinematic terms, but in largely studio-bound television live production, it was by no means common or easy to achieve at that time. We wanted to make it move, and the excellent cameramen and their cable-bashers at ABC were demonstrating their athletic prowess, showing the way to change the style of TV drama – breaking away from the old BBC concept of the static theatrical style where the pedestal-mounted camera was considered to be fixed. At ABC (largely because of the Canadian, CBC, influences) the 'ped' was used as a travelling hand-held, covering endless shot-cards, pushing and pulling to the next position, selecting the lens from four alternatives on the turret, checking focus. And all the while being encouraged by the director in the control room to "get in closer", and at the same time avoid all the other cameras dancing around – not to mention the sound booms, and the set!

Emphasising the broad scope of contributors to the launch of this new series, for the first twenty-six episodes we used nineteen different writers (or teams). Only seven wrote two scripts each; no one wrote more than two. We needed them all to be able to keep up with transmission – and we only just kept up, never getting ahead.

We were well into the scripting before an actual title was agreed. There were many suggestions, long since forgotten. Having scoured the dictionary and thesaurus, I favoured 'The Avengers' – but when I tried this on Sydney Newman he was not sure about it. He thought it smacked of revenge, and had to be convinced that avenging was something different. I got the dictionary and described for him that avenging was "retribution on behalf of another....", and, I believe this Robin Hood element convinced him.

Apart from the running characters, over 150 actors were used in featured roles – remembered with pleasure, and all deserving credit. 'Luvvies all' as the parlance goes.

The Avengers – First season (Hendry and Macnee as Keel and Steed)
26 episodes – running from January 7 to December 30, 1961*.

Story Editor
Patrick Brawn
Writers
Geoffrey Belman
& John Whitney (2)
Patrick Campbell (1)
Brian Clemens (2)
Lewis Davidson (1)
Fred Edge (1)
Terence Feely (2)
Richard Harris (2)
John Kruse (1)
Peter Ling & Sheila Ward (2)
John Lucarotti (1)
Max Marquis (1)
Berkeley Mather (1)
James Mitchell (2)
Eric Paice (1)
Lester Powell (1)
Ray Rigby
& Patrick Brawn (1)
Dennis Spooner (2)
Bill Strutton (1)
Gerald Verner (1)
Running Characters
Ian Hendry
Patrick Macnee
Directors
Peter Hammond (9)
Roger Jenkins (2)
John Knight (2)
Don Leaver (10)
Robert Tronson (1)
Dennis Vance (1)
Guy Verney (1)
Designers
Paul Bernard (2)
Patrick Downing (3)
Robert Fuest (9)
James Goddard (4)
Douglas James (1)
Robert Macgowan (1)
Alpho O'Reilly (5)
Voytek (1)

Don Leaver and Peter Hammond, between them, directed 19 of the first 26 episodes These two stalwarts were, throughout, the main strength of the team pulling together the on-air style of the series – always (often madly) working against the clock. But they never dropped their standards and, more often than not, extended the limits of live production possibilities. I was a fortunate producer to have them with me. Patrick Brawn was also the first story editor of the series, and played an important part in the creative team.

The first episode of *The Avengers* was transmitted at 10pm (not the best slot) on Saturday January 7, 1961 in the Midlands and the North, the two areas for which ABC had the weekend franchise. *Hot Snow* was written by Ray Rigby, based on a story by Patrick Brawn. It was directed by Don Leaver and designed by Alpho O'Reilly.

After the launch, the series ran for nine weeks in the Midlands and the North, and then made the grade for London (literally, as ATV's Lew Grade held the power in London for ITV's weekend programming). Not that Lew (Lord) Grade gave away the Saturday slot entirely. He was anxious to get his *Deadline Midnight* on the Network, and so a deal was done for *The Avengers* to network (all except Central Scotland) on alternate weeks with ATV's *Deadline Midnight*. Not ideal scheduling for either production, with each show having to carry its audience in fortnightly jumps – but seemingly sufficient unto the day.

And so, on March 18, 1961, while viewers in the Midlands and the North were watching episodes 10 and 11 of *The Avengers*, London and the rest of the network (except Central

* See Appendix II

Left: London edition cover
First *Avengers* in London
Episode 1. *Hot Snow* – March 18, 1961
Start of fortnightly transmissions

TV Times
Mar 12–18 1961

10.0 THE AVENGERS
starring
IAN HENDRY
in
HUNT THE MAN DOWN
Teleplay by
Richard Harris
Melissa Stribling
Also starring
PATRICK MACNEE
Cast includes:
John Steed .... **Patrick Macnee**
Paul Stacey .... **Maurice Good**
Dr. David Keel .... **Ian Hendry**
Carol Wilson .... **Ingrid Hafner**
Stella Preston .... **Melissa Stribling**
Nurse Wyatt .... **Susan Castle**
"The Avengers" theme composed and played by ***Johnny Dankworth***
Designed by ***Robert Fuest***
Produced by ***LEONARD WHITE***
Directed by ***PETER HAMMOND***
A woman's secret and a double-cross involve David Keel and Carol in a man-hunt under the city streets
An ABC Television Network Production

Above: Northern Edition listing
Episode 10. *Hunt The Man Down*
March 18, 1961 Weekly transmissions

Scotland) started to view episodes 1 and 2. This was necessary to show the new audiences how the relationship between Keel and Steed began.

By April 15, the new network audience came together to view the same episode, the twelfth to be made – *Dance with Death* – written by Peter Ling and Sheila Ward. It was directed by Don Leaver, and designed by James Goddard, another ABC Television designer who later became a fine director.

From that moment on, all working on the programme were watching the ratings. Nowadays, a show is regarded as a failure if it doesn't hit the jackpot right away. In the 1960s, there was an opportunity to nurse a show, to build an audience, to grow. The important element was to note the reaction from the inherited viewing figures for the previous show. If between 10pm and 11pm on a Saturday night the show held the inherited audience – no one had switched off – then that was positive at least. If the audience figures held, or grew from the inherited figure, then we were cheerful. If not, then worries began.

It is interesting to note, in respect of this opportuinuty to nurse a show in this environment, that *Coronation Street* did not make the Top Ten programmes for the network at that time, and it only appeared in the Top Ten for two of the ten regions.

On the network, *The Avengers* started slowly in this 'one-on, one-off', fortnightly schedule, gradually creeping into individual regional Top Tens. The critics started to look at it, but not all that enthusiastically. Philip Purser (*Sunday Telegraph*, 19/3/1961) wrote describing the John Steed role of Patrick Macnee as—

> the unlikeliest undercover agent in the annals of fiction … a whoopee cop whose expense sheet for call-girls and bottles of brandy alone would mean 1½d on the Westminster City rate.

He described the first episode, *Hot Snow,* as—

> a preposterous, camped-up bit of make-believe … more dispiriting than anything are the bloodless performances ... Ian Hendry [plays] as if he's hatching the 'flu.

However, after seven episodes on the Network, the series was brought forward from 10pm to the earlier transmission on Saturdays at 8.50pm for the high summer schedule. After four more episodes at this new time, the show crept into TAM's Network Top Twenty programmes at No.13, with just over 10 million viewers. That episode – *The Tunnel of Fear* – was written by John Kruse (the only episode he wrote of the twenty-six made with Keel and Steed). It was directed by Guy Verney and designed by James Goddard.

The Avengers
20. *The Tunnel of Fear*
Patrick Macnee as Steed in disguise

In that particular week, the top ratings were shared between Associated Rediffusion's *No Hiding Place* and ATV's *Harpers West One*, with just over 14 million viewers each. Even the Prime Minister broadcasting (week ending August 6) on both BBC and ITV could not make higher than the bottom of the Top Twenty programmes!

By the end of the summer schedule, 22 episodes of *The Avengers* had been made and transmitted in eight months. The first nine had been seen only in the Midlands and the North regions, and thirteen on the Network (Central Scotland joining later).

A welcome break of a few weeks ensued during that autumn. But on December 9, 1961, *The Avengers* was back on-air, with a long run planned. Now, however, it returned to weekly transmissions on Saturdays at 10pm, with a better opportunity to test the Network viewing.

By the second week of this run, *The Avengers* was at No.10 in the Top Ten of all programmes, with some 12 million viewers (even though Central Scotland still did not take the programme). The following episode rose to No.8 in the charts, and the next actually beat *Armchair Theatre*, which was a regular in the top placings. Thus, Sydney Newman had won the double with both of ABC's weekend drama productions – the single play and the series – achieving Top Ten acclaim: one on Saturday and one on Sunday.

Alas, Fate again took a hand. At the end of 1961, productions came to a halt when the British Equity union called the actors out on strike against the ITV Companies.

We seized the chance to get ahead with scripting, assuming that the strike would not last for long and that all would resume as before. A rare opportunity, a blessing in disguise – or, so we thought. But it was not to be so. The actors were out on strike for a long time, and with all the year's work building up, *The Avengers* lost momentum.

We were into 1962, and as the weeks and months passed, with no new production being possible, our hold on the leading actors began to slip. We could not count on them being available to us when the strike ended, so this script preparation time, at first so welcome, was now in danger of being wasted, considering that Hendry and Macnee might not be playing the leads. Indeed, several months into the strike it became known that Ian Hendry had secured himself a nice film contract – an offer that he couldn't refuse – and so he would not be playing Dr Keel any more.

We were not able to get it back on-air until eight months later. And things had to change. The curtain had come down on the original *Avengers*.

History repeated itself (echoes of the end of *Police Surgeon*) in that Sydney Newman again summoned us to one of his 'feet up on the desk' meetings and declared that we had to dream up a new character to play opposite Patrick Macnee's John Steed.

Patrick was only too pleased to take up the reins of his Steed. The dream factory was on the go again.

The necessity for the new character in *The Avengers* brought fresh ideas. It also presented problems in that further scripting had to await the creation of the new character to play opposite Steed.

The departure of Ian Hendry meant that Patrick Macnee would now take over top billing. That event has been Patrick's 'calling card' ever since, in fact for most of his professional life.

But what of this new character? Just about everyone in the department chipped in with suggestions. Even the Chairman, Sir Philip Warter, sent a memo at this time with his thoughts on drama series in general. Headed "Crime Series and Westerns", it read—

> No story programme can go far wrong if it contains, amongst others, the following ingredients:
>
> (1) a predominance of attractive, recognisably human characters
>
> (2) some wit, humour, and grace in the dialogue
>
> (3) something in the story to intrigue the intelligence, and
>
> (4) a constant awareness of the viewers' capacity for friendly affection for the screen characters.
>
> Violence sinks into place in such a context.

Whether those words actually were Sir Philip's own, or whether they might have been part of the Warner Brothers philosophy, they were good sense; and I nailed them to the masthead (pinned them up on the wall facing my desk), with copies sent to the team. A pity that such an instruction is not pinned up in the offices of drama producers and editors today.

The easy option was to replace the Dr Keel character with another similar male; but frankly that was to ignore the opportunity that presented itself to try something different.

I had nursed the idea that I'd like to try an actress in what, hitherto, had been almost entirely male territory.

We had some scripts prepared, expecting to continue with the Keel/Steed format, and I wondered – just idly wondered – how it would be if we cast an actress (changing the character name of course) to play that Keel role; with perhaps some minor adjustments but largely keeping to the role written for a man? In other words, a woman leading, and not supporting – active, not passive.

In respect of women, Shaw and Ibsen had long been breaking the mould in theatre. However, this was not at all obvious in mainstream television or even most theatre drama at that time. Ask any actress back then about the imbalance of 'M' roles to 'F' roles in the Samuel French catalogues of plays!

Sydney Newman had role models that inspired this development. He kept talking of Margaret Mead, the anthropologist. Also, it was the period of the horrors of the Mau Mau atrocities in Kenya, which hit the headlines with tales of women taking on the male roles in running and defending their homesteads in that country. A character more in that mode seemed attractive for us. That was a starting point, but a far cry from the character that eventually evolved, a character that was never the product of one creator. No one writer ever played god in that respect.

New-Zealander Marie Donaldson, our Press Officer, often augmented regular meetings of the team, in Sydney Newman's office (in the days when the drinks cabinet was not uncommon). Marie was a stalwart worker for the series and a great help to me, committed totally to this new format. She later played a large part in the successful fashion element publicity.

My basic concept of 'a woman playing the male role' could have gone very wrong without feminine input and points of view. It was necessary that a woman, an outside influence, was there to consider our deliberations and try to pull together our combined thoughts into a cohesive character description.

So, writer/editor Doreen Montgomery was brought in to attempt this task. It seems now that her time with us was no more than a few days, but I believe that actually it was a few weeks. But whatever, it did not work. She insisted on working from her home, which was inconvenient for us, as we needed instant recourse to her at any time. Her not being available in the studios meant that we wasted time. Her work with us quickly concluded when she put in a claim for expenses "for a new carpet" because "a writer" she was interviewing had burned a hole in her carpet with cigarette ash.

Michael Chapman (later of *The Bill* fame) who had by now taken over as Administrator of the Drama Department (in place of Arthur Johnston) was never, as Sydney Newman used to say, one to "give a sucker an even break". Michael took perverse pleasure in dealing with

Doreen Montgomery's claim for a new carpet. He exhibited a wicked sense of humour (greatly appreciated by me). I trust he will relate – perhaps with the help of his secretary of the time, Marion McDougall – some of his exploits when he writes his own memoirs. Doreen Montgomery left behind some notes, which we considered in our discussions.

Dave Rogers, in his book *The Complete Avengers* (Boxtree 1989) which had no input from me, published some of my internal memos at that time! It is interesting that Thames Television (who had presumably taken over the archives of ABC) allowed access to my memos, and for Dave Rogers to use them in his book, without as much as a word to me. Had I been consulted I might have been able to correct some of the inaccuracies in that book.

However, at this time of the conjuring of this new character to play opposite Steed, I am credited with "a new updated directive", which stated—

> Name: CATHERINE GALE [Cathy] Age 28/30.
>
> A widow. She is very attractive, intelligent and has a vital personality.
>
> Her BACKGROUND includes a good education. She has been to a University and gained an honours degree – BA/Anthropology.
>
> Her intention was to continue research for her PhD but she met and fell in love with a young farmer on holiday in London from his farm in Africa. The idea of sharing his life abroad appealed to her lively spirit of adventure.
>
> She married him.
>
> Her experiences during several years on their isolated homestead in Africa toughened her and she came to accept and thrive in their new environment. Carrying firearms was second nature to her and she became expert in their use. She learned to cope with the practicalities of isolated living as well as any man. She could equally well deal with the mechanics of a car engine as with the delivery of a baby.
>
> After several years her husband was killed on their farm.
>
> Cathy returned to this country and resumed her studies to pick up the threads of her original career. She gained a PhD in Anthropology.
>
> She has become a first-class photographer. She has presented a paper to the Royal Geographical Society on her recent photographic expedition to the Amazon. During this expedition she was separated from the party and attacked by natives: she escaped only after shooting three of them.
>
> She is essentially a strong lively personality. She is an individualist. She doesn't make friends too easily but such as she may have are friends for life. Her experiences may have made her a little withdrawn: she may even appear to be a somewhat lonely person. She may repress the sensual side of her nature but nevertheless all these characteristics only enhance our desire to get to know her better.
>
> She is sophisticated but not upper-class.
>
> She has a strong sense of humour.

Her flat reflects her personality and interests. There are some special firearms: some prizes of her expeditions: some of her African treasure and examples of her photography and equipment. There is nothing flambuoyant and the effect is not of luxury. It is obviously a woman's flat and strong touches of femininity are seen. In all good taste is evident.

In her 'undercover' activities she is fired by the desire to fight against evil and essentially help those who are victims of crime.

During her joint missions with Steed she will, more often than not, provide the moral attitude. She may not always approve of Steed's methods. His is the attitude of the ruthless professional and hers may be that of the crusading 'amateur', who cares deeply for the people involved.

We will care deeply about her.

So much for the directive before the event. The flesh and bones achieved in the casting, and the eventual playing of the role, created something a great deal more human.

This casting of Cathy Gale was critical. Having given up the easy option, the new character, replacing Keel – complete with change of sex – was to be tested in the casting. It was a make or break situation for the series, and no one knew that better than Sydney Newman, who had his usual strong views on the subject. The team, all of whom contributed, included: Dodo Watts, Head of Casting (who had been with ABC's Drama Department from the start, and a great expert); Tony Arnell (who had recently joined her staff); the directors; the story editors (John Bryce was the new energy in that department and was enormously helpful to me); Marie Donaldson (Press); and myself; and others. The net was spread wide. It had to be. No one was obvious for the role.

Honor Blackman as Cathy Gale in *The Avengers*

Eventually it came down to a short-list, which I presented to Sydney Newman for his consideration. This list consisted of about five names, which was a distillation of my long discussions and interviews, and particularly had the approval of the two directors – Peter Hammond and Don Leaver – who had done the bulk of the work on the series so far. At the top of my list was Honor Blackman, and at the bottom was Nyree Dawn Porter. Apart from these, they were not in any preferential order, and all on the list were strong contenders. However, Sydney certainly turned it into an order of his preference, putting Nyree Dawn Porter as his first choice and Honor Blackman at the bottom.

It looked like a head-on clash or back to find a compromise. Not that compromise ever fitted Sydney Newman's personality. But he did have an ear for sound argument, and he was big enough to delegate. As Head of Department, I always thought his great strength lay in his ability to give responsibility to the individual members of his team, and to support them. Of course, he would bawl and shout and harangue better than most – especially when he'd been proven right – but he did respect the talents of those he had engaged and gave them full responsibility in their respective areas.

This decision time for casting Cathy Gale coincided with Sydney Newman going on holiday. He left feeling, I'm sure, that I would cast Nyree Dawn Porter – or possibly that he would return to find us still discussing it. But I was left in no doubt that it was my decision, one for which I would carry the can. I cast Honor Blackman. When Sydney returned from his holiday to discover that Honor had been contracted, he was surprised – to put it mildly. However, with all his misgivings about the decision, from that moment on he gave his whole-hearted support and indeed led the development of that character until all of us – especially, Honor herself – made it succeed.

For me that casting was only the start of a mad dash to get the series back on-air. We could now go ahead with getting the scripts written; and, as ever, time was too short. The major problem was that we were due to start a continuous weekly run with production only just ahead of being on-air: and with no editing possibilities (except in dire emergency).

We had no way of knowing if this major change of style in the series would be acceptable to the audience that had approved of the Hendry/Macnee format. Winning an audience would have to start all over again.

Also, we had to hedge our bets in respect of the size of the roles that could be carried in each successive episode by the leading actors. We spread the load by introducing two further characters. Dr Martin King served as a bridge to cover the role of the Doctor from the earlier format until Cathy Gale took over. The other, who went by the professional name of Venus Smith, was a quite different female character in the form of a nightclub singer who would be useful in taking Steed into a world not likely to be frequented by Cathy Gale.

Dave Rogers, again in his *The Complete Avengers* (Boxtree), quotes a directive from me regarding this character—

> Name: VENUS SMITH.
>
> She is a vivacious nightclub singer.
>
> Her father was a barge owner and her early years were spent with her family on a barge travelling the canals of England. She is the youngest of three children. Her two brothers, much older than she, both emigrated when she was 12 years old. Her formal education was rather sporadic but her lack of academic prowess is compensated by her alert commonsense.

At 17 she decided to leave 'home'. In London she found ways of developing her natural talent to entertain. At first with amateur and semi-pro jazz groups and then, recently, club work.

The nature of her formative years has created a resilient character quite able and eager to cope with the rough and tumble of her career in show-business.

Her character is NOT that of a corny 'sex bombshell' type of entertainer. She is well able to put over a sexy number if necessary, but essentially she is a warm hearted, lovable girl. She may be earthy, but NEVER coarse or jaded.

Others feel they would like to take care of her.

She makes friends easily. She accepts people as she finds them. This does not mean that she is lacking in perception, but that she prefers to think well of people. She hates gossip.

She is by no means a 'goody-goody'; but she *is* a good person.

She has a special radiant quality which is her great attraction both on-stage and off.

She does not know anything of the true nature of Steed's work.

She is NOT an undercover agent. She is involved in Steed's escapades for several reasons. She does it for the excitement, for the opportunity to go places and do things otherwise not possible for her.

She likes Steed, and the aura of mystery surrounding him is an intriguing attraction for her.

There is NO suggestion of any 'affair' between them. If anything, she probably regards Steed as a 'special' elder brother. This attitude he finds flattering and he may feel that she 'needs looking after'. Very often, in fact, on her adventures she may indeed NEED Steed's timely aid to get her out of trouble.

Steed usually calls her 'Smith', but to her friends and associates at the club she is known as 'Vee'. 'Vee' for vitality!

The detail of such a directive indicated that the character wasn't just to be a convenient filler, but to be very capable of being the double with Steed as an alternative to Cathy Gale.

The casting of Venus Smith involved the connection of ABC Television (Iris Productions, the production arm) and the parent company, Associated British Picture Corporation. This was still the era when film studios maintained star contract artistes. And it was still the time when the film studio empires regarded television as little more than an irritation that would never be a threat to the cinema. Among the contract artistes was Julie Stevens. She had become something of a household name as the hostess in *The Sunday Break*.

Julie was a good young actress and very attractive. I was happy to provide her debut in television drama by casting her as Venus Smith. Indeed, I had intentions to build this character into a long-running element of *The Avengers*. However, after I ceased to be producer of the series, Venus Smith started to slip out of the stories. A missed opportunity.

In order to keep some sort of occasional contact with Steed's authority, above and behind him, some ill-defined characters were built in, known only by their code numbers. Each was used only sporadically: One-Ten (Douglas Muir) a few times; very rare appearances of One-Twelve (Arthur Hewlett); and One-Seven (Frederick Farley).

So much for directives. It was now over to the writers under the energetic guidance of Story Editor John Bryce. Of the first 14 episodes of this new format – introducing Cathy Gale, Venus Smith and Dr Martin King – no less than nine different writers (or teams) were used. Eric Paice – the only one to write for all three of the new characters – greatly contributed to this critical re-launch of the series

The Avengers – Second season (with Honor Blackman as Cathy Gale – launch run)
14 episodes – running from September 29 to December 29, 1962*

Story editor
John Bryce
Writers
Leonard Fincham (1)
John Gilbert (1)
Malcolm Hulke & Terrance Dicks (1)
Roger Marshall & Jeremy Scott (1)
Eric Paice (2)
Lester Powell (1)
Anthony Terpiloff & Brandon Brady (1)
John Manchip-White (1)
Martin Woodhouse (2)
Running Characters
Honor Blackman
Patrick Macnee
Julie Stevens

Directors
Jonathan Alwyn (3)
Peter Hammond (2)
Richmond Harding (4)
Don Leaver (4)
Kim Mills (1)
Designers
Paul Bernard (I)
Patrick Downing (2)
Robert Fuest (I)
James Goddard (2)
Terry Green (5)
Philip Harrison (I)
Robert Macgowan (I)
Timothy O'Brien (Head of Design)
Anne Spavin (I)

By late September 1962, following the actors' strike, we were back on-air – some nine months after the end of the Hendry/Macnee avenging. The first episode – *Mr Teddy Bear* – was transmitted on Saturday September 29, 1962, at 10.05pm. Written by Martin Woodhouse and directed by Richmond Harding, it introduced Honor Blackman as Cathy Gale. This episode was not transmitted at the same time throughout the network. The second was, but the whole of Scotland and the Border region were not included.

By the end of that run of 14 episodes, on December 29, 1962, *The Avengers* achieved, without full networking, No.8 in the TAM Top Twenty network programmes, with some 14 million viewers – beating *Armchair Theatre* (all networks) at No.13 that week. It was a week in which ABC had three programmes in the TAM Top Twenty, the other being *Thank Your*

* See Appendix II

Lucky Stars. All of which made Brian Tesler a happy New Year. By now, Brian had become Programme Controller and he wrote a memo—

> Please convey my congratulations to the entire AVENGERS team for getting the December 29th show into the TAM TOP TEN. To be placed 8th in spite of not being taken by the two Scottish stations is pretty good going...

It is interesting to look at the Top Twenty for that week. *Coronation Street* (Monday) was No.1, but its Wednesday edition was down at No.14. The BBC's *Hedda Gabler*, of all plays, beat *The Tommy Steele Show* (ATV). And *Christmas Night With The Stars* (BBC) only made No.20

The reviewers took a new look at the show.

Maurice Wiggin (*Sunday Times,* 7/10/1962) dismissed that week's *Armchair Theatre* play, *Afternoon of a Nymph,* as "a pretentious affair" – but described *The Avengers* as an—

> innocent little thing ... like 'em or leave 'em, they don't take themselves too seriously

Tony Gruner (*Kinematograph Weekly*, 11/10/1962) found it—

> excellent of its kind ... an outstandingly good tongue-in-cheek adventure thriller ... can be relied on to smother all BBC opposition...

American Variety thought that—

> Honor Blackman scored as the cucumber-cool Cathy, provocatively clad … energetic and satisfying

Television Mail ('Professional Eye on Programmes', 26/10/1962)—

> A further instance of the power of a good story emerges from a scan of the network ratings ... where, for the week in question Granada's only two entries, Coronation Street and ABC's two top-twenty items, *Armchair Theatre* and *The Avengers* are consistent with the trend ... drama is in the commanding position overall.

Peter Evans (*Sunday Express,* 10/12/1962) declared that—

> Honor Blackman has become the most sensuous actress on British television. As Catherine Gale, the judo-hep heroine … she has found an unsuspected earthiness and a brand of vitality that not only has melted her own dewy image but led television sex out of the playpen.

Barry Norman, in his TV column, considered Honor Blackman as one of only two—

> Lively Birds [who attract a] mass following every week … [having] so much impact that viewers automatically switch on whenever they appear.

(The other was Millicent Martin of *That Was The Week That Was* fame.)

Mark Gregory (*Today*, 3/11/1962) wrote—

> Patrick Macnee, as suave undercover-man John Steed … has been making the American TV private-eyes look as though they needed an eyebath.

And Tony Gruner thought Patrick's John Steed the—

> best adventure hero of them all.

The series also attracted attention for extending the technical boundaries at that time. Certainly, a great strength in the studio operation at Teddington was the close-knit working of both the programme departments and the technicians who were always happily challenging each other. Under such excellent heads of the technical operations as Bernard Greenhead, and later Howard Steele, all were united in the creative effort, a first-rate example of a continuing studio team, which is greatly missed today.

R. Howard Cricks, Hon FBKS, FRPS described his visit to Studio One at Teddington at the time of making an episode of *The Avengers*, comparing the old Warner Brothers film days with 1962 and video. He wrote—

> I sat in the control room and watched the crew at work. Bearded director, Don Leaver – vision mixer, Gordon Heskith – camera racks, Bob Godfrey – sound, John Tasker – Lighting, Peter Kew. The spacious floor was crowded with sets designed by Pat Downing, ranging from a cafe to a sandy beach ... Never a dull moment: while one set was being shot the (EMI) cameras on their (Vinten) pedestals, and the (Mole-Richardson) booms, were being moved for the next shot...
> Costumes were changed, make-up, hairdressers and wardrobe were kept busy ... And the result was that instead or taking months in production as a one-hour film would, "*The Avengers*" took weeks: instead of taking weeks on the floor, the stage was occupied only for days...

More than forty years later, the trend has reverted to taking months instead of weeks! Therefore more expensive, therefore less production, therefore less people employed, and thereby the unique 'life' of television drama is gradually throttled.

By the end of 1962, I had produced and broadcast forty episodes of *The Avengers* over two years – at which point (half way through the third season) I handed over to John Bryce who, up until then, had been story editor. All forty episodes* – from *Hot Snow* to *Dead on Course* – were introduced by that excellent theme music composed and recorded for us by the unique Johnny Dankworth.

*See Appendix II

Later connections with *The Avengers* – 1964-65

Elizabeth Shepherd – who had starred in a short run of *Armchair Mystery Theatre* in John Hopkins' *Time Out Of Mind,* July 19, 1964 – had been first choice to replace Honor Blackman when she left *The Avengers* in March 1964 at the end of the third season. (Honor changed from the peaches-and-cream, J. Arthur Rank, Worthing repish-charm-school starlet, to become, after her great success in *The Avengers*, the match for James Bond in *Goldfinger*, and much more.) Elizabeth Shepherd was cast, costumed and built into the newly created character of Emma Peel (M-appeal, the 'M' being for male!) and was into production – then dropped. The reasons for this have never been explained.

The Avengers had by this time moved into film production at Elstree and, with the exception of John Bryce, consisted of a new team under the charge of film producer, Julian Wintle. How the wheel turns! Julian had been, in my actor days, my staunchest supporter in getting me into film roles. He gave me my first and only screen test, and cast me in several of his productions. His early death was a great loss to British film making.

With Elizabeth Shepherd out of *The Avengers*, casting started all over again and there was a halt to production for many months. During that time, I produced an *Armchair Theatre* teleplay – *The Hothouse* by Donald Churchill – which included Diana Rigg's television debut. Duly impressed, Howard Thomas saw Diana Rigg as right for the role of Emma Peel. Her legendry success in that is now history.

The fourth season of *the Avengers* – introducing Emma Peel – started October 2, 1965.

That piece of casting and re-casting highlights the enormous differences in attitude and practice between the film studios and the television methods of that time. In television, we would never have considered many months of lay-off just waiting to make up our minds about casting. We had to deliver. It was eggs in the basket, and they had to be delivered, fresh, unbroken, on time, on-air. Cinemas could wait for their films but the unblinking eye of the 'box' in the homes throughout the land, had to be live each day.

CHAPTER 6

Out of this World – 1962

At the same time as looking after *The Avengers*, I was responsible for ITV's first science fiction series, an anthology called *Out of this World*, which ran on the Network on Saturday evenings at 10pm during the summer from June 30 to September 22, 1962.

While *The Avengers* was giving me headaches, this sci-fi series provided a welcome antidote. It was a great pleasure to make, getting away from today and exploring the unrealities (or so we thought) of tomorrow. An opportunity for the suspension of disbelief even in the here-and-now ambience of television.

We had the good fortune to get Boris Karloff (in real life the genial William Pratt) to introduce each episode. Not, I hasten to add, as a monster, but as Boris himself, with a touch of 'other worldliness'.

The preceding *Armchair Theatre* season had included a sci-fi story, *The Dumb Martian*, as an introduction to the *Out of this World* season following. (Originally, this was intended for my sci-fi series, but Sydney Newman decided he'd like it in his *Armchair Theatre*). Boris Karloff spoke a promo for my anthology—

> Tonight's play has taken us to Jupiter 4-2, the second moon of Callisto! A mere pebble in space, about forty miles across; four hundred and eighty-three million miles out of this world. "OUT OF THIS WORLD" the first play next Saturday evening, is called The Yellow Pill. If you do not find it a most unusual story, then my name isn't Boris Karloff

Irene Shubik was the story editor for this series, which she, like me, much enjoyed. I believe it must have been so, because later on when she joined the BBC, one of the first things she did was to make another sci-fi series (and indeed used one of the same stories again!).

The Yellow Pill was the first of the series, and it achieved over 11 million viewers, being also No.11 in the Network Top Twenty. The much-acclaimed *Z Cars* could only attain equal No.18, with a million less viewers, that week.

The Yellow Pill	June 30, 1962
Story by	Rog Phillips
Teleplay by	Leon Griffiths
Cast included	Nigel Stock, Richard Pasco, Peter Dyneley and Pauline Yates – with Gerald Turner and Robert Pitt
Director	Jonathan Alwyn
Designer	Robert Macgowan

The second in this series:

Little Lost Robot July 7, 1962

Story by	Isaac Asimov
Teleplay by	Leo Lehman
Cast included	Maxine Audley and Clifford Evans – with Gerald Flood, Roger Snowden, Murray Hayne and Haydn Jones
Director	Guy Verney
Designer	Douglas James

The next introduced a young actress, Jane Asher, who at sixteen had been acting since she was five. She played a teenager who stows away aboard a rocket into space in order to visit her brother on another planet.

***Cold Equations* – Peter Wyngarde as an astronaut, and Jane Asher as the girl who discovers that there is a rule which says all stowaways must be jettisoned!**

Cold Equations July 14, 1962

Story by	Tom Goodwin
Teleplay by	Clive Exton
Cast included	Peter Wyngarde and Jane Asher – with William Marlowe, Godfrey James, Patrick Holt, Peter Williams and Richard Gale
Director	Peter Hammond
Designer	Paul Bernard

We moved on with a play set among an Earth community living under a protective dome after years of nuclear war with the Outspace people. The fate of the planet depends on the success of a project headed by a scientist, when a warning is received that his personality may have been "taken over" by an enemy robot-bomb.

Impostor
Patrick Allen and John Carson

Impostor	July 21, 1962
Story by	Philip K. Dick
Teleplay by	Terry Nation
Cast included	John Carson, Glyn Owen, Patrick Allen and Angela Browne – with Keith Anderson, Philip Anthony, Colin Rix, Paul Bacon, Louida Vaughan, Alec Ross and June Shaw
Director	Peter Hammond
Designer	Robert Fuest

The following play – described as a "Take-over bid for the World!" – was the first that we had specially written for this series.

Botany Bay July 28, 1962

Teleplay by	Terry Nation
Cast included	Ann Lynn, Julian Glover, Jerry Stovin and Anthony Bate – with Aubrey Morris, William Gaunt, Storm Durr and Virginia Stride
Director	Guy Verney
Designer	Douglas James

Terry Nation went on to write for the *Dr Who* series, and became particularly famous for his creation of the Daleks.

Guy Verney was one of the earliest ABC directors doing (as we all had to in those days) almost any sort of programming before he could get into drama. I had known Guy from his early acting career and indeed, he had acted in Noel Coward's *Relative Values*, which I directed for its Canadian premiere at the Royal Alexandra Theatre in Toronto in the fifties. Alas, Guy died too young.

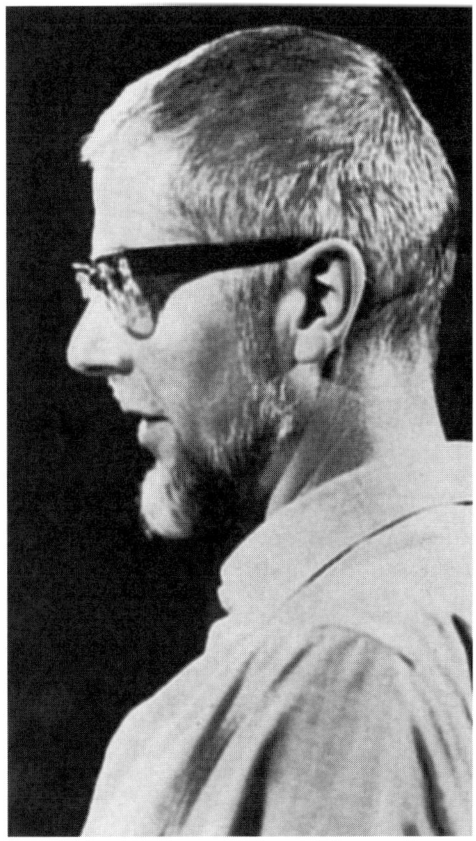

Director Guy Verney

A week later we presented:

Medicine Show August 4, 1962

Story by	Robert Moore Williams
Teleplay by	Julian Bond
Cast included	Alan MacNaughton, Carl Bernard and Jacqueline Hill – with Peter Madden, Vic Wise, Madeleine Burgess, Nigel Arkwright, Natalie Lynn, Elaine Millar, Ken Wayne, Margo Cunningham, Rory MacDermot, Martin Wyldeck and Raymond Adamson
Director	Richmond Harding
Designer	Adrian Vaux

Pictures Don't Lie August 11, 1962

Story by	Katherine Maclean
Teleplay by	Bruce Stewart
Cast included	Milo O'Shea and Gary Watson – with Roger Avon, Reginald Marsh, Blake Hunter, Madi Hedd, Kenneth Watson, David Hemmings, Richard Wilding, Frank Gatliff, Norman Claridge and Judy Cornwell
Director	John Knight
Settings by	Brian Currah

Judy Cornwell, playing a character called Butch, I imagine was not too worried about the misprint of her name (as "July") in *TV Times*. Also, for the first (of only two, I believe) in ABC's drama design credits, Brian Currah's design is described as "Settings by…" Brian, of course, has many excellent theatre credits to his name.

Pictures Don't Lie was one of the series that long remained in the memory of at least one viewer, for when I drove into my local garage thirty years later, the owner continued to remind me of that production, saying that he wished that he could get a video of it. Alas, unless anyone has harboured, under the bed or in the back of a cupboard, anything of *Out of this World*, I know of none in existence. A great pity. Had videos of that series been available, they would have had continuing interest, I feel sure. But, of course, in those days wiping the tape was more the norm than storing anything. Oh, ephemera!

This next play was the second of only two written specially for the series.

Vanishing Act August 18, 1962

Teleplay by	Richard Waring
Cast included	Maurice Denham and Jennifer Wilson – with William Job, Philip Grout, Joan Heath, Edward Dentith, Barry Wilsher, Ivor Bean, Cameron Miller, Terence Woodfield, John Frawley, Evan Thomas, William Buck, Richard Klee, Robert Lankesheer, David Lander, Sheena Marshe, Donald Webster, Derek Newark and Godfrey Quigley
Director	Don Leaver
Designer	Robert Fuest

Edward Dentith was a fellow thesp from my old acting days in the Arts Council company in Coventry.

Don Leaver had a large cast of some twenty for his sci-fi directing debut (like Peter Hammond and others he was waiting for *The Avengers* to get rolling again).

This story, set in the year 2033, posed the problem of not being able to distinguish between real and synthetic humans. A pretty classy clone! Who's your friend?

Divided We Fall August 25, 1962

Story by	Raymond F. Jones
Teleplay by	Leon Griffiths
Cast included	Ronald Radd, Bernard Horsfall, Ann Bell and Clive Morton – with John Barcroft, Norman Scace and Gerald Harper
Director	John Knight
Designer	Anne Spavin

Ape of London was adapted for television and renamed.

The Dark Star September 1, 1962

Novel by	Frank Crisp
Teleplay by	Denis Butler
Cast included	William Dexter – with Bruce Beeby, Rosemary Miller – also Barrie Cookson, Michael Hawkins, Vanessa Thornton, Jerome Willis, Ronald Wilson, Yvette Rees, Keith Pyott and John Moore
Director	Peter Hammond
Designer	Philip Harrison

The cast list had a strong commonwealth flavour about it, including Bruce Beeby (Australia), Rosemary Miller and Barrie Cookson (New Zealand).

The Dark Star gave Peter Hammond his third directing credit in this series, and another opportunity to entertain us with his distinctive visual style, working with designer Philip Harrison.

"Selective immigration to the newly-discovered planet, Kimon, the richest in this or any other galaxy – the new Klondike" was the environment of the following production, simply called:

Immigrant September 8, 1962

Story by	Clifford Simak
Teleplay by	Terry Nation
Cast included	Gary Raymond and Vivienne Drummond – with Jill Melford, Penelope Lee, Christine Shaw, Walter Glennie, Gary Hope, Ann Saker, John Horsley, Ian Shand, Bruce Boa, Frank Singuineau, Peter Layton, Jo Rowbottom and Donald Eccles
Director	Jonathan Alwyn
Designer	Voytek

The very special talent, Voytek, gave us his singular design version of the planet 'Kimon'.

The next is set in a community that has been several generations in space – set apart from Earth – and knowing of no other existence than their own. One of my favourites:

Target Generation		September 15, 1962
Story by	Clifford Simak	
Teleplay by	Clive Exton	
Cast included	Dinsdale Landen, Susan Maryott and Paul Eddington – with Michael Golden, Hugh Janes, Ann Tirard, Philip Madoc and Bert Palmer	
Director	Alan Cooke	
Designer	Douglas James	

It provided my first opportnity to work with Director Alan Cooke.

This anthology bowed out with a lighter comedy sci-fi to relieve the seriousness of the genre.

The Tycoons		September 22, 1962
Story by	Arthur Sellings	
Teleplay by	Bruce Stewart	
Cast included	Geraldine McEwan – with Charles Gray and Ronald Fraser – also John Cater, Patricia Mort, Edwin Apps, Sheree Winton, Jill Curzon and Alastair Williamson	
Director	Charles Jarrott	
Designer	Patrick Downing	

Patrick Downing later became the Head of the Design department.

Sci-fi is an acquired taste, but fortunately, with Irene Shubik's story guidance, the mix of *Out of this World*, worked well. And the reviewers liked it.

H.F. Hall (*Yorkshire Evening Post,* 25/7/1962) wrote—

> If there is any handing out of prizes after the present crop of space-fiction series, the only question will be which of the BBC's two efforts, The Andromeda Breakthrough and The Big Pull will come second to ITV's Out Of This World, the most accomplished thing of its kind TV has yet produced… well-schemed scripting and disciplined production … In shape, form, lucidity and sheer ingenuity it could not provide a greater contrast to The Andromeda Breakthrough, a tortuous tale which left me bewildered.

Tony Gruner (*Kinematograph Weekly*, 9/8/1962)—

> …the series is certainly the most intelligent and best written of its genre since Quatermass … and Leonard White, producer of the series, justifies an accolade for providing rich production values from what might appear to have been a limited budget…

And referring to the budget for the series, it is revealing to see that the average above the line cost for each episode was just over £5,000. Today, a comparable one-hour drama would be budgeted at least thirty times as much, and likely much more. Of the average ('above the line') total per episode, the cast took just under half that cost, and the writing slightly over one-tenth (ranging from just ovcr £400 to around £750 each).

Peter Black wrote in the *Daily Mail* (17/9/1962)—

> The whole of this series has been tremendously better than expectations of a Saturday night entertainment.

In *The Times* (4/8/1962) 'From our Special Correspondent' wrote—

> ...the level of writing and direction has been encouragingly high ... Out Of This World may well help to banish forever the view of summer as a time when just anything will do.

But on a personal level, and a message I have cherished ever since, came in the form of the old-time telegram, which read—

> WONDERFUL SHOW OUT OF THIS WORLD PLEASE CONVEY
> JOYOUS CONGRATULATIONS FOR WONDERFUL
> ENTERTAINMENT AND KEEP SOME FOR YOURSELF
> SINCERELY – MICHAEL BENTINE

That was accolade enough for me.

So, as 1962 drew to a close, and in less than three years of drama at Teddington, I had produced seventy-six one-hour shows. It hadn't all been sweetness and light. I got very close to throwing it all in at one stage.

I was nursing a show through to recording, and things were pretty tense. We had just reached the final run-through. That was the stage when time was critical. Final adjustments had to be made, and all was delicately poised. Peter Hammond was directing, and as always with his unique style he was stretching the limits. However, that somewhat unreal calm reigned in the control room, when Sydney Newman arrived on the scene, and sounded off about some shots to which he objected. Not to me quietly; not to Peter Hammond directly; but for all and sundry to hear. Sydney was noisy. And unsubtle.

The delicate association of Producer and Director, at a crucial time, was destroyed in a few moments. I was livid, and I walked out.

I got into my car and drove like a bat out of hell away from Teddington to breathe the fresh air of Sussex-by-the-Sea. As I got home, I realised that, even though my authority had been usurped, I had done an unforgivable thing in walking away from my responsibility.

I did not expect to return to ABC, and did not go back the next morning. Soon the phone rang and Michael Chapman (Sydney Newman's Administrator) was calling, telling me not to be an idiot and to forget it: "You know Sydney by now!"

After persuasion – Michael was being the perfect diplomat (a role not natural to him but he could act it very well, and he was a good friend) – I agreed to meet with him and talk, but I would not immediately go back to the Studios. We met in the pub next door and, sitting on the banks of Teddington Weir, Michael finally persuaded me to return and carry on.

No other person ever mentioned the incident. Sydney Newman carried on exactly as though nothing had happened between us, and indeed, I wonder if he ever did know what had happened!

To the day he died, he has certainly never recalled my walkout – and I'm sure that Peter Hammond never changed the shots.

In retrospect, I often wonder whether Sydney had a bad day, because it was not typical of him to behave like that. Certainly, we had 'words' from time to time, not always subdued, but generally kept between just the two of us and in good spirits. And, as I've said before, Sydney did pay me the greatest compliment by delegating authority.

On that one occasion, I thought my walkout was the end of an association. If I had stayed away, I would have missed the next and very exciting development: and I'm thankful that Michael Chapman persuaded me otherwise.

In 1962, considerable changes had been taking place at ABC. 1963 was going to be different. Sydney Newman was leaving ABC to join the BBC!

PART TWO

Armchair Theatre

The Leonard White Years

CHAPTER 7

Armchair Theatre – 1963 – Seventh Season

I Take the Hot Seat

Sydney Newman had been used to working directly under Howard Thomas (Managing Director), but by now Brian Tesler, who had been brought in specially to develop 'Light Entertainment', had been made Programme Controller.

Although I believe that Howard Thomas had been quite happy to continue with ABC being dominantly a drama producing company for the Network, leaving Lew Grade's ATV to be the major provider of light entertainment, the situation altered when ATV started to want some of the drama slots as well. ABC responded by wanting some of the LE programming, and Brian Tesler was the man to lead this change of emphasis at ABC.

It was a change of emphasis obviously noted when, while away on holiday, Sydney Newman lost his weekly slots and *Armchair Theatre* was changed to fortnightly transmissions. I believe that was the point where Sydney began to look elsewhere. When he left at the end of 1962, it was quite sudden. He had been invited to be Head of Drama Group at BBC Television.

It is reported that he took a drop in salary – but, whatever, he now headed the largest TV drama-producing group, and that was indeed a fitting appointment to mark his successes at CBC in Canada and ABC in the UK. He was the most talked about producer of television drama in the country, and now he was in the position to influence the largest output.

Changes at ABC came quickly. Brian Tesler decided that the Drama department would have a separate head and separate producer of *Armchair Theatre*. Sydney Newman, under Howard Thomas, had combined these two functions very successfully. It was a 'tight ship' (though not in the sense of organisation at Associated Rediffusion, where all was run from the 'poop deck').

Brian gave me the option to be Head of Department or Producer in charge of *Armchair Theatre*. I had a choice! As I did not want to move further into the administration side of things, it was an easy decision. Moving from being a director to being a producer was far enough, and I'd managed to hold on to my concept of being an 'Artistic Producer': (a term now much later adopted by impresario, Bill Kenwright, in theatre). I surely wanted to keep as close as possible to the creative elements of making individual programmes.

I was very grateful for the opportunity to be in charge of what was at that time ITV's major single teleplay series. Also, I saw that when Sydney Newman got into his stride at the BBC, the competition would be fiercer, and I welcomed that challenge. (It wasn't long before Sydney got even with me for casting Honor Blackman instead of Nyree Dawn Porter in *The Avengers*, when he had Nyree starring in the very successful *Forsyte Saga*).

The new Head of Department was George Kerr. George was a successful writer and editor from the earliest days of ABC, when the Drama Supervisor was Dennis Vance. Indeed, he adapted for television Dorothy Brandon's *The Outsider*, the very first *Armchair Theatre*, transmitted on July 8, 1956. I believe I got on very well with George (though I never knew what he thought of me) and I was sorry and surprised when after not too long he left ABC. I don't know the reason for this. He was entirely helpful and we put together some excellent shows under his headship.

There were one or two productions already in the pipeline of *Armchair Theatre*, and only a day or so after Sydney left I found myself in the control room, Studio One at Teddington, in my new role – or at least looking after this new challenge.

By the end of the first week in 1963, I saw Kenneth Jupp's *Blue and White* recorded. We left Sydney Newman's credit intact.

Blue and White		January 6, 1963 (9.35pm)
Teleplay by	Kenneth Jupp	
Cast included	James Villiers, Frances White and David Saire	
Director	Philip Saville	
Designer	Voytek	(Produced by Sydney Newman)

I had more to do with the next two productions, but as they had already been in the pipeline, I took no credit.

The Hot Potato Boys		January 20, 1963 (9.35pm)
Teleplay by	Alun Richards	
Cast included	Gerald James, Paul Curran, John Bluthal, Mary Miller, Betty Baskcomb, Anthony Sharp, Margery Mason and Danvers Walker	
Director	Charles Jarrott	
Designer	Terry Green	(No Producer credit given)

Into The Dark		February 3, 1963 (9.35pm)
Teleplay by	Ken Taylor	
Cast included	Peter Sallis, Norman Rossington and Wendy Craig	
Director	William T. Kotcheff	
Designer	Timothy O'Brien (Head of Design)	(No Producer credit given)

Norman Kay, who contributed considerably to *Armchair Theatre*, composed the special music for this production.

Into The Dark achieved No.6 in the national ratings with over 6.9 million homes. (Nowadays the ratings are in 'viewers' not 'homes').

I had taken over a production schedule which stipulated just 35 days from 'Availability of Script' to the drama being completed ready for transmission. The pattern was:–

Day 1	Script available/legal security/budgets
Day 7	Director discusses script with Designer
Day 11	Billings
Day 16	Synopsis to ITA
Day 22	Rehearsals start
Day 35	Recording date

That was the standard. Any extension of the pattern was a rarity and undesirable. With the on-air schedule as it was, it meant that generally several productions were in progress simultaneously, but at different stages.

I got into my stride with the third production of that year.

It all began on January 3, when we welcomed Carroll Baker to the UK with a meeting at the Connaught Hotel. She had arrived from the USA.

The Paradise Suite February 17, 1963 (9.35pm)

Teleplay by	Robert Muller
Cast included	Carroll Baker, Sam Wanamaker – with Ian Holm, Derek Smith and special guest Jess Conrad
Director	Philip Saville
Designer	Voytek

A glossy lift-off for my first year of nearly seven in charge of *Armchair Theatre*. Carroll Baker made the front cover of *TV Times*, and the press had copy galore, this being her first TV role since her Oscar-winning performance in Tennessee Williams' film *Baby Doll*. And it was here in England, for us, at *Armchair Theatre*.

Robert Muller's screenplay was dubbed "this thinly-disguised story of Marilyn Monroe" but Muller just considered his leading character 'Lena Roland' as an amalgam of film stars, who suffer from the loneliness of self-love.

We recorded the production on January 23, 1963 and, as perhaps to be expected in such a show, rehearsals didn't always go smoothly. Carroll Baker, deeply into her character, transferring her part to real life "stormed out of rehearsals" (vide *Daily Express*). But not for long. Philip Saville, using his best camera-side manner, harnessed the temperaments to great advantage and (with some help from George Kerr and myself playing the diplomats) created a show that the audience obviously liked. The ratings built on its inherited figure, being viewed in some 7,308,000 homes (something over 18 million viewers) and was No.5 in the Top Ten programmes for that week.

Robert Tee (*Daily Sketch* 18/2/1963) put it all in context—

> When TV tries its hand at beating the big drum of Hollywood-style ballyhoo, it often falls flat on its 405-line behind [we were still black-and-white]
> ... numerous offerings ... which appeared to have the same three-letter word in common. Ugh! So, when last night's "Armchair Theatre" play "The Paradise Suite" skimmed over the horizon it seemed reasonable to reach for the anti-ballyhoo goggles and start dusting out the TV fallout shelter. It had all the suspicious signs. Beautiful Hollywood star Carroll Baker, with "Oscar" in handbag; play by Robert Muller; gowns by Balmain; hairstyle by Francke. I'm happy to say the suspicions went unconfirmed. Here was a clever small-screen portrait of a big-screen subject ...
> Blonde Baker was everything she was ballyhooed up to be—and more. Subtly aided by a shrewd cast and smooth-as-smooth production. Briefly, this was one built-up bombshell that went off.

Clifford Davis, in the *Daily Mirror* (18/2/63) wrote—

> No wonder Carroll Baker agreed to fly over here and make her television debut in Robert Muller's play ...
> She had only the script to go on—ABC-TV sent it to her in New York. One reading was enough for the astute Miss Baker to make up her mind. For this thinly disguised story of Marilyn Monroe gave her, as an actress, a tremendous role as a mixed-up, insecure Hollywood star in love with herself ...
> Her love scene on a couch with Sam Wanamaker (a shrewdly restrained performance here as a Press photographer who really understood her dilemma) was searing stuff. Off-hand, I can't think of any English actress who could have put over such a performance—uninhibited, reckless and savage in its penetrating truth. Pop-singer, Jess Conrad, made an impressive debut.

James Green (*London Evening News,* 18/2/1963) in his 'Watching Brief'—

> Whatever four figure sum ABC paid for Carroll Baker to star in "Paradise Suite" they got value for money. Easy on the eye, she gave a hypnotic performance as Lena Roland, full-chested and empty-headed Hollywood siren. Philip Saville's direction was outstanding and Voytek's set, a masterpiece...

But Mr Green wasn't so sure about the script, describing it as—

> A phoney story about phoney people. Leonard White's production was Hollywood glossy and actors Sam Wanamaker and Jess Conrad merit some of the honours. But it was Miss Baker's night.

The Paradise Suite
Carroll Baker (as Lena Roland) with Sam Wanamaker (as photographer Frank Adler)

Internally, in ABC, it was appreciated by 'top brass'. A memo from Brian Tesler read—

> ... Sir Philip Warter [Chairman] told Howard Thomas and myself that this was in his opinion the best television play production for years, and passed on his warm congratulations.

I still cherish the book (*Cape Cod Lighter* by John O'Hara) that Carroll Baker and her husband Jack Garfein gave me as they left to return to the USA.

After that, I got back to the more usual fortnightly fare. Norman King's *The Cruel Kind* admirably made the adjustment from Hollywood gloss to the firmly grounded Midlands milieu. This script was the last of a trilogy by Norman King, all directed by Alan Cooke, and all set in Midlands pubs. The other two – *Night Stop* and *The Fishing Match* – had been transmitted in 1962.

The Cruel Kind
Fanny Carby and Percy Herbert (as the publican and his wife), Ronald Radd (as the gypsy) and Michel Ray (as a boy being hunted by local men). A disused cock-pit in an old country inn is the setting for much of the action in this story

The Cruel Kind	March 17, 1963 (9.35pm)
Teleplay by	Norman King
Cast included	Percy Herbert, Fanny Carby, Ronald Radd – with Paul Dawkins, Michael Robbins, Tracey Lloyd, Charles Denville – and introducing Michel Ray
Director	Alan Cooke
Designer	Assheton Gorton

Ronald Radd's appearance in this play followed his four years as Doolittle in *My Fair Lady* on Broadway.

Then came a rare excursion into television by author Angus Wilson (ABC had an 'exclusive' on his television work). Written specially for *Armchair Theatre*, this play was described as "a tongue-in-cheek romp with a satirical bite".

The Invasion
Frances Rowe, Athene Seyler, Eleanor Summerfield and Patrick Wymark – with the ashes of the Earl of Swent

The Invasion	March 31, 1963 (9.35pm)
Teleplay by	Angus Wilson
Cast included	Frances Rowe, Athene Seyler, Patrick Wymark and Eleanor Summerfield – and Clive Morton – with Bill Shine, Gordon Phillott and James Cossins
Director	Charles Jarrott
Designer	James Goddard

Character names such as Charles and Clarissa Hedge-Hacking and W/Cdr Flighty signposted a style that was not the norm for *Armchair Theatre*, and certainly not in the vogue of the 'angry young men' of the time. It was perhaps a tentative move to widen the brand image of this anthology, but the audience was not too sure about the satirical style.

Our next transmission date coincided with Easter Sunday, and something 'a little more serious' befitting that anniversary was called for. This was one of those rare occasions when *Armchair Theatre* presented a teleplay that was not specially commissioned.

Power and Glory
Alfred Marks as the Marshal who rules a dictator state

Power and Glory	April 14, 1963 (9.35pm)
Written by	Karel Capek
Cast included	Alfred Marks, Paul Daneman, Alfred Burke and Gerald Cross – with Gerald Sim, Alun Edwards, Philip Stone, Mavis Walker, Paul Bacon, Daniel Thorndike, Edward Kelsey and Lynn Redgrave
Director	Jonathan Alwyn
Designer	Assheton Gorton

Lynn Redgrave made her television debut.

This play had impressed me greatly in earlier days, and I had made an adaptation. It seemed particularly suitable as an Easter plea for peace. Alfred Marks – playing a very different role from his 'comic' image – took the lead of 'the Marshal', which had been played by Oscar Homolka in the original London stage production.

Easter over, we moved into the homely atmosphere of a Stephen Lewis script in which the author also played the lead of the London East Ender that he knew so well. Don Leaver was in his element directing this production with a cast who demonstrated that 'sparrers can sing'. It achieved No.4 in the ratings.

Wagger April 28, 1963 (9.35pm)

Teleplay by	Stephen Lewis
Cast included	Stephen Lewis, Jennifer Wilson, Bert Palmer, George Moon and guest star Juliet Mills – with Tim Pearce, Jo Rowbottom, Ann Tirard and Clare Kelly
Director	Don Leaver
Designer	Douglas James

Maintaining variety in the Sunday night ITV drama, we presented a story set in Queensland.

Jungle Juice
Derek Godfrey (National Theatre contract player making his first appearence in an ITV play) as the bank manager suffering from the effects of the illicit brew – with Jane Barrett holding his head

Jungle Juice May 12, 1963 (9.35pm)

Teleplay by	Bruce Stewart
Cast included	Derek Godfrey, Kenneth J. Warren, Jane Barrett, Redmond Phillips, Bill Kerr, Lloyd Lamble – with Morris Perry, Walter Sparrow, Gwenda Wilson and Ed Devereaux
Director	Guy Verney
Designer	Assheton Gorton

Armchair Theatre's production of *The Blood Knot* by Athol Fugard – recorded May 18, 1963 – was never transmitted. A great disappointment to me. The BBC picked up the rights and made their own version, which was screened.*

Australian connections continued in the next production: 74-year-old Ethel Gabriel travelled from Sydney to play the lead.

The Wednesday Caller	May 26, 1963 (9.35pm)
Teleplay by	Lynne Reid Banks
Cast included	Ethel Gabriel and Fiona Hartford – with Jeremy Lloyd, Derek Nimmo, Gwynne Whitby, Rita Webb, Patricia Samuels, Jeremy Wilkin and Suzanne Vasey
Director	Charles Jarrott
Designer	Voytek

It was a lovely performance, introducing a young and very talented actress, Fiona Hartford, 19 years old and just out of drama school.

This production marked the first time during my period with *Armchair Theatre* that the story editor achieved a credit in the *TV Times* billing. (Many years later, we still have to fight to get important credits recognised.) Irene Shubik was described as 'Script Editor', which was not accurate. When Sydney Newman set up his story editors (and they were the basic strength of the department) he insisted that essentially they were the seekers after new writing, new writers... the stories. They were not there to re-write. Therefore, the job title of Story Editor was very important.

Those story editors who worked throughout the years with me – John Bryce, Richard Bates, Norman Bogner (an American who eventually returned to the USA to become a successful novelist), Brian Brooke, Clive Hirshhorn, Robert Banks Stewart, Terence Feely, and Irene Shubik – continued to work in this way. I always regarded them as the writers' friends: playing advocate, representing the writer and 'selling' them to me. Certainly they were not acting as representatives of me and my ideas, or even their own, but always searching for broader concepts and encouraging creative talent.

So far as I was concerned, the story editors had to be my 'open door', and it always was open. It had to be, to maintain the continuing on-air commitments. If at any one time I did not have at least five new scripts ready to 'go' (or as near as damn it) stacked in my office, I had sleepless nights. The nightmare was always of not having a script – not having a show – having nothing for 'on-air'. And I carried the can.

*See Appendix I

This, my first season of '*Armchair*', ran on through the summer without the conventional break for the end-of-pier popular (or the "lets get rid of it in the summer schedule" philosophy) and fortunately maintained its healthy place in the ratings. (ATV, on alternative weekends was now providing *Love Story*.)

In his his debut for us, Christopher Morahan directed a rare story of rivalry between a steeplejack and a boastful spiderman of the Mohawk Club (able to climb over 1,500 feet).

The Monkey and the Mohawk	June 9 1963 (9.35pm)
Teleplay by	Donal Giltinan
Cast included	Ron Moody, Brenda Bruce and Harry Locke
Director	Christopher Morahan
Designer	Roy Stannard

Next: a young man plays a sly confidence trick on two old ladies and their brother in a play by actress Gwen Cherrell.

The Push-Over
Frank Pettingell as the joke-loving brother and Jane Eccles as his long-suffering sister

The Push-Over	June 23, 1963 (9.35pm)
Teleplay by	Gwen Cherrell
Cast included	Frank Pettingell, Gillian Lind, Jane Eccles and James Beckett – with David Warner, Nan Braunton, Pauline Delaney and Beatrice Shaw
Director	Peter Hammond
Designer	Assheton Gorton

With a setting in the South of France, our next story focussed on an older woman falling in love with a much younger man. Unusual for that time; not so earth-moving now.

Late Summer **International star Constance Cummings as the woman who escapes for a holiday in France with her best friend's son, and John Stride as the young man**

Late Summer July 7, 1963 (9.35pm)

Teleplay by	Alexander Baron
Cast included	John Stride and Constance Cummings – with Yvonne Coulette, Makki Marseilles, Joan Heath, Gerard Heinz, Denis Carey, Roland Brand and David Futcher
Director	Reginald Collin
Designer	Voytek

Late Summer hit the front cover of *TV Times* with the young John Stride and the international star, Constance Cummings.

Reginald Collin had been working in the Features department of ABC for some time, and this gave him his first opportunity to move into *Armchair Theatre*.

A musical evening in middle-class Edinburgh came next. Actor Paul Curran described this story of 'behind the lace curtains and facade of gentility – a place that beats with furious passion', as being "a bubble of fun. One of the funniest plays I've ever been in". It was by Ronald Mavor (son of the famous Scottish doctor-playwright, James Bridie) once a doctor himself, then a journalist – now turned playwright.

A Little Night Music
Paul Curran, Lally Bowers, Barbara Couper, Geoffrey Whitehead and Fulton Mackay

A Little Night Music July 22, 1963 (9.35pm)

Teleplay by	Ronald Mavor
Cast included	Barbara Couper, Paul Curran, Lally Bowers, Fulton Mackay and Geoffrey Whitehead
Director	Alan Cooke
Designer	Paul Bernard

A Little Night Music provided an unexpected lesson. It went over big in Scotland, getting to the unheard of heights for a single play of being No.1 in the Top Ten of all programmes for that week in Central Scotland, while the rest of the UK didn't agree. Overall, it was No.18 – a clear indication of the differences north and south of the network in respect of entertainment. Because of that imbalance of audiences, I later turned down a fine play from Bill Bryden – *Willie Rough* – which was set in his native land. I suggested that it ought to be made by one of the Scottish companies. Needless to say, his work went on to great success elsewhere.

For the August Bank Holiday weekend – one of the black spots of the year for drama – we tried a "happily farcical, no-message comedy" by Donal Giltinan (his second work for me in *Armchair Theatre*). The setting was a corsetiere's salon, 'The Firm Foundation'!

The Snag
Barry Ingham and June Barry

The Snag August 4, 1963 (9.35pm)

Teleplay by	Donal Giltinan
Cast included	Derek Francis, Gwen Nelson and Barrie Ingham – with Patsy Rowlands, Judith Furse, June Barry and Arthur Lowe
Director	Jonathan Alwyn
Designer	Anne Spavin

However, farce – here played by a cast of experts – is a very difficult target to hit on television, particularly when recorded 'as live' and without benefit of audience (actual or canned). And with the normal Bank Holiday dip in viewing, we dropped to No.19 in the ratings. Even that, however, was something like just under 10 million viewers.

Following that, we returned to rather more serious subject matter: a generation clash in the art world between a famous father and his son.

Living Image
Alexis Kanner, Elizabeth MacLennan and James Villiers

Living Image August 18, 1963 (9.35pm)

Teleplay by	James Broom Lynne
Cast included	Alec Clunes, James Villiers, Alexis Kanner and Elizabeth MacLennan – with Kynaston Reeves and Clive Colin Bowler
Director	Philip Saville
Designer	James Goddard

Philip Saville directed in his unique, great style, while James Goddard provided excellent settings. The viewers started to come back from their holidays.

A Kind of Kingdom September 2, 1963 (9.35pm)

Teleplay by	Hugh Leonard
Cast included	Norman Rodway, Patrick Bedford, Maureen Davis, Pauline Delaney and Patrick McAlinney – with Brian Waldron, Jim Fitzgerald, Kevin McHugh, Desmond Perry and Sheena Marshe
Director	Guy Verney
Designer	Terry Green

I was particularly pleased to do this play because in September 1960 Sydney Newman had sent me to Ireland to view the Dublin International Theatre Festival and to look at the new writers and writing. There, at the Eblana Theatre, I saw a Dublin Group Theatre Company production of a new play by Hugh Leonard – *A Walk on the Water* – co-directed by Godfrey Quigley and Jim Fitzgerald. I was much impressed with the writing and the performances, but at that time did not think it suitable for a TV version. But in my report to Sydney Newman, I strongly recommended "this author might well be encouraged to do something specifically for us". Looking back at my old memo I also see the Group Company was finding it impossible to continue, and I wished "that it could come under one of ABC's schemes to give assistance". It didn't, but certainly, this writer, and several of the Irish actors, did benefit from working many times with ABC later.

A Kind of Kingdom
Maureen Davis and Norman Rodway

In his last season of *Armchair Theatre*, Sydney produced *The Irish Boys*, which he had commissioned Hugh Leonard to write. *A Kind of Kingdom* was a sequel to that story, using the same lead characters 'four years later', and it was the first of three by Hugh Leonard that I produced.

I had to struggle to persuade Philip Saville to direct this next play. Always looking for the more spunky and active script, he found this one not at all attractive with its house-proud North Country husband-and-wife conflict stuck in the confines of one room. However, I felt that Philip would enhance the very restrictions of this script with its deep, introverted revelations of character. He did, and provided a high-rated (No.5 in the Top Ten) Sunday night drama to finish the seventh season.

For Assheton Gorton – used to working with big and impressive settings – this seemed a puny task. Together with Philip Saville, he conceived a set that enabled the shooting of direct reversals, even in a recording 'as live'. That in itself was innovative at that time.

The Front Room: **Betty Baskcomb and Richard Pearson in a marriage threatened by the wife's obsession with cleaning the house – with [centre] Bryan Mosley and Mary Chester**

The Front Room September 15, 1963 (9.35pm)

Teleplay by	Robert Storey
Cast included	Richard Pearson, Betty Baskcomb, Betty Marsden, Bert Palmer, Bryan Mosley, Mary Chester and Richard Turner
Director	Philip Saville
Designer	Assheton Gorton

Actor Richard Pearson was never honoured enough. Brian Mosley, thirty years later, still gave us that essential touch of truth in Coronation Street.

CHAPTER 8

Armchair Theatre – 1963-64 – Eighth Season

Just About the Best Team...

The new season of *Armchair Theatre* opened without a break at the start of the autumn schedule. As usual it was marked by a welcome get-together with the press at one of those 'launch' affairs – often in Hanover Square – that starts about lunchtime and peters out around 4.30pm. I always enjoyed meeting the press on those occasions. Whether for or against, it was constructive and upbeat, and there were always good stories going around. Invariably we had the excellent and attractive talents of the thesps and writers with us to engage the cameras and make early copy. This was in the time when advance viewing of the shows was not possible, as it is now. Therefore, the whole session was based upon handouts, chat and interviews – laced with as much refreshment as anyone wanted. The skills of our Publicity and PR department under Barry Wynne, Marie Donaldson, George Spackman and Joan Davey made these affairs work well.

Unusually, we opened this season with an adaptation rather than a specially commissioned work. I was much attracted to the stories of Ray Bradbury – bizarre tales but always with a human face. Originally called *The Dwarf*, it was adapted and renamed *Mr Big* (short for Mr Bignell). Mr Big enriches his life in a Hall of Mirrors…

Mr Big	September 29, 1963 (9.35pm)
Story by	Ray Bradbury
Teleplay by	Ken Taylor
Cast included	George Claydon, Peter Vaughan and Rosemary Leach – with Aubrey Morris, Hilary Martyn, Clive Colin Bowler and Frank Seton
Director	Philip Saville
Designer	Voytek

George Claydon, making his debut as a straight actor, was first-rate as Mr Big, with Rosemary Leach playing her first major television role, giving a lovely performance. Peter Vaughan also starred (how the world turns: Peter was my understudy in the days when I was still trying to be an actor).

Philip Saville, let loose among the Hall of Mirrors, found his release from *The Front Room* and directed a most sensitive production; and with Voytek's design made certain that we didn't look through a glass darkly. With hindsight, *Mr Big* was one of my favourites. But, at the time, of course, I could not afford the luxury of favourites. Every production had to have equal emphasis.

George Claydon
and Rosemary Leach
in *Mr Big*

FESTIVAL OF
WORLD TELEVISION
LONDON

Mr Big A·B·C TELEVISION LTD.

was selected for showing
at the Festival
1963

David Perry – tried, tested and successful – wrote the second production. *Little Doris* was even more outrageous than his previous intriguing macabre piece, *The Trouble With Our Ivy*, written for Sydney Newman. Little Doris – a sea-monster, kept as a house pet – devours Auntie Flo!

Gladys Henson, Vivienne Martin, Bryan Mosley, Charles Lamb and Gretchen Franklin as the family having a conference about Little Doris

Little Doris	October 13, 1963 (9.35pm)
Teleplay by	David Perry
Cast included	Vivienne Martin, Gladys Henson, Gretchen Franklin, Bryan Mosley, Charles Lamb, Royston Tickner, John Crocker, Malcolm Knight and Ian Wilson
Director	Charles Jarrott
Designer	Assheton Gorton

An ideal cast for this story telling. As with all black comedies, it wasn't everyone's cuppa, but it was excellent of its genre, and achieved a healthy No.5 in the Top Ten.

Established authors made their television writing debuts with the next two plays.

The first, *The Chocolate Tree* by Andrew Sinclair, was a keenly observed story of the "snuffing out of a great Anglo-African trading family" – an unusual and challenging piece about 'the wind of change' in Africa.

The Chocolate Tree
Above: Paul Rogers – with Zena Walker and Arthur Pentelow as his son and daughter-in-law

Right: Paul Rogers (in the wheelchair) as the head of the family in an argument with the head of the new African state, played by Earl Cameron

The Chocolate Tree October 27, 1963 (9.35pm)

Teleplay by	Andrew Sinclair
Cast included	Paul Rogers, Zena Walker and Peter McEnery – with Arthur Pentelow, Earl Cameron, Yemi Ajibade and Willie Payne
Director	Alan Cooke
Designer	Assheton Gorton

Great performances from the leads.

The second debut was by ace novelist Len Deighton (also writer of a weekly cookery column for a Sunday newspaper). It was originally called *Pests*, but we suggested that another title might be more attractive. And, as it happened, the eventual title of *Long Past Glory* had a touch of irony that fitted this story very well.

Long Past Glory
Maurice Denham and David Andrews

Long Past Glory November 17, 1963 (9.35pm)

Teleplay by	Len Deighton
Cast included	Maurice Denham, John Le Mesurier and David Andrews
Director	Charles Jarrott
Designer	Assheton Gorton

The design for this production was crucial. Almost throughout, the minimal action took place in what, to all intents and purposes, was a small underground hideout. However, it was necessary to reveal at the end that the exterior environment was an enormous empty no-mans-land on a battlefield. The studio was chock-full with this expansive setting, used only for the final moments of the entire show. A most impressive ending.

David Andrews, many moons later, worked with me as a director at STV and the BBC.

Jarrott delivered excellent performances, as ever, in this mystery and menace of "talking liberals".

I cherish the appreciation I received from Len Deighton after the production when he wrote thanking me "for kind words and encouragement". Expressions like that put some warmth into the factory.

The Higher They Fly was an adaptation from the writer's own book – an early airliner drama dealing with a mid-air near disaster.

The Higher They Fly	December 1, 1963 (9.35pm)
Teleplay by	Christopher Hodder-Williams
Cast included	Andrew Faulds, Michael Goodliffe, Frederick Jaeger, John Paul, Jill Dixon, June Thorburn and Mark Eden – with Richard Coleman, Michael Gaunt and Barry Letts
Director	Guy Verney
Designer	Terry Green

The cast, who made up the 'crew', had the rare experience of rehearsing in a flight simulator of BEA, and for which they got full marks from their true-life pilot-trainer, Captain Stanley Jones, DSO, DFC. He thought that "there must be something of the actor in every airline pilot".

Not exactly the sort of story to try to tell in a 'studio-bound' production! But it worked very well with the viewers, and achieved No.3 in the Top Ten.

Andrew Faulds, who played the fictional pilot in this story, went on to become a Labour Member of Parliament.

Armchair Theatre held its audience in the run-up to Christmas (always a dodgy time for the ratings, especially for single teleplays). *The Swindler* had over 7.7 million homes viewing – over 15 million people – the fourth highest rating for any programme that week.

The Swindler	December 15, 1963 (9.35pm)
Teleplay by	John Hall
Cast included	Ronald Lewis, William Lucas, Denis Quilley, Petra Davis, Betty McDowall – with Jan Holden, Victor Platt and Howard Goorney
Director	Jonathan Alwyn
Designer	James Goddard

A Way of Living
Rosemary Nicols and David Buck

We ended my first year in charge of *Armchair Theatre* with another notable 'first' – a play written by David Mercer specially for television and commissioned for us.

A Way of Living	December 29, 1963 (10.05pm)
Teleplay by	David Mercer
Cast included	David Buck and David Davies – with Rosemary Nicols, Beatrice Varley, Geoffrey Whitehead, Bert Palmer, Ruth Kettlewell and Annette Robertson
Director	Alan Cooke
Designer	Assheton Gorton

Set in a small northeast fishing and coal-mining town, it demanded the inclusion of location sequences – rare at that time. This necessitated sending the whole Outside Broadcast Unit to Newbiggin-by-the-Sea in Northumberland. Although the love story had the clash between different families, Mercer centred on the additional complication of the young girl breaking the mould and seeking higher education elsewhere.

This was Rosemary Nicol's first full-length TV drama. She later played H.G. Wells' 'Ann Veronica' for BBC 2.

A Way of Living
David Buck with Geoffrey Whitehead and Rosemary Nicols

A Way of Living was one of the very few *Armchair Theatre* productions of the period 1963-69 to have been seen in any of the archival programmes screened by the British Film Institute – in this case a David Mercer retrospective. Had it not been for a friend, Paul Lewis (who was responsible for the music – his first for *Armchair Theatre*) – telephoning me on the day, I would have missed this screening. The BFI probably thought I was dead!

So, some twenty years after the original transmission – in some trepidation – I went to the National Film Theatre. Frankly, I expected it to look extremely out of date (quite apart from the black-and-white and multi-camera techniques) but that the performances would still be very good (as they were at the time we made it). I prepared myself by getting a seat at the end of a row close to a door, for a quick exit.

But, sadly, it was the performances that came off worst with the passing of time – not because they were poor in any way, but because that way of casting had become unacceptable. A salutary experience, and not entirely a happy one.

1963 ended as a very successful year for *Armchair Theatre*. The strong department that Sydney Newman had built at ABC Television withstood the first year of his leaving his drama anthology in the hands of a successor – myself.

I had the great good fortune to have just about the best team around me.

Above: Design by Voytek
***The Paradise Suite* by Robert Muller**
Pictured: Carroll Baker and Ian Holm
(February 1963)

Right: Design by Assheton Gorton
***The Chocolate Tree* by Andrew Sinclair**
Pictured: Paul Rogers, Arthur Pentelow and Zena Walker
(October 1963)

STRANG
RULE BRITANNIA
ELIJAH STRANG

Design by Assheton Gorton
Long Past Glory **by Len Deighton (November 1963)**

Stars from *Armchair Theatre* — 1963

Above: Betty Marsden as the sympathetic barmaid in *The Front Room*

Left: Famous London hair stylist Alexandre Francke giving the finishing touches to Carroll Baker's hair just before she recorded *The Paradise Suite* – February 1963

Continuing the eighth season, 1964 opened strongly, with a comedy:

Sharp at Four	January 12, 1964 (9.35pm)
Teleplay by	Donald Churchill
Cast included	Derek Godfrey, Rosemary Leach and John Standing – with Mona Bruce, Lynne Ashcroft, Murray Hayne and Valerie Bell
Director	Guy Verney
Designer	Patrick Downing

Donald Churchill was establishing a highly successful run of teleplays for *Armchair Theatre*, in which he had the knack of balancing social observation in the comedy form. Churchill took a serious subject – the problems facing a working one-parent family in the early sixties – and dealt with it discerningly and humorously.

Our writing strength continued with the next. Concentrating on rich characters – and that being the very essence of television drama – this mystery story had added depth.

Last Word On Julie January 26, 1964 (9.35pm)

Teleplay by	Lynne Reid Banks
Cast included	Joan Miller, John Bonney, Bill Owen, David Sumner and Patricia Garwood – with Jessica Dunning and Sue Lloyd
Director	Jonathan Alwyn
Designer	Patrick Downing

This was the time of the renewal of ABC Television's contract and, more significantly for television drama, it was announced that *Armchair Theatre* transmissions would be increased from 26 to 39 (two out of every three weeks) during the year. Evidence enough that this unique anthology worked with audiences on the national network and indeed with the ITA. I cannot understand why such an open skein of single teleplays has not maintained its place in programme scheduling throughout the years, thus ensuring that the 'new' has an opportunity to be seen and tested on a regular basis. It is the lifeblood of TV drama.

With this increase in the number of productions of *Armchair Theatre* needed on the Network, we introduced some directors new to ABC. Herbert Wise, Eric Till (from Canada, and with whom I'd worked during my time at CBC), John Hale (from the Bristol Old Vic Theatre company) and Basil Coleman (who also had worked at CBC in Toronto and who had just produced *Billy Budd* at Covent Garden). These four enlarged my team. Also, Alvin Rakoff returned on an exclusive contract for a year. At this time too, Norman Bogner, a young American, was wooed from the book-publishing world to story-edit.

John Hopkins made his debut with us, with a stylish and unusual thriller – a far cry from Agatha Christie. He deals with the rising culture of the freedom to travel: "Two young and independent, attractive English secretaries, run into dangers, while on a holiday abroad…"

The Pretty English Girls February 16, 1964 (9.35pm)

Teleplay by	John Hopkins
Cast included	Caroline Mortimer, Jennie Linden and Jack Hedley – with Jonathan Elsom, Peter Bowles and Paul Whitsun-Jones
Director	Peter Hammond
Designer	Terry Green

The Pretty English Girls
Caroline Mortimer, Jack Hedley and Jennie Linden

Described as a "strong warning of the dangers of undisciplined dabbling in the occult" *Realm of Error* was based, so the writer told me, on a true experience of a friend of his. But simply dubbed 'a ghost story' in the handout.

Realm of Error March 1, 1964 (9.35pm)

Teleplay by	Hugh Leonard
Cast included	Andrew Faulds, Gwen Cherrell, Derek Smith and Helen Lindsay
Director	Guy Verney
Designer	Stan Woodward

Although some 12 million watched it, the ratings were down. Clearly the audience were not so keen on the 'dabble in the occult' as entertainment.

Jumping back into the Top Ten at No.6 came *Always Ask For The Best*, Stephen Lewis's second commission for *Armchair Theatre*. Set among London's East End shopkeepers, it certainly came from the Stratford-East school, and most welcome.

Always Ask For The Best March 15, 1964 (9.35pm)

Teleplay by	Stephen Lewis
Cast included	Warren Mitchell, Eira Heath, Irene Hamilton and Stephen Lewis – with Lila Kaye and Harry Ross
Director	Don Leaver
Designer	Patrick Downing

Tip-top casting for Stephen Lewis's comedy.

The following play was the first in an increased run, with two out of every three weeks being an *Armchair Theatre* production on the ITV Network – some thirty-five separate teleplays a year.

Mug's Game March 29, 1964 (9.35pm)

Teleplay by	Robert Storey
Cast included	Michael Craig, Rosemary Leach, Walter Fitzgerald and David Langton – with Donald Hewlett and Bert Palmer
Director	Don Leaver
Designer	Philip Harrison

The *TV Times* preview by Sarah Snow described it thus—

> Starting your own business . . . being independent . . . making a go of it. It's many a man's dream. But the man who throws up his job to be his own boss can burn his fingers.

Mug's Game might well have been written for the much later Thatcher era.

The next production was described as being "experimental". Not exactly a word to entice viewers and one that must have caused Controller Brian Tesler to pause and wonder. He might even have felt the need to read the script to keep an eye on what I was up to. "Is it accessible?" was his usual question.

Charles Wood's *Prisoner and Escort* presented similar problems to those with *The Front Room* and *The Blood Knot* in that they are all essentially theatre pieces, and the accent with *Armchair Theatre* was to get away from the old BBC television drama of static cameras and stand-back-and-observe-from-the-fourth-wall. But, for all that, Charles Wood was an excellent new writer of that time whom we surely could not ignore, and whom we intended would write specially for us.

Prisoner and Escort was one of a trilogy written under the general title of *Cockade*, which had been running very successfully at the Arts Theatre in London, and indeed had won the *Evening Standard* Drama Award for Charles Wood as—

The Most Promising New Playwright of 1963

We certainly could not ignore that.

Phillip Saville once again took up the challenge, and although he did not accept the description 'experimental', it is true to say that nothing in his hands could ever be conventional, and he described it as "provocative". He and Voytek, together, created a release from the theatre convention. *Huis Clos* on the move, imaginatively?

The story is about Charles Wood's prisoner being transported on a long journey on a train in a compartment that is also a cell.

Prisoner and Escort		April 5, 1964 (9.35pm)
Teleplay by	Charles Wood	
Cast included	Alfred Lynch, Norman Rossington, June Barry and Tim Preece	
Director	Philip Saville	
Designer	Voytek	

The cast gave their original best. The characters created by Charles Wood were certainly 'accessible', the audience figures being only just below block-busters like Val Parnell's *Sunday Palladium* and *Big Night Out*.

We continued the Army theme with an "unusual love-story". It was a period play – unusual for us – set just twenty years back, during the weekend before D-Day, 1944.

Cradle Song	April 12, 1964 (9.35pm)
Teleplay by	Hugo Charteris
Cast included	Fay Compton, Rosalie Crutchley, John Phillips and Suzan Farmer – with Fiona Hartford, Graham James, Susan Tracy and Nadine Hanwell
Director	Basil Coleman
Designer	Patrick Downing

This production involved two more *Armchair Theatre* debuts: the novelist Hugo Charteris' teleplay; and Basil Coleman as Director.

Cradle Song introduced Suzan Farmer. Also in the cast was Fiona Hartford who had been very impressive in the previous season's *The Wednesday Caller*.

This achieved equal ratings with the *Palladium Show* earlier that Sunday evening.

Guy Compton's *The Bandstand* – recorded on April 16, 1964 – was never transmitted*

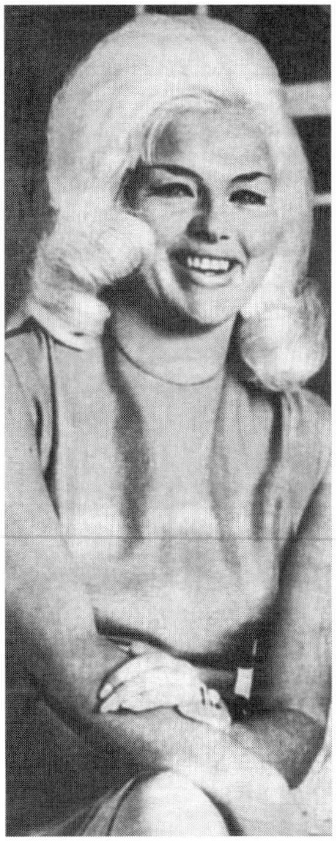

Diana Dors

Things lit up when the notable Miss Fluck of Swindon – better known as Diana Dors – was enticed from America to star in:

A Nice Little Business	April 26, 1964 (9.35pm)
Teleplay by	Marc Brandel
Cast included	Diana Dors, William Franklyn, Anthony Bate and Arthur Lowe – with Mona Bruce, Haydn Jones, Mavis Walker and Rowena Ingram
Director	Guy Verney
Designer	Assheton Gorton

With a mixture of glamour and notoriety *A Nice Little Business* turned out to be 'a nice little earner'. It beat Val Parnell's variety show by some 1.5 million viewers.

The "platinum and provocative, svelte and swinging" Diana Dors (as *TV Times* described her) was making her second *Armchair Theatre* appearance (the first, and her ITV drama debut, having been during the Sydney Newman era). For this play, she was directed by Guy Verney, who was in his element having once run the J. Arthur Rank Charm School for film starlets at the Connaught Theatre, Worthing.

*See Appendix I

After that, the schedulers altered *Armchair Theatre* to start half an hour later at 10.05pm. This put more strain on the single play to compete in the ratings, and although the programme held its own and even built on the inherited figures from the previous programme, the figures began to slip overall.

Pleasure Where She Finds It May 3, 1964 (10.05pm)

Teleplay by	Robert Muller
Cast included	Nigel Stock, Richard Pasco, Rosemary Leach and Anthony Bate
Director	Charles Jarrott
Designer	Assheton Gorton

Richard Pasco made one of his rare television appearances: he was steeped in Shakespeare with the Bristol Old Vic Company.

Jack Malton, another new writer to television drama – having been encouraged by Peter Cheeseman at the 'Vic' Theatre in Stoke-on-Trent, and whose work I had noted there – gave us this 'Midlands comedy'. A gentle 'slice of life', where a win on the pools is the catalyst in the environment of the 'kitchen sink', did not compulsively hold the audience that Sunday night, accessible though it was. The cast included Jerry Verno, changing from music-hall and going straight.

A Jug of Bread May 17, 1964 (10.05pm)

Teleplay by	Jack Malton
Cast included	John Hurt and Annette Robertson – with Jerry Verno and Fulton Mackay, Ruth Kettlewell, Walter Macken, Doreen Andrew, Bob Grant and Jill Thompson
Director	Don Leaver
Designer	David Marshall

Next, our first script from Alan Gosling – another comedy, but this one was of the 'black' variety.

St Ernie Leatherbound May 24, 1964 (10.05pm)

Teleplay by	Alan Gosling
Cast included	Harry Andrews, Peter Woodthorpe and David Andrews – with Margery Mason, Gladys Henson, Julie Samuels, Patsy Smart and Avril Fane
Director	John Hale
Designer	Voytek

Harry Andrews led as 'Leatherbound', a grocer and founder of a one-man religion, who paraded a sandwich board, which declared "Doom to Jezebels – Women the Devil's bait" on one side, and an advert for his grocery shop on the other.

John Hale, from the Bristol Old Vic, made his debut at Teddington directing this production.

St Ernie Leatherbound maintained *Armchair Theatre* as the top ABC rated programme on the Network, but the later time of transmission was making it harder for us to compete with the larger audience for Val Parnell's *Sunday Palladium*. And it provided unwelcome ammunition for all those anti-single play lobbyists who wanted, for their own reasons, to get shot of the 'problems' of this drama anthology.

Now for change of scene to a "small mid-western town" in the USA, with a very successful American television writer.

That's Where The Town's Going! June 7, 1964 (10.05pm)

Teleplay by	Tad Mosel
Cast included	Margaret Johnston, Patricia Marmont, David Bauer and Larry Cross – with Monica Merlin
Director	Charles Jarrott
Designer	Assheton Gorton

Charles Jarrott was gearing up for his eventual move to Hollywood and the big screen.

Margaret Johnston and Patricia Marmont, both moved into casting other actors when they became very successful artists' agents.

Another first for us – writer John Hall joined director Christopher Morahan. Out of the marked contrasts of life at Oxford (graduation) and Keele (Gulbenkian Fellowship), John Hall was provoked to write *Exit Joe—Running*. The leading character – within a few months of leaving academia – writes a paper titled '39 Reasons Why University Is No Good'. This gains him the dual role of both idol and rebel.

Exit Joe—Running June 14, 1964 (9.35pm)

Teleplay by	John Hall
Cast included	Tim Preece and Keith Barron – with Neville Smith, Arthur Pentelow, Katherine Schofield, Catherine Griller, Wendy Varnals, Ewen Roberts, Yvonne Coulette, Edward Burnham, Terence Woodfield and Marcus Hammond
Director	Christopher Morahan
Designer	Philip Harrison

We ended this run of *Armchair Theatre* in the long daylight hours with another specially written teleplay by a novelist.

A Certain Kind of Silence June 28,1964 (10.05pm)

Teleplay by	Hugo Charteris
Cast included	Judy Campbell, Laurence Hardy, Robin Palmer, Patricia Garwood – with Peter Bowles and guest star Henry Oscar – also Susan Peters and Peter Hoar
Director	Don Leaver
Designer	Patrick Downing

In my first eighteen months in charge of *Armchair Theatre* 'proper' I had produced forty teleplays, thirty-five of which were original for television, and involving thirty-two writers.

For the short summer season of 1964, we launched a run of six *Armchair Mystery* plays – with an earlier and better transmission time. An ACTT strike of technicians having delayed the first by two weeks, we kicked off with another thriller:

Time Out Of Mind July 19, 1964 (9.35pm)

Teleplay by	John Hopkins
Cast included	Ian Hendry, Miranda Connell, John Bentley and Elizabeth Shepherd – with Maurice Good, Morris Perry and Billy Cornelius
Director	Guy Verney
Designer	Voytek

Elizabeth Shepherd had been first choice to replace Honor Blackman when she left *The Avengers* this year. But for reasons never made clear she was dropped*.

Ian Hendry was back in our television orbit after making five films. He and his wife, lovely actress Janet Munro, were living in their home on one of the River Thames islands, having during this production had their baby daughter. Ian was firing on all cylinders!

A week later we presented:

The Blackmailing of Mr S. July 26, 1964 (9.35pm)

Teleplay by	Michael Gilbert
Cast included	John Le Mesurier, Peter Vaughan, Peter Butterworth and Jo Rowbottom – with Sheila Keith, Robert James, Winifred Dennis, Graham Squire and Marcus Hammond
Director	Robert Tronson
Designer	Philip Harrison

*See Chapter 5 *The Avengers*

Our excellent Head of Casting, Dodo Watts yet again put together a strong team of actors resulting in this next production nudging the ratings still further up in the Top Twenty. *The Lonely Crime* came top in four of the ITV regions, and overall No.3 on the network. Fortunate for us, but disappointing for those waiting in the wings to put down the importance of the single play in the schedules. We could hold off that onslaught for a few years, but we had to watch our backs!

The Lonely Crime August 9, 1964 (9.35pm)

Teleplay by	James Mitchell
Cast included	John Ronane, J.G. Devlin, Terence Scully and guest star Marian Spencer – with June Brown, Arthur Pentelow, Robert Arnold, Bert Palmer, Alethea Charlton, Peggy Marshall
Director	Toby Robertson
Designer	Patrick Downing

We followed with a German mystery, set in 1933 on the Hamburg-Kiel express – another rare excursion into period for *Armchair Theatre* – with a play and setting that pre-dated other notable television drama excursions on trains. This train, and in particular 'the last coach', was the trap – the 'no escape' – in which to probe guilty secrets. Voytek designed this moving yet studio-bound setting.

The Last Coach August 16, 1964 (9.35pm)

Teleplay by	Paul Erickson
Cast included	Richard Pearson, Mary Merrall, Donald Eccles – with Mike Pratt and Robert James – also Clive Cleghorn and Janet McIntire
Director	Alan Cooke
Designer	Voytek

Richard Pearson was as always worth his weight in gold as a character actor. Mike Pratt had recently been an Award-winning song writer with Lionel Bart and Tommy Steele.

Actress turned successful writer, Virginia Hewett, wrote *Admirer At Number Eight*, providing a strong starring role for Diana Churchill. That cast was studded with names due for promotion later on.

Admirer at Number Eight August 30, 1964 (9.35pm)

Teleplay by	Virginia Hewett
Cast included	Diana Churchill – with Sally Geeson, Mitzi Rogers, Gwendolyn Watts, Bryan Pringle, William Victor, Sean Lynch, Doris Hare, Ronnie Brody, Reg Whitehead and Janet Rowsell
Director	Peter Hammond
Designer	Terry Green

The last scheduled *Mystery* play of this short summer season was specially written for *Armchair Theatre* by Richard Harris, later to become one of the most successful writers in both television and theatre.

You Must Be Virginia September 6, 1964 (9.35pm)

Teleplay by	Richard Harris
Cast included	Richard Johnson, Nigel Stock and Toby Robins
Director	Don Leaver
Designer	David Marshall

Richard Johnson appeared by permission of Metro Goldwyn-Meyer, a rare credit! This play included the lovely Canadian actress, Toby Robins, making a very successful break into British television. With the traditional holiday month over, *You Must Be Virginia* was a real winner, breaking the barrier of 7 million homes viewing (about 17 million viewers). It was later turned into a stage play and performed in London's West End.

A week later, ABC Television had an additional transmission slot. *The Trial of Dr Fancy* had been made while Sydney Newman was producer of *Armchair Theatre*. At that time – two years earlier – it was considered that "the comedy in this strong, black satirical vein might possibly offend" and the play was withheld. Now there was an opportunity for transmission. The public were 'allowed' to see it. *The Trial of Dr Fancy* was described as a "satire of life in the 1960s", and certainly there is no doubt that Sydney Newman found nothing offensive in it and indeed was in admiration of Exton's story, which was directed with enthusiasm by Ted Kotcheff.

The Trial of Dr Fancy September 13, 1964 (9.35pm)

Teleplay by	Clive Exton
Cast included	Kynaston Reeves, Barry Jones, Nigel Stock, Ronald Hines, Walter Hudd, Dandy Nichols, Norman Bird, John Paul, Peter Sallis, Susan Richards, John Lee, John Boyd-Brent, Langley Howard and Malcolm Watson
Director	William T. Kotcheff
Designer	Timothy O'Brien (Produced by Sydney Newman in 1962)

As well as 'Dr Fancy' there was an issue on trial: individual freedom. A patient who had lost his self-confidence, because he was abnormally tall, desperately wanted to be ordinary by having his legs shortened by a surgeon in order that he might fit in with the crowd. The patient dies in the fashionable nursing home. Is it murder? Should the law allow such practice?

As I remember, Sydney Newman took the controversial withdrawal calmly. It was always 'on with the next' and there was never any time for worrying about 'yesterday's production'.

So, at the end of the eighth season of *Armchair Theatre*, it was demonstrated again that television drama needs the life-blood of the sharp commentary of the social issues of the time.

CHAPTER 9

Armchair Theatre – 1964-65 – Ninth Season

"Wilde and Blackpool Rock"

We launched the ninth season of *Armchair Theatre* with a sharp-edged comedy: the story of the serio-comic lengths to which a Women's Royal Air Force officer will go in order to get herself discharged from an unfulfilling life in the Services.

The Cherry on the Top
Pauline Yates and Robert Lang

The Cherry on the Top		September 27, 1964 (9.35pm)
Teleplay by	Donald Churchill	
Cast included	Pauline Yates and Robert Lang – with Peggy Sinclair, Anthony Dawes, Vivien Lloyd, Gay Gallie, Judy Franklin, Mona Bruce, Ernest Hare and Jerry Verno	
Director	Guy Verney	
Designer	Patrick Downing	

The story editor was Norman Bogner, the young American who had joined the team a few months before. *The Cherry on the Top* fell just short of the previous target of 7 million homes viewing, but it beat the *Sunday Palladium* by several places in the Top Ten.

Comedy is a particularly difficult form of drama to achieve on television, especially in the single play format. There is no immediate audience feedback, as in traditional theatre. The sit-com audience is told how to react by the use of 'warm-ups', or a 'laugh track' is used.

What worked in the production stages of comedy did not necessarily work as well for the viewers watching at home. Therefore, it was with no little apprehension that we decided to give more emphasis to comedy while keeping the focus on 'reality' and the social issues.

The next offering to our audience – *Something to Declare* – introduced several new talents to our team. Newcomers were Director Toby Robertson and Designer Trevor Williams. Terence Feely, playwright and journalist, joined us as one of our story editors. He set the scene each day by his impeccable sartorial taste, arriving at the studio wearing a fresh flower in his lapel duly delivered each morning from Harrods. He introduced this American screen and theatre writer's first play for television.

Something to Declare	October 4, 1964 (9.35pm)
Teleplay by	William Marchant
Cast included	Sylvia Sims and Jeremy Brett – with Georgio Piazzi and Robert Arnold
Director	Toby Robertson
Designer	Trevor Williams

Sylvia Sims and Jeremy Brett

The play – a welcome debut – was described by the caption writers as a "high class romantic comedy … of the kind that cinema does so well … and takes an American to write the crackling sophisticated and laconic dialogue that such subjects need". The contrast in the expert writing styles of Donald Churchill (for the UK) and William Marchant (for the USA) made for a lively interest at the start of this new season.

Top of the bill for this production was Sylvia Sims, who had been a contract film star for Associated British Pictures for eight years, making her first appearance in *Armchair Theatre*. Co-star Jeremy Brett was no stranger to ABC Television drama, but he had just returned from the USA after filming *My Fair Lady*, and being on Broadway. A very strong duo in the leads.

Our audiences liked it. Rediffusion's *No Hiding Place* was at No.3 in the week's National Top Twenty, but *Armchair Theatre* at No.5 beat Val Parnell's *Sunday Palladium* again and was well ahead of ATV's *Love Story* anthology and other popular series such as *Emergency-Ward Ten* and *Steptoe and Son*. It is interesting to note that, at that time, *Z Cars* did not even rate in the Top Twenty.

Television Audience Measurement (TAM)
Week ending Sunday October 4, 1964

Top Twenty Programmes		– Homes in Millions	
1	Coronation Street (Mon)	Granada	8.559
2	Coronation Street (Wed)	Granada	8.559
3	No Hiding Place	Rediffusion	7.756
4	Take Your Pick	Rediffusion	7.355
5	Something to Declare (AT)	ABC	6.954
6	Opportunity Knocks!	ABC	6.820
6=	Sunday Palladium	ATV	6.820
8	Bring on the Girls	Rediffusion	6.687
9	Love Story	ATV	6.152
9=	Double Your Money	Rediffusion	6.152
9=	The Rogues	BBC1	6.152
9=	Emergency-Ward Ten (Fri)	ATV	6.152
13	Emergency-Ward Ten (Tue)	ATV	6.018
13=	Steptoe and Son	BBC1	6.018
15	Cinema	Granada	5.861
16	Call in on Carroll (Tue)	ATV	5.750
17	A Whole Lotta Shakin'	Granada	5.617
17=	Thank Your Lucky Stars	ABC	5.617
19	Call in on Carroll (Wed)	ATV	5.483
20	Paris 1900	Granada	5.349

***Something to Declare* at No.5**

A fortnight later, we were back with a serious examination of the problems of a middle-aged Army major adjusting to civvie-street and domesticity.

Kenneth More in *Old Soldiers*

Old Soldiers	October 18, 1964 (9.35pm)
Teleplay by	Andrew Sinclair
Cast included	Kenneth More – with Rachel Kempson, Derek Fowlds, Basil Dignam and Francesca Annis
Director	Jonathan Alwyn
Designer	Stan Woodward

It was seen in over 7 million homes.

This season included a special event: Allan Prior's trilogy of teleplays. The common theme was the people of the unique resort of Blackpool and its Golden Mile – "that incredible magnetic stretch of arcades, booths and sideshows, of hot dog and candy-floss stands".

They Throw It At You	October 25, 1964 (9.35pm ABC) (10.05pm ATV)
Teleplay by	Allan Prior
Cast included	Julia Foster and Terry Palmer – with Megs Jenkins, Jack Smethurst, Pauline Munro, Bert Palmer and Leonard Pearce
Director	Alvin Rakoff
Designer	Voytek

They Throw It At You was led by the young and lovely Julia Foster, and introduced another budding talent in Terry Palmer. This production re-introduced Canadian director Alvin Rakoff to *Armchair Theatre.* He and designer Voytek combined to make all three of the Allan Prior Golden Mile teleplays for this season.

That Sunday night our ratings increased over the previous week by nearly half-a-million homes. *They Throw It At You* – at No.4 – was the only single play in the National Top Ten.

A closer look at the viewing figures for this essentially 'regional' story reveals interesting variations throughout the country. In London *They Throw It At You* was equal 4th, having built strongly on the inherited audience. In the Midlands it was No.3 (only beaten by two episodes of *Coronation Street* which was now well established at the top of the league). But in the North (the setting for the story) it was down at No.10. A story of Blackpool's Golden Mile was seemingly of less interest for the locals of the North, than for those in the South.

It was no virtue of expert scheduling at that time, but just the plain pattern of getting the productions made, that meant the trilogy was not transmitted sequentially over three consecutive weeks. No such thing as stock-piling in those days. From 'concept' to 'on-air' was quick. It had to be (and the better for it) to provide the 35 productions needed that year.

We followed up with something of an aberration in *Armchair Theatre*. To make as big a change as possible, we went for a 90-minute slot, a period piece, and a classic! We decided to make Oscar Wilde's quintessential comedy, *The Importance of Being Earnest*.

Just why we made this departure from the usual style of *Armchair Theatre* at that time is not helped by my hindsight. True the 70-year old play was regarded as being 'the most famous comedy in the English language', and therefore a perfect example of that genre. But, it was certainly not written for television, and Oscar Wilde was not commissioned by ABC!

It was Programme Controller Brian Tesler's suggestion to Drama Executive George Kerr that we should do it; but there was a name attached to it. Ian Carmichael would play John Worthing – he had "always wanted to do it". And apart from that, it would attract a star cast throughout, which certainly found favour with George Kerr.

Coincidentally, Patrick Macnee (who was continuing to play his alter-ego John Steed in *The Avengers*) wanted an opportunity to make a change – to remind the 'biz' and probably himself that he could do other roles. At that time it was thought that being successful in a drama series on TV, and playing to an audience of many millions weekly, had less prestige than a lead in a single classic drama, especially if it was in a limited run in theatre in London's West End.

The Importance of Being Earnest
Recording on location somewhere in Staffordshire

In the foreground: Director Bill Bain and Producer Leonard White

So, Patrick Mcnee as Algernon Moncrieff, joined Ian Carmichael as Oscar Wilde's two 'luvvies' in *The Importance of Being Earnest.* Cathlccn Nesbitt (making a rare visit back to the UK from America) was to play Lady Bracknell, but the technicians Union, ACTT, called a strike and our production schedule was held up. That resulted in Cathleen Nesbitt having to return to Hollywood where she was contracted to start a television series.

The Importance of Being Earnest

Clockwise from the top-left: Fenella Fielding, Pamela Brown, Patrick Macnee, Irene Handl, Wilfred Brambell, Ian Carmichael and [centre] Susannah Yorke

But we were very lucky, and delighted, when Pamela Brown took up the challenge of the 'handbag' line and all the rest of the glorious Lady Bracknell role. The star line-up continued with Susannah York as Cecily, Fenella Fielding as Gwendolyn, Irene Handl as Miss Prism. Wilfred Brambell played Canon Chasuble (what a transformation for him from the junkyard of *Steptoe and Son*). Charles Lloyd Pack and William Redmond were Merriman and Lane.

These were reported at the time as the—

> most enticing band of players that has ever swapped lines in a television studio…

To give this classic special fresh approach for *Armchair Theatre* I selected Antipodean Bill Bain to direct, and Assheton Gorton for a new 'look' to design.

It was a rare occurrence (for *Armchair Theatre*) when credits for Costumes (Audrey Brock, Ambren Garland and Margaret Morris) and Make-up Supervisor (Launa Bradish) were rightly given prominence.

The Importance of Being Earnest **Susannah York as Cecily**

Rare too, was the move to break the mould of the all-studio video-tape production, started earlier by us with David Mercer's *A Way of Living* (recorded partly on location in Northumberland), and furthered by Allan Prior's Blackpool trilogy.

We opened up the scenes by moving out with the OB circus to Maer Hall in Staffordshire. Visually very attractive, but a gamble in respect of the taut theatrical text – and particularly groundbreaking since the Wilde play was essentially an interior theatre piece.

The Importance of Being Earnest
Patrick Macnee, Susannah York, Ian Carmichael

The Importance of Being Earnest	November 15, 1964 (9.35pm)
Written by	Oscar Wilde
Cast included	Patrick Mcnee – with Ian Carmichael, Pamela Brown, Susannah York, Fenella Fielding, Irene Handl, Wilfred Brambell, Charles Lloyd Pack and William Redmond
Director	Bill Bain
Designer	Assheton Gorton

Despite the worthiness of the play, our audience was not wild about this change of fare. From the previous week, the rating dropped by a million homes. Even so, it was a good turn-out for a play, described by the author whilst writing it, as "quite nonsensical" and of "no serious interest". It probably entertained, at a single performance, a larger audience on that occasion than ever before – or, possibly, since.

The BBC (the natural provider of classical drama) had only two shows in the Top Twenty that week – one being *Miss World 1964* (at No.7), and the other the imported American *Perry Mason* (at No.18). At No.12 in the National Top Twenty – with 6,498,000 homes viewing – our excursion into the classics had done comparatively well. *The Importance of Being Earnest* was the only single-play in the Top Twenty that week.

Armchair Theatre from now on, starting half-an-hour later at 10.05pm on Sunday evenings, was presenting the single play with an added burden we could well do without in this challenge for the ratings. Single-plays, written to provoke the viewers, require the audience to be fully awake; not with an eye on the clock, thinking of switching on the electric-blanket, and anticipating the Monday morning grind.

It was about this time, as I remember, that Controller Brian Tesler had a little chat with me. He had just won the fight for ABC to provide no less than 35 plays a year to the Network, and we were discussing the scripts that were in the pipe-line, including one or two that might be a 'little difficult'. Brian, rightly considering the challenge to the single-play on ITV – especially as a continuing series – gently suggested that I should arrange for five scripts to be 'accessible' for every one that might be 'difficult'. In other words, if we had subjects that were not likely to be as popular (but well-worth doing) we were to sandwich them into the schedule carefully.

Following the Wilde aberration, it was back to normal with our next production – the second of the Blackpool trilogy.

The Girl in the Picture	November 29, 1964 (10.05pm)
Teleplay by	Allan Prior
Cast included	Ruth Dunning and Richard Butler – with Nicola Pagett, Peter Purves, Seymour Green, Naomi Chance, Vic Wise, Walter Sparrow, Kathleen Heath, Margie Young and Margaret Read – and a large number of local extras including 'Miss *TV Times*' Valerie Martin
Director	Alvin Rakoff
Designer	Voytek

This play introduced Nicola Pagett (said to be then "19 years-old and just out of RADA") in her first television performance. She played the role of a girl from Oldham on holiday in Blackpool, who was cajoled by a flashy photographer – not to mention her scheming mother – into entering a competition for the 'Northern Personality Girl of the Year'. Allan Prior described the character that Nicola played as "singularly lovely". Another piece of excellent casting by our Dodo Watts.

This production also introduced the young actor, Peter Purves. The large number of local extras included a line-up of Beauty Queen hopefuls, together with their scheming Mums. To give this line-up some authenticity we were graced by the presence of 'Miss *TV Times*' herself, Valerie Martin.

Before shooting the beauty competition scenes at the Winter Gardens in Blackpool, fact took over from the fiction when the selection of the extras to be in the line-up on camera became

The Girl in the Picture
Nicola Pagett with Ruth Dunning playing the role of the mother who has ambitions to see her daughter as the local beauty queen – and Richard Butler as the father

a realistic competition. Certainly fierce, tense, and not inappropriately named the 'cat-walk'! Reality was certainly hotter than the fiction. If Prior had written the real stuff into the play, in those days we would never have got away with it.

The Golden Mile story clawed back the ratings, adding about 2 million viewers to that of the classic adventure previously, and getting to No.8 in the Top Twenty.

Shooting on location – especially with the whole of the OB multi VT camera circus trying to get the set-ups on the pier and the promenade at Blackpool – provided more than enough problems in controlling the enthusiasm of the inquisitive summertime crowds. On one occasion, we had to create a diversion to get anything done at all. We formed an entirely fake camera crew and set-up, and had designer Voytek acting as a director working with fake actors making as much of an exhibition of themselves as possible to attract the crowds, while at another part of the pier Alvin Rakoff could get on with the real thing without being noticed! Voytek always wanted to direct, so now he got his chance! Later on in his career, he did it for real.

This was the time when we were looking for new directors. Sydney Newman, now established as Head of BBC Drama, was inviting some of his old team at ABC to join him at Television Centre. Fortunately for me, not many followed him, but we needed new blood and it was obvious that we would look out for talent at the BBC. We wanted James McTaggart, an outstanding director, but we couldn't woo him away from Auntie. Of course, his judgment was right. In spite of ITV beating the BBC with popular teleplays, and *Armchair Theatre* in particular achieving an enviable reputation, there is no doubt that working for BBC television drama had particular prestige. I doubt that there would now be a 'McTaggart Lecture' as the keynote of the annual International Television Festival in Edinburgh if James had moved to direct ITV's *Armchair Theatre*. Commercial television had to work twice as hard and for a long time to break this 'prestige credit' monopoly held by the BBC. But we did break it, of course.

We didn't get McTaggart, but we did get Patrick Dromgoole. He has recounted several times since then that I "offered him a contract that he couldn't refuse". I didn't think his contract was anything out of the ordinary for us. (McTaggart had found himself able to refuse it). We always demanded TV exclusivity, of course, but restricted the number of productions per year in order to give the directors opportunities to work in other media if they wanted. In Dromgoole's case, he had the opportunity to work in theatre in any given year. This he did with some notoriety.

Having been poached from the BBC, Dromgoole made his debut with us (and ITV) as director of *Sally*.

A special highlight came with this production when Vanessa Redgrave – giving a fine performance – made her ITV debut with us. A taut theatrical piece, this play, with a cast of only three, examined two women's views of the same man: those of his mother and his mistress. Not ideal for television drama, but it provided excellent character studies in some depth.

Sally	December 6, 1964 (10.05pm ABC) (9.35pm ATV)
Teleplay by	William Wood
Cast included	Vanessa Redgrave, Joyce Carey and Nigel Stock
Director	Patrick Dromgoole
Designer	Patrick Downing

Sally beat *Sunday Palladium* and the popular drama series, *The Plane Makers,* in the Top Twenty.

Unexpected Summer by Gwendolyn Gazeley – recorded on December 10, 1964 – was never transmitted.*

*See Appendix I

In the run-up to Christmas, we entered the festive season with another Donald Churchill comedy. The potted story was described in *TV Times* as, "An ailing mango, two wives and an ambitious employee all help to upset a youthful tycoon's weekend in the hothouse".

The Hothouse
Harry H. Corbett (as the youthful tycoon) and Miranda Connell (as the wife of one of his managers)

The Hothouse December 13, 1964 (10.05pm ABC) (9.35pm ATV)

Teleplay by	Donald Churchill
Cast included	Harry H. Corbett, Donald Churchill, Miranda Connell and Diana Rigg
Director	Guy Verney
Designer	Assheton Gorton

The Hothouse
This play provided Harry H. Corbett with a role quite distant from his famous Harold Steptoe character. Pictured here with Miranda Connell in the hothouse

Below: Diana Rigg and Harry H. Corbett

It was also Diana Rigg's television debut. Her move from the rarefied drama of the Royal Shakespeare Company to, what she described as, the "reality" of an *Armchair Theatre* production, led directly to her being cast as Emma Peel* in *The Avengers* later on.

Playing a small part was Michael Darlow, who later became better known as both a director and a producer, running his own company.

The Hothouse achieved exceptional success, gaining third place in the Top Twenty ratings with some 20.5 million viewers (8.26 million homes).

*See Chapter 5 *The Avengers*

TAM top 20 network television programmes

week ending 13th DEC. 1964

	NETWORK*TOP TWENTY	Originating Programme Company	ITV Areas †	Homes Viewing (000's)
1	CORONATION STREET (MONDAY 7th DECEMBER)	GRANADA	ALL	9210
1=	CORONATION STREET (WEDNESDAY 9th DECEMBER)	GRANADA	ALL	9210
3	ARMCHAIR THEATRE (THE HOTHOUSE)	ABC	ALL	8260
4	TAKE YOUR PICK	REDIFFUSION	ALL	8130
5	VAL PARNELL'S SUNDAY PALLADIUM	ATV	ALL	7590
6	CRANE	REDIFFUSION	ALL	7450
7	DOUBLE YOUR MONEY	REDIFFUSION	ALL	7320
8	THE VILLAINS	GRANADA	ALL	7180
9	THE PLANE MAKERS	ATV	ALL	6910
9=	EMERGENCY-WARD 10 (FRIDAY 11th DECEMBER)	ATV	ALL	6910
11	EMERGENCY-WARD 10 (TUESDAY 8th DECEMBER)	ATV	ALL	6770
12	ALL OUR YESTERDAYS	GRANADA	ALL	6640
13	THE ARTHUR HAYNES SHOW	ATV	ALL	6370
14	CINEMA	GRANADA	ALL EXCEPT CS/SW/U/B	6210
15	PERRY MASON	BBC 1	ALL	6100
15=	DAVE'S KINGDOM	ATV	ALL	6100
17	THE SULLAVAN BROTHERS	ATV	ALL EXCEPT CS	5910
18	WORLD IN ACTION	GRANADA	ALL	5830
19	THANK YOUR LUCKY STARS	ABC	ALL	5690
20	MEET THE WIFE	BBC 1	ALL	5420
20=	DR. KILDARE	BBC 1	ALL	5420

***The Hothouse* at No. 3**

Television Audience Measurement (TAM) – weeking ending December 13, 1964

Old Man's Fancy by Evan Jones, recorded on New Year's Eve, 1964, was never transmitted.*

1964 had been a good year for *Armchair Theatre*, gaining no less than thirteen out of the Top Twenty television plays for the year. Of those, we had the first three: two written by Donald Churchill and directed by Guy Verney, and the third written by John Hopkins and directed by Peter Hammond. Story editors Norman Bogner and Terence Feely had delivered a great package.

Then into 1965. We tackled the after-Christmas lull with the third of Allan Prior's trilogy about the people of Blackpool's Golden Mile.

I've Got a System
Kika Markham and Keith Baxter play two young people involved in the operations of a betting shop

I've Got a System January 3, 1965 (10.05pm)

Teleplay by	Allan Prior
Cast included	Derek Francis, Avis Bunnage, Keith Baxter and Kika Markham
Director	Alvin Rakoff
Designer	Voytek

I've Got a System – with an echo of the tipster 'Ras Prince Monolulu' and his cry, "I've gotta hosse" – had betting and gambling as its theme. In the cast were Keith Baxter (just prior to filming in Spain with Orson Welles) and Kika Markham (as a sociology student!) working

*See Appendix I

in a bingo stall. Derek Francis was the man trying to beat the system, and Avis Bunnage, as ever, giving us more than value for money as his wife, a boarding house landlady.

The New Year started with a dip in our ratings. The Christmas week had, naturally, had an accent on light entertainment with *It's Tarbuck*, *Take Your Pick*, *Double Your Money*, *The Gang Show*, and, of course, *Sunday Night at the London Palladium* taking the higher places in the Top Twenty. *Armchair Theatre* shared 10th place in the ratings with *Emergency-Ward Ten*, but still with some 13 million viewers.

We reverted to something more serious, and the ratings wobble continued, at least in comparison with recent very high figures. Set in the Officers' Mess of a British regiment in Germany *The Gaming Book* dealt with an experiment in posting a subaltern from a working class background to join a 'fashionable regiment' stuffed with aristocratic officers. The guinea pig is not up to the class competition. A thought-provoking, fine piece of writing.

The Gaming Book January 10, 1965 (9.35pm)

Teleplay by	Simon Raven
Cast included	Derek Fowlds – with Geoffrey Keen, Liam Redmond, Derrick Sherwin, Jerome Willis, Geoffrey Whitehead, Seymour Green, Lauriston Shaw, David Futcher, Anthony Baird, Fanny Rowe and Penelope Horner
Director	Eric Till
Designer	Assheton Gorton

The Gaming Book

The young subaltern was played by Derek Fowlds who had served as a radio-operator in the RAF in Malta.

The Gaming Book provided a debut on *Armchair Theatre* for director Eric Till from Canada. He made a beautiful work of this drama, but seemingly its hard edge couldn't hold the viewers until eleven o'clock at night on a Sunday. Even so – at No.18 – it still had some 11 million watching. That sort of rating, which we regarded as slipping, would now be hailed as a triumph for a single play.

What would have been our next – *Putty Medal* – had to be postponed because of schedule changes due to the death of Sir Winston Churchill.

Three weeks later, director Herbert Wise made his *Armchair Theatre* debut.

The Lady With The Albatross	February 14, 1965 (10.05pm)
Teleplay by	Robert Storey
Cast included	Katharine Blake, Tim Preece, Carole Mowlam and Anthony Roye
Director	Herbert Wise
Designer	Philip Harrison

Katharine Blake – 'Television Actress of the Year'– cut short her holiday in Capri to fly home to take this part. Most welcome by me.

I first saw Kate Blake in the cast of the famous Laurence Olivier double-bill of *Anthony and Cleopatra* and *Caesar and Cleopatra* on Broadway in New York in 1952. Then, a year later, I had the pleasure of staying with her and her (then) husband David Greene at their home in Toronto when I paid my first visit to that city.

Putty Medal was the play that had been postponed because of the re-scheduling caused by the death of Winston Churchill. It was described as "one of the few successful contemporary visits to a middle-class home paid by TV drama".

Putty Medal	February 21, 1965 (10.05pm)
Teleplay by	Robert Storey
Cast included	Jack Hawkins and Angela Baddeley – with Eira Heath and Barry McGregor
Director	Jonathan Alwyn
Designer	Robert Fuest

Jack Hawkins and Angela Baddeley paid tribute to the standard of *Armchair Theatre*, when they played the two leads, both welcoming the opportunity to do 'something different' – he getting away from the 'rugged hero', and she from the 'Noel Coward aura'.

Barry McGregor (son of Hector McGregor, with whom I'd given my 'Malcolm' and he his 'Ross' in Michael Redgrave's *Macbeth* at the Aldwych Theatre, London in 1947) had spent four years with the Royal Shakespeare Company, and then later joined the company at the Stratford (Ontario) Festival, where he remained for many years.

Edna O'Brien wrote the following play – another coup for *Armchair Theatre.*

The Keys of the Café	March 7, 1965 (10.05pm)
Written by	Edna O'Brien
Cast included	Ronnie Barker, Margaret Whiting, Peter Barkworth and Lois Dane – with Constance Chapman and David Garth
Director	Patrick Dromgoole
Designer	Stuart Durant

Ronnie Barker – perhaps not quite the comedian playing Hamlet, but proving that he could successfully play a straight part.

Designer Stuart Durant was new to the team. Another memorable aspect of this production was that the cast included twenty pigs, which Patrick Dromgoole kept too long in the studio without recourse to the toilets!

Before John Hopkins went to work on the script of the James Bond film *Thunderball*, he delivered another for *Armchair Theatre*. Written in what was described as "Hopkins' pared-down style", this play fell into the 'difficult' category.

I Took My Little World Away **Susannah York plays a girl on the knife-edge of suicide. With her is John Ronane**

I Took My Little World Away March 14, 1965 (10.05pm)

Teleplay by	John Hopkins
Cast included	Susannah York, John Robinson and John Ronane – with Gary Watson, Clemence Bettany, Neil Robertson and Janet Rowsell
Director	Peter Hammond
Designer	Voytek

Peter Hammond was the ideal director for *I Took My Little World Away*, his second Hopkins' drama during my time in the hot-seat. And Voytek was the obvious designer for it.

Susannah York, an international star at twenty-two, headed the cast beautifully. A 'dark' play from a fine writer, which challenged us to find its audience.

Following that, Story Editor Terence Feely came up with something more accessible – a fantasy-thriller in the space-age environment, but not so disturbing as to give our viewers bad dreams that Sunday night.

A Voice in the Sky March 21, 1965 (10.05pm)

Teleplay by	Christopher Hodder-Williams
Cast included	Jack Hedley – with Ann Bell, David Bauer, Paul Maxwell – and Denis Goacher, Roberta Huby, Jolyon Booth, Morris Perry, Lloyd Lamble, Richard Coleman, Paul Danquah, Michael Newell, Michael Finlayson, James Darwin and Jack Niles
Director	Guy Verney
Designer	Patrick Downing

Jack Hedley had the biggest fan mail of any actor on television for his 'Tim Frazer' days.

We continued the stories set around the character of Mick Daly, which started in *The Irish Boys* nearly three years earlier. That character had been in *A Kind of Kingdom* (1963) and was now seen again in this new work by Hugh Leonard – *I Loved You Last Summer*.

As before, the role of Mick Daly was played by Brian Bedford.

"Take the Three Musketeers and change them into Irish Labourers and set them in Birmingham" is how the play was described. Hugh Leonard saw it as "A real send-up of the Alexandre Dumas stories". A strong Dublin team made up the cast, including the Abbey Theatre's own Marie Keen.

I Loved You Last Summer April 4, 1965 (10.05pm)

Teleplay by	Hugh Leonard
Cast included	Brian Bedford, Marie Keen, Margaret Anderson and John Cowley – with Dermot Tuohy, John McCarthy, David Kelly, Elizabeth Davis, James Kerry, Angela Lovell and Billy Cornelius
Director	Guy Verney
Designer	Philip Harrison

Easter Sunday was our next transmission date that year. Not the best day in the calendar to woo a big audience. If the weather is good, they're not at home, and if bad, then they want light entertainment.

So, we tried with a thriller, originally a successful theatre play, which I had seen at the Theatre Royal, Windsor. Although the good reputation of *Armchair Theatre* was built on original works – preferably commissioned – *The Man Who Came To Die* was popular fare needed for a holiday season. An adaptation was written for us by the author.

The Man Who Came To Die April 11, 1965 (10.05pm)

Written by	Reginald Marsh
Cast included	Reginald Marsh, Toby Robins, Ronald Leigh-Hunt and Peter Copley – with Gretchen Franklin, John Gabriel, Michael Stainton and Viola Keats
Director	Jonathan Alwyn
Designer	David Marshall

Toby Robins

Toby Robins was one of the impressive talents to come out of Canada in the early days of ITV and make such an enormous impact upon television here. (A great loss when she died so young.)

Actor Reginald Marsh (having become a household name in *The Plane Makers*) took a lead in his own play, the role of "a believable copper".

We languished only briefly in the adaptation business. Two weeks later, we were back on line with another important *Armchair Theatre* first from Alan Plater. This commissioned teleplay featured a subject ahead of its time: the division of the Northlands from the south of England. Plater called it "a macabre comedy". Certainly it had a hard centre to contemplate – bureaucracy gone mad.

The Incident April 25, 1965 (10.05pm)

Teleplay by	Alan Plater
Cast included	Pauline Munro, Alan Dobie, Norman Rossington and Bryan Pringle – with Victor Winding and Alan Rowe
Director	Alvin Rakoff
Designer	Assheton Gorton

We then moved into another short season of *Armchair Mystery* stories for the summer of 1965, opening with acknowledgements to several anniversaries. *The Last Reunion* was a work from the first year of ITV drama. Appropriately, this revival marked the 25th anniversary of the 'Battle of Britain'. Esmond Knight, who played one of the leads, was himself a war veteran and victim of the 'Bismark action'. A harrowing ghost story evolves at the annual reunion dinner of a bomber crew. Esmond Knight, especially, must have been hard-put to separate his own painful experiences from those relating to the role of Commanding Officer.

The Last Reunion
Walter Carr, Jeremy Kemp and Esmond Knight as the flight engineer, the pilot and the station commander, respectively

The Last Reunion May 9, 1965 (10.05pm)

Teleplay by	Kenneth Hyde
Cast included	Esmond Knight and Jeremy Kemp – with guest star Nora Swinburne – also Robin Hawdon, Bryan Mosley, Walter Carr, Kenneth Farringdon, Roger Croucher, Griffith Davies and Ronald Brandon
Director	Bill Bain
Designer	Philip Harrison

The *Television Mail* reviewer (21/5/1965) described it as—

> at once exciting, gripping and moving ... Bill Bain, Jeremy Kemp, Esmond Knight, and the rest of the cast brought a mysterious reunion to vivid life...

The Last Reunion also had resonances for four people at ABC at that time. George Kerr (our dedicated Drama Executive) had been the story editor when the play was first produced by High Definition Films. Bernard Greenhead (our Technical Controller), Dodo Watts (Casting Director) and Michael Baldock (Senior Cameraman – and what a super cameraman he was) had all been on the team that made the first production almost ten years before.

The next production brought me special pleasure in that I was able to present the fine Canadian star, John Colicos, to our UK television audience. John had served his apprenticeship some fifteen years earlier at the Old Vic in London when he must have been the youngest actor ever to play King Lear! He took over the role from Stephen Murray, and received much acclaim for it.

Licence to Murder had been seen some three years earlier at the Vaudeville Theatre in London. Because the theme was so topical (if not ahead of its time), which certainly suited the style of our TV drama, we departed once more from our usual practise of concentrating on new dramas specially written for us.

This play revolved around the psychological drama confronting the owner of a nuclear fall-out shelter who is forced to take extreme action in defence when a neighbour seeks safety during an emergency. It was described by one reviewer at the time as, "One of the best productions in the American idiom".

Licence to Murder May 16, 1965 (10.05pm)

Teleplay by Elaine Morgan
Cast included John Colicos, Paul Maxwell, June Tobin, Clement McCallin – with Jerry Stovin, Robert Arden, Tucker McGuire – and John McLaren, James Dyrenforth, Robert Arden, Hester Cameron, Riggs O'Hara and David Cargill
Director Basil Coleman
Designer Voytek

Raymond Menmuir was another director new to us and, like Bill Bain, was from the Antipodes.

The Hunter June 6, 1965 (10.05pm)

Teleplay by N.J. Crisp
Cast included Ronald Fraser, John Meillon and Keith Barron – with Camilla Hasse, Ann Kennedy – and David Beale
Director Raymond Menmuir
Designer Assheton Gorton

Robert Muller made a rare excursion into the mystery genre, providing us with the next production in this summer season. *Man and Mirror* attracted no less than Sybil Thorndike to play the lead (illustrating how far the anthology had departed from its earlier tag of 'kitchen sink drama'). The great Dame Sybil was 82 when she played this 70 year-old character, and yet she had to be made-up to look old enough for the part!

Man and Mirror	June 13, 1965 (10.05pm)
Teleplay by	Robert Muller
Cast included	Sybil Thorndike, Denholm Elliott and Richard Pasco – with Kathleen Michael, Anne Cunningham, Thomas Heathcote – also Constance Chapman, Campbell Singer and Edwin Apps
Director	Patrick Dromgoole
Designer	David Marshall

Although co-star Denholm Elliot had appeared in an *Armchair Theatre* production in the early days of 1958 (Dennis Vance's period) his participation for me at this time was a special occasion. It was the first time I'd had an opportunity in my new role as Producer to work with him since we had been together in my acting days (Christopher Fry's *A Sleep of Prisoners* – 1951) in which I had to attempt to strangle him nightly!

As early as June 1965, the knives were being sharpened to spill the lifeblood of television drama: the single play. The ITA deemed it necessary to conduct a 'Consultation on Television Drama'. The Report eventually issued was considered 'Confidential'. Goodness knows why such a consultation had to be kept under wraps. Who was frightened? We at ABC certainly were not.

Earlier, the ITA had commissioned two outside research and assessment groups (with the cooperation of members of the ITCA Research Liaison Committee) to "Study Television Play Viewing" and, in April 1965, they delivered a Report of some 150 pages. This report "in written form, with supporting Statistical Tables, Appendices, and Questionnaires" started with just a couple of pages with a heading—

> **Very Briefly: This Report Shows That:–**
> No play studied was completely 'good' or completely 'bad' to all its viewers

Hardly a startling revelation! Further—

> ...even plays of a similar type do yield perceived differences along some dimensions...

Thus, some 150 pages, all the time spent on research and doubtless a lot of money, revealed only the obvious. And it didn't stop there. In June of that year, the ITA called a consultation on Television Drama. Over eighty people were summoned to Brompton Road for the two days to discuss this report. Over a quarter of those attending were ITA's own staff/personnel.

Thirteen ITV companies were represented (only little "Channel" was not there). Of those attending, only twenty-eight were in the actual business of making television drama programmes, of which six were authors, and one an actor.

As an aid to the discussions, the participants were bidden to watch ten drama productions (three from the BBC; two from ABC; two from ATV, and one each from Rediffusion, Granada and Anglia) that had been selected as a focus for the research.

These ten had all been transmitted during a three-week period (Sundays, Mondays and Wednesdays): nine in April, one in May. Other information available was made up of the TAM Ratings (network and regional) and the press comments about the plays.

Whereas any random selection of a group of plays to be researched might be justified, the period that included the Easter holiday, as this did, could hardly be regarded as typical.

The press coverage was also less than scientific as a basis for analysis. None of the thirteen newspapers selected covered all of the ten productions. Indeed, only one (*Daily Telegraph*) covered nine. Another (*Stage and Television Today*) covered five. Eight of the thirteen covered three or less. To add weight, there were three separate 'general' articles (from *The People*, *The Mirror* and *TV Mail*).

The stated object of the ITA consultation was—

> To exchange information, discuss mutual problems and consider future possibilities

And, of course, they were to consider the 150 pages of the commissioned report by the outside researchers.

However the two days (June 23 and 24) were largely concerned with a number of addresses, and in the subsequent Report issued by the ITA to record this event, these addresses took up over twenty pages of the total twenty-eight. True some 'discussion' was scheduled, but as reported, this element was supplementary, and in no instances were any of the discussion points credited to a specific individual.

Professor Hugh Hunt based his opening address on the premise that—

> the television play is under heavy criticism [from] television viewers in general [and from the] television play audience

No one will deny the changes of popularity from one play to another will vary – sometimes greatly – as part of the natural form of such a series of one-offs. With different styles of writing, acting, directing and designing there is little continuity. Because the very nature of a continuing series of single plays is difficult, it represents a whole lot more hard work and commitment than, say, the preferred easy option of the cosy long-running soap opera. The single original play is just too much trouble.

Of the ten drama productions selected to be the guinea-pigs for the 'Study' in 1965, the two *Armchair Theatre* presentations, *The Man Who Came To Die* (by Reginald Marsh) and *The Incident* (by Alan Plater) came ahead of all the rest in the TAM ratings. And this in spite of the fact that both shows were transmitted later (after 10pm) than all the rest, as well as having split transmission days (some of the network transmitted on Saturday rather than Sunday).

Brian Tesler (Programme Controller, ABC and a member of the ITA/ITCA Research) in making his comments stated that—

> the judgment and perception of viewers had been sharpened rather than dulled by years of television drama.

Meaning, of course, that we had succeeded in gaining an enormous mass audience for 'television theatre' and in the process had 'educated' that audience to become more choosey: to demand more of their separate likes and dislikes.

Personally, I felt the cold draught blowing around our endeavours at that time, and I saw the signs of inevitable change of philosophy in programming rather than any serious desire to 'improve' the single play. After all, breaking up the very successful pattern of *Sunday Night at the London Palladium* and *Armchair Theatre* as a double act cannot be regarded as likely to help the single play! Certainly not ABC's contribution to the weekend network.

Bemused and undaunted, we continued our summer season.

At this time we welcomed Robert Love to join our team at Teddington Studios. I first met him at Nottingham Playhouse where he worked with John Neville. That Playhouse was on my regular visiting list to watch the progress of the then trainee-director, Michael Rudman who was there under our 'Regional Theatre Trainee Director Scheme' sponsorship – a unique and highly respected opportunity for training in those days and for many years, which we ran. Robert Love, then with us, worked enthusiastically as Co-ordinator to Head of Drama, Lloyd Shirley.

The Teddington experience must have taught him well: it wasn't long before he started to produce. He eventually moved to his homeland to be Head of Drama at Scottish Telelvision, where he was notable for launching the *Taggart* series among STV's many successes.

We moved on with a play described as an "Art World Thriller".

Time and Mr Madingley June 27, 1965

Teleplay by	Richard Harris
Cast included	Charles Gray and Peter Jeffrey – with John Barron, Juliet Harmer and Ric Hutton
Director	Raymond Menmuir
Designer	Assheton Gorton

According to Kari Anderson of *Television Today*—

> Once again Assheton Gorton let his imagination run away with him in the design.

Perhaps, in an "Art World Thriller", Assheton Gorton was justified in the effort to move far away from the old 'kitchen sink' label.

This play was written for the summer season *Mystery* grouping.

The Welcome July 4, 1965

Teleplay by	Allan Prior
Cast included	Mark Eden, Maureen Pryor, Richard Butler, Robert MacLeod and Fidelma Murphy – with Colin Douglas and Patricia Shakesby
Director	Don Leaver
Designer	Patrick Downing

Criticism concerning 'over-kill design' continued with Patrick Downing's setting for this play, and probably indicates just how high was the expectation of television drama to have all the ambiance of 'reality'. Suspension of disbelief, a norm for theatregoers was, seemingly, harder to come by in television viewers, including the critics.

Described as being in the "classic detective story tradition":

The Finishing Touch July 18, 1965 (10.15pm)

Teleplay by	Julian Symons
Cast included	Laurence Hardy, Gary Watson, Jennie Linden and Faith Kent – with Nicola Pagett, David Dodimead, Susan Field, Robert Russell, Terry Hedley, and Jane Birkin
Director	Basil Coleman
Designer	William McCrow

This production included several more 'firsts' for *Armchair Theatre*: Julian Symons, William McCrow, and the TV debut for the 18 year-old Jane Birkin.

Very unusually for *Armchair Theatre* with its first-rate technical staff at Teddington Studios, one reviewer, Marjorie Norris, questioning camera focus on occasions and sound balance, reported that—

> Technically speaking, the production was not all it should have been.

How risky it was to experiment with changing the style of conventional television drama production. While still harnessed in the live method of recording productions, we were pushing all the time for the fast-moving style of film cutting (editing) with many and shorter scenes in the format – especially in this type of drama. All of which constantly challenged the dexterity of the cameramen (and cable bashers), the boom operators and the 'switcher', and crew in the control room. We had broken down the old static norm of early UK television drama production. Director Basil Coleman had also worked in Toronto and he (like me) had seen how the camera-style, set by the CBC crews there some years before, had radically changed our concept of the camera-work on drama productions. However, within the constraints of live recording we were living dangerously. We certainly didn't shrink from that, but, of course, we didn't always entirely succeed. Nevertheless, we continued not to opt for safety, but to try to stretch the considered limits of multi-camera live production.

Our next production was not an original text, but a new dramatisation of a work of fiction.

The Lodger	July 25, 1965 (10.15pm)
Novel by	Mrs Belloc Lowndes
Teleplay by	Anthony Skene
Cast included	Brenda Bruce, Charles Gray and Angela Douglas – with Victor Platt and Stacy Davies
Director	Don Leaver
Designer	Patrick Downing

Unlike the usual focus of *Armchair Theatre* upon 'drama of today', it was a nineteenth century period piece – a classic example of the 'mystery' genre (Jack the Ripper).

Gwen Cherrell, still better known as an actress at that time, continued her writing career and concentration on providing good parts for women with her second teleplay for *Armchair Theatre*. Out of a cast of five, the four leading characters were women.

The Madam	Aug 8, 1965
Teleplay by	Gwen Cherrell
Cast included	Rosalie Crutchley, Gwen Watford, Alethea Charlton and Angela Pleasance – with Paul Williamson
Director	Raymond Menmuir
Designer	Royston Carss

Dame Flora Robson was reported to have declared, "I'm fed up with reading plays, because they are all written with men in mind. Parts for women are meagre".

Gwen Cherrell was beginning to correct that imbalance. Indeed, we of the Drama department of ABC Television were helping that change with writers like Elaine Morgan, Edna O'Brien, Virginia Hewett, Lynne Reid Banks and Sophie Treadwell. Not to mention the shift in the emphasis upon male leading actors as being the 'norm', when in *The Avengers* earlier, Honor Blackman was the powerful catalyst.

A change of environment came from the American writer, William Marchant (then living in London). His play involved sophisticated characters in an Italian setting – described as "a romantic mystery". Again a woman calling the shots, albeit pistols at dawn!

The Challenge	August 15, 1965
Teleplay by	William Marchant
Cast included	Moira Redmond and Gerald Flood – with Gabriella Pascoli, Deborah Stanford, Simon Gough and Stewart Guidotti
Director	Guy Verney
Designer	Kenneth Mellor

We continued with a hospital thriller:

Wake a Stranger	August 29, 1965
Teleplay by	Donald and Derek Ford
Cast included	Nyree Dawn Porter, Edward Woodward and Anthony Newlands – with Mark Burns and Peter Halliday, Hannah Gordon, Susan Dowdall, Delia Corrie, Julian D'Albie, Harry Littlewood and Terry Hedley
Director	Basil Coleman
Designer	William McCrow

Nyree Dawn Porter's role 'Lisa' was described as "blonde and beautiful, travelling light; all she has goes into a hatbox – brimful of money…" The role called for a strong drunken scene, and Nyree revealed her trick to assist in such performances: a splash of brandy on her arms!

Yet another 'first' for *Armchair Theatre* came next with an original teleplay, a black comedy thriller, a taut encounter with just three characters: two undistinguished buskers and a deranged gunman. Programme Controller Brian Tesler had reservations about this one, voicing concerns to me about its 'black' element overriding any comedy, but Herbert Wise steered three strong performances in a fine balancing act.

Charlie Never Warned Us	September 5, 1965
Teleplay by	Douglas Livingstone
Cast included	Ron Moody, Jack MacGowran and Fulton Mackay
Director	Herbert Wise
Designer	William McCrow

Tony Williamson, another new writer to us, provided the original teleplay for the next production.

Ask Any Neighbour	September 19, 1965 (10.05pm ABC) (10.45pm ATV)
Teleplay by	Tony Williamson
Cast included	Jack Hedley, Ronald Lewis, Barry Ingham, Margaret Whiting and Angela Browne
Director	Patrick Dromgoole
Designer	David Marshall

For the last of the fourteen dramas in the mystery genre, for this session, we tried something different – a double-bill of two separate short plays. A thirty-minute drama had not been done in *Armchair Theatre* since the first season (1956-57) under Dennis Vance some ten years earlier.

This double-bill came about because of another 'first' – the decision to make an *improvised* television drama. Certainly a unique challenge. A few weeks earlier, I had received a note from the MD, Howard Thomas, together with a short story from a woman's magazine. He was suggesting that the writer, Mary Hocking, was "one to watch and maybe use".

I read the story and liked it, but it was clearly not suitable for a full one-hour teleplay. However, I was in the mood to try to break the mould – but time was short (the last slot in the season). I ventured with the seemingly crackpot idea of trying to get two actors of such calibre that they might take this written story and, without a script as such, to rehearse an improvisation of it. They would have only a story line in narrative form to work with.

Besides two suitable actors, I needed a director. I could only think of one such who might be excited by it, and willing to have a go: Peter Hammond. I put my idea to him and his response was that if we could get the right actors then, yes, he would take the challenge with relish. Peter Hammond was always extending the limits – right from the early days of putting a unique style on *The Avengers*.

Of the very few actors considered, one stood out as ideal: Donald Pleasance, a unique talent. Peter hooked him. There were some reservations, but I believe that Donald was quite fascinated by the zany idea.

Having got that far, it mattered immensely who would play opposite him. The balance was delicate. We were able to get Elizabeth Begley – herself a very special talent – to team with Donald Pleasance and 'create' this teleplay. Simply named, it was certainly inspirational.

Ambrose
Donald Pleasance and Elizabeth Begley with Peter Reeves (standing)

Ambrose September 26, 1965

Story by	Mary Hocking
Cast included	Donald Pleasance and Elizabeth Begley – with Peter Reeves
Director	Peter Hammond
Designer	Patrick Downing

The Stairway
Gary Watson and Bernard Bresslaw moving successfully from his *Army Game* image into straight acting

The other half of the double-bill was a good contrast – a highly acclaimed short thriller.

The Stairway	September 26, 1965(10.05pm ABC) (11pm ATV)
Written by	John Whiting
Cast included	Bernard Bresslaw, Gary Watson and Walter Gotell
Designer	Michael Hall
Director	Patrick Dromgoole

According to reviewer Sarah Snow (*TV Times*) it all added up to—

> first-class suspense.

Thus, the ninth season of *Armchair Theatre* ended having endured some unhelpful scheduling. Apart from sharing the 'slot' (every third week ATV took over), productions were transmitted at different times in different areas. The last presentation was shown at 10.05pm in our own ABC Television areas (Midlands and the North) and as late as 11pm in the London area by ATV. This break with continuity, especially in a single-play anthology where each and every play has to fight for its audience, is especially difficult to overcome. Something had to be done.

CHAPTER 10

Armchair Theatre – 1965-66 – Tenth Season

High Drama! We Have to Cut the Tape...

The press-handout (dated December 1, 1965) heralded my fourth season—

> ABC's ARMCHAIR THEATRE opens its Tenth Season this Saturday (4th December) with a new network screening policy and a new look to its future plans. ...
> For the next twenty weeks (not counting Christmas weekend) ABC TELEVISION will present the Saturday night play on the full ITV Network.

That looked impressive enough, but the "Saturday night play" in this run from ABC was to be shared between two anthology titles. *Armchair Theatre* was to present thirteen, and those to be split in the middle by a run of seven plays under the title of *Mystery and Imagination*.

The change from the previous transmission pattern of two dramas from ABC (*Armchair Theatre*) and one from ATV now allowed more continuity and relationship with our audience, and that was to be welcomed. And better still, we were back to full-networking on the same night, rather than split between Saturdays and Sundays. But I wasn't happy about losing our Sunday night date with our audience.

These improvements, engineered by Brian Tesler and Lloyd Shirley (now putting his own stamp on affairs as Drama Supervisor) were described as being—

> to get the best possible network exposure for the programme and to give added vitality to the development of the single play.

Lloyd Shirley went on record saying—

> By grouping our plays in short seasons we can use methods of presentation that will enhance the sense of occasion and stimulate the public's interest afresh each time. There is so much series drama on television now that the single play must be made to seem an event to be anticipated with special interest.

So, the single play was under threat. Gone was the highly successful scheduling format of *Armchair Theatre* as the drama event of Sunday nights, following a top-flight light-entertainment variety hour. It was now becoming self-evident that scheduling a successful drama series over fifty-two weeks of the year was a lot less work than having to worry about the changing content of runs of single plays fighting for the audience afresh each time.

The fact that in the previous year, *Armchair Theatre* had occupied thirteen places out of the 'Drama Top Twenty', and crowned it by taking the first three places, this impressive rating and popular success was discounted in the search for format schedule-fillers.

We launched our tenth season with a “sly, ever so slightly naughty play” (*Television Mail*), the comedy with a darker side which was Donald Churchill’s particular style, and his fifth for *Armchair Theatre*.

The Paraffin Season
George Baker and Pauline Yates

The Paraffin Season December 4, 1965 (10.05pm)

Teleplay by	Donald Churchill
Cast included	Norman Rossington, Pauline Yates, George Baker and Joss Ackland – with Tessa Wyatt, Richard Coleman, Mona Bruce and Maureen Davis
Director	Guy Verney
Designer	Stan Woodward

Philip Purser selected Donald Churchill as a writer he highlights from his many years experience as a television critic.

An accident of scheduling resulted in the excellent actress Tessa Wyatt appearing in this and the following week’s play.

The Paraffin Season
Maureen Davis, Norman Rossington and Tessa Wyatt

Story editor Terence Feely discovered the work of Michael Harald. His play was a strong story of a "VC wartime hero who is a peacetime failure", which had been written especially for Leslie Phillips who, in playing this role, demonstrated excellently that he was not just a 'Boeing-Boeing, Carry On' light comedian.

The Gong Game December 11, 1965 (10.05pm)

Teleplay by	Michael Harald
Cast included	Leslie Phillips – with Caroline Mortimer, Denis Quilley, Nora Swinburne, James Kerry, Margaret Robertson, Frank Gatliff, P.G. Stephens, Annette Kerr and Tessa Wyatt
Director	Bill Bain
Designer	Peter Le Page

Bill Bain, directed this "subtle examination of class in British society" which provoked stimulating opposing comments from viewers. One letter from Amersham, finding it "not very interesting", posed a question concerning some dialogue. The leading character had remarked that "opportunities had slipped through his fingers", and the girl had replied, "As the actress said to the Bishop". The correspondent wrote that his son, who considered himself to be 'with it', asked what this meant, and as he, the parent, couldn't explain "some modern humour" would we "kindly explain"! Naturally, I replied to educate the son.

A Mr Rattigan of Coventry declared that he had only once before written to congratulate actors and that was "some years ago". He called *The Gong Game*—

> first class entertainment in every department.

Our next production made the front cover of *TV Times* with a stunning photograph of Britt Ekland. She was starring and making her first appearance in a British television play. It was also the first TV performance of Roy Dotrice (a member of the Royal Shakespeare Company at that time).

Muller, an ex-journalist, had written a powerful play, using his experience to write about a journalist colleague – thinly veiled as the leading character.

Marjorie Norris (*Stage and Television Today,* 23/12/1965) described it as—

> so painfully real that at times it seemed indecent to be watching it in armchair comfort.

She also said that this play, set in the south of France, was—

> one of the rare occasions when a setting referred to in the script as being opulent has come over as exactly that, thanks to designer Patrick Downing.

A Cold Peace
Britt Ekland and Ian Hendry: he plays a writer who has thrown up his responsibilties; she plays the beautiful girl who is his consolation

A Cold Peace

December 18, 1965 (10.05pm)

Teleplay by	Robert Muller
Cast included	Britt Ekland, Ian Hendry, Roy Dotrice, Isabel Dean – with Kathleen Breck and David Phethean
Director	Don Leaver
Designer	Patrick Downing

A Cold Peace
Isabel Dean and Roy Dotrice play the couple whose marriage is in crisis

The production was notable for two particular problems. Firstly, the opulent setting called for a large swimming pool to be built in the studio, and secondly because the ITA suggested some changes when they viewed the production.

The technical problem (and a higher than average design cost) was due to the need to provide a large swimming pool in Studio One at Teddington – a challenge not at all attractive to the studio management. Nevertheless, it was achieved, and was a considerable visual plus. Unfortunately, as the days of rehearsal and recording went on, the great weight of the water in the pool tested the studio flooring (possibly weakened from the bombing it had suffered during the war) to a degree that it began to leak. The leaks were plugged (Heath Robinson-style) with only partial success. The tempo of shooting during that recording was raised considerably! The show had to go on. Buckets to the ready (if not the fire brigade). We got the show in the can but not all the water!

The ITA reaction after seeing the show ready for transmission created a few obvious headlines (and as ever on these occasions didn't do the ratings any harm):

Britt Ekland

Daily Telegraph—

ITA CENSORS BRITT EKLAND PLAY

Daily Mail—

BRITT EKLAND'S TV DEBUT CENSORED

Daily Express—

TV CENSOR CUTS BRITT'S LOVE SCENE

It was reported that the objections were that Ian Hendry—

fondled Miss Ekland a little too fondly

And that elsewhere a man is—

on a bed fully dressed and the woman walked towards him with part of her back bared

How times have changed since those cautious days.

All this has to be remembered as being in the times when to cut a tape was sacrilege – because if a tape was cut it could not be wiped and used again, and therefore became a charge against the programme cost. This was the first time that I had to commit such vandalism. I have a vivid memory of sitting with the editor (well, hardly that, we never used such film crafts in live tape production) watching his hand poised uncertainly... "You really do want me to do this?"

I still have in my scrapbook that piece of severed tape, just twelve inches long! That's all we cut.

New Year's Day 1966, *Armchair Theatre* presented a tough but excellent play. The setting was in an Army camp in Malaysia.

The Sweet War Man
Neil Stacy and Kenneth More. More plays a major under arrest after going berserk due to too much guerilla fighting in the Far East. Stacy plays the raw subaltern set to guard the old sweat

The Sweet War Man January 1, 1966 (10.05pm)

Teleplay by	Barry England
Cast included	Kenneth More and Neil Stacy
Director	Alvin Rakoff
Designer	Michael Hall

The story editor was Robert Banks Stewart, who later went on to become a successful producer.

From the Army to the Navy. Alun Richards – who wrote the following week's play *Ready for the Glory* – had a naval background, and made one of his characters an old sailor. The female lead was "a three-time married titled lady with a drink problem, who writes to a marriage bureau for a new husband". A surprising candidate turns up at her Gibraltar villa.

Ready for the Glory **Colin Blakely and Ann Todd**

Ready for the Glory January 8, 1966 (10.05pm)

Teleplay by	Alun Richards
Cast included	Ann Todd and Colin Blakely – with Stephen Murray, Terence Alexander and Frances White
Director	Jonathan Alwyn
Designer	David Marshall

No one could accuse Alun Richards of not knowing his subject. Again, rich characters and a human situation just right for the 'box', attracted fine actors and fine performances, which provoked audience appreciation from both the ordinary viewers and from inside the 'biz'.

A plea from Mrs Elizabeth O'Brien of Ilkley—

> More plays of this type with this great acting please.

Herbert Wise of Birmingham agreed—

> This was first-class entertainment, brisk, revealing dialogue, good situations, splendidly cast and sensitively acted. More plays of this nature please!

The pace of production in those days didn't give us much time to reflect but such reactions gave a lift to all concerned. We were hitting the spot every now and then.

"A comedy with a kick like a rifle" was how one pre-viewer described this next play by an American writer. An *Armchair Theatre* debut.

Toby Robins, Dick Gregory, Ruby Dee and Donald Harron in *Neighbours*
A white couple living in an American suburb decide to sell their house to a black couple

Neighbours	January 15, 1966 (10.05pm)
Teleplay by	Arkady Leokum
Cast included	Ruby Dee and Dick Gregory – with Toby Robins and Donald Harron
Director	Paul Almond
Designer	Philip Harrison

Truly American in style and situation, yet accessible to a British television audience.

With just four characters, the play needed accurate casting. We had the great good fortune to line-up a first-rate quartet to deal with a very sensitive issue.

Dick Gregory in *Neighbours*

Two artistes from America – Ruby Dee and Dick Gregory – besides being fine actors were both strongly involved in Civil Rights work. Dick Gregory was best known as a comedian, and had become a cabaret star who used his sardonic humour as a weapon for his active crusading. Indeed, his very active crusading almost frustrated our casting and stopped the production. He only just got out of gaol in time to join us! I was mightily thankful we were able to present his first dramatic role on UK television in *Armchair Theatre*.

To balance these two very strong characters, casting the white couple to play opposite them was going to be difficult and delicate. Canadians Toby Robins and Donald Harron fitted these roles admirably. A rare quartet of talent.

I had greatly admired the work of Toby Robins since her earlier days in Toronto, and I had worked with Donald Harron in New York. By the time of Arkady Leokum's teleplay *Neighbours,* they had both made a considerable impact in London.

Canadian Paul Almond directed – working in one of my productions for the first time, and assuring a true North American understanding of Leokum's script.

Philip Harrison's design very well supported the special environment, being described by Kari Anderson (*Stage and Television Today*) as—

> more accurate in all details ... than any American setting I've seen on British television

The controversial nature of the drama did raise some adverse comments as to its intention. A viewer from Kent considered that this play—

> certainly excelled if it was shown with the express purpose of inciting further racial prejudice and hatred.

Which of course could not have been further from the intentions of Arkady Leokum, or indeed Dick Gregory or Ruby Dee – or any of the team.

A Mr Hewlett of Chingford wrote—

> This was an extremely good play...

The Pity of it All
Billie Whitelaw and Nigel Stock: she plays a young widow who falls in love with the man who has accidentally run over her only child; he plays the man in the case

The following week our audience was brought back to the realities of northern England and no mistaking.

The Pity of it All January 22, 1966 (10.05pm)

Teleplay by	Stan Barstow
Cast included	Billie Whitelaw and Nigel Stock – with Ann Firbank, Jack Watson, Maureen Pryor, John McKelvey and Patricia Shakesby
Director	Patrick Dromgoole
Designer	David Marshall

"Back to the headscarf" is how Billie Whitelaw described it. She was returning after two years working on stage with the National Theatre to star in this *Armchair Theatre* ('television's National Theatre') production. She exchanged Desdemona's love story for that of another tragedy confronting 'a backstreet young widow of a miner'. As ever the audience loved her work – all of more than 15 million of them.

The *Television Mail* (28/1/1966) reviewer said of Billie Whitelaw—

> This was superb performance.

Man Without A Mortgage
Margaret Anderson and Donald Churchill

A further run started with another notable comedy, in which the author played the central character in his own play about an engineering draughtsman who tries to get a rise in salary in order to buy a larger house to accomodate his family and inlaws.

Man Without a Mortgage March 19, 1966 (10.10pm)

Teleplay by	Donald Churchill
Cast included	Donald Churchill – with Terence Alexander, Sally Bazely, Fabia Drake, Margaret Anderson, Anne Godfrey, Ernest Hare, Leslie Sarony, Rowena Ingram, Carmen Dene and Richard Curnock
Director	Guy Verney
Designer	Patrick Downing

Director Guy Verney continued his association with Churchill to great effect.

Marjorie Norris (*Stage and Television Today,* 24/3/1966)—

> Funny though the play was—and it was very funny—it was tinged with sadness. ... Guy Verney's direction ensured that the fun never obscured the underlying truths.

Looking at press cuttings of this production, I see that Pauline Yates – Donald Churchill's wife – is quoted as describing Donald's escape to the loft rafters at the top of the house, "whenever he feels a play coming on..." and pulling up the ladder behind him.

And here I am some thirty years later doing the same, sitting in my loft re-living another time and another place. However, whereas Donald was creating, I am only *re*-creating – struggling to be true to warm memories of his and other talents that I have had the honour to work with.

Armchair Theatre, no matter how successful, was being pushed later and later in the evening. The following week we presented what ought to have been a very attractive event – a teleplay, described as "an Allegorical Comedy", with a popular comedian playing the lead.

The Battersea Miracle
Charlie Drake plays a failed highwire artiste who turns clown and discovers a talking flea called Pete which aims to influence national politics

The Battersea Miracle March 26, 1966 (10.20pm)

Teleplay by	Wolf Mankowitz
Cast included	Charlie Drake – with Edward Burnham, John Barron, Robert James, Patrick Troughton, George Woodbridge, Gerald Turner, Rex Garner, Monica Merlin, Keith Pyott, Brian Osborne, Robert Russell and David Neal
Director	Shaun O'Riordan
Designer	Assheton Gorton

I should have seen the red lights flashing when it became obvious that Charlie Drake needed to approve the director. For years the strength of the Drama Department at ABC Television had been its internal mechanism; a group with lots of in-house experience and similar aims. Agree or disagree, we did work well as a team. Now with *The Battersea Miracle*, this production was beginning to look like something 'bought in'. I was unable to apply a director to it that I knew.

Charlie Drake in *The Battersea Miracle*

Charlie Drake wanted Shaun O'Riordan to direct his first straight dramatic role. O'Riordan worked mostly with ATV and was with Drake on *The Worker* series. Eventually we agreed.

The combination of a Mankowitz script and Charlie Drake as straight actor in the lead was very attractive. The quirky nature of the whole project – which was now being described as a 'satirical comedy' rather than 'allegorical' – tickled my perverse nature, and appealed to story editor Terence Feely's particular sense of humour. It was a different challenge, and we liked challenges at Teddington.

Alas, it didn't succeed with the critics who, to put it mildly, didn't like it at all.

Kenneth Easthaugh of the *Daily Mirror* (28/3/1966) said—

> The theme of a talking flea who wants to be God is (if you'll pardon the expression) jumping with biting possibilites. But brother, how they loused it up ... Presumably writer Wolf Mankowitz wrote it with insecticide, not ink

However, he went on to say—

> Certainly, on this showing, he [Charlie Drake] should do more plays.

The 'Battersea miracle' is that this super-flea has a message of 'Peace for the World' and is able to speak to Joey the clown.

Outrageous, difficult stuff, especially for television drama that was stuck in the 'reality' groove. We attempted something different but failed in this case.

We moved on to firmer ground with a "marriage comedy" by another new writer for *Armchair Theatre*. More, perhaps, in the style of sit-coms of the future – but having the extra quality of Jack Rosenthal's acute observation.

The Night Before the Morning After
Rodney Bewes, Trevor Bannister and Coral Atkins

The Night Before the Morning After April 2, 1966 (10.05pm)

Teleplay by	Jack Rosenthal
Cast included	Bernard Lee, Julia Foster, Rodney Bewes, Betty Marsden – with Trevor Bannister and Coral Atkins
Director	Kim Mills
Designer	Peter Le Page

Kim Mills was directing his first for *Armchair Theatre* – a play that had all the ingredients of accessibility.

Story Editor Terence Feely also bounced back with yet another new writer for us, Anton Delmar, providing a happy vehicle for the youthful duo Dame Sybil Thorndike (83) and Athene Seyler (77) playing two daffy spinsters, shady operators not averse to counterfeiting. Nothing satirical this time, or allegorical – just honest to goodness wholesome escapism. Armchairs were drawn up for:

Don't Utter a Note
with Peter Copley
and Sybil Thorndike

Athene Seyler
and Sidney James

Don't Utter A Note April 9, 1966 (10.15pm)

Teleplay by	Anton Delmar
Cast included	Sybil Thorndike and Athene Seyler – with Sidney James, Peter Bowles, Peter Copley, Kathleen Breck, Tim Preece and Jack Watson
Director	Patrick Dromgoole
Designer	Voytek

Voytek, despite still having trouble with the English language, spoke volumes with his designs.

Was television drama, at last, beginning to be taken seriously? Theatre was the place for glamour and prestige, but more people saw an actor in a single TV play than would see him/her in ten years on the boards.

A quote from that time in the mid-sixties—

> Television is the fame-maker of show business these days.

And so it was that Alfie Bass (of TV fame) teamed with Robert Stephens (best stage actor of 1965, star of the National Theatre, but little known to our audiences). They made an unlikely partnership, but worked happily in tandem as a couple of Cockney plumbers.

Daughter of the House
Robert Stephens plays a plumber. Sharing his tandem is Alfie Bass as the plumber's mate

Daughter of the House April 16, 1966 (10.0pm)

Teleplay by	Guy Clark
Cast included	Alfie Bass, Robert Stephens and Wanda Ventham – with Gerald James, Anthony Dawes, Gordon Rollings, Richard Davies, Ann Kennedy, Paul Whitsun-Jones and Frank Thornton
Director	Jonathan Alwyn
Designer	Stan Woodward

Director Jonathan Alwyn had some light relief with this one, but I'm sure he preferred meatier yarns.

Daughter of the House

Left: Wanda Ventham plays the daughter sunbathing on the roof when she is interrupted by the plumber who comes to mend the guttering

Below left: Wanda Ventham and Robert Stephens, the romantically-minded plumber

Below right: Paul Whitsun-Jones as the police constable marooned on the roof with with Robert Stephens

Critics seemed unable to reconcile 'farcical complications' with the play not being a farce. They expected a farce and didn't get it. The old problem of hitting the right style was made more difficult by the very special nature of live television performance and cutting the shots.

Story Editor Robert Banks Stewart again had an opportunity to concentrate on a series of comedy plays. I now believe it was unwise to tamper with *Armchair Theatre*'s tradition of providing a running anthology of differing teleplays, a healthy mix which had worked well for us in the past.

The Walls Came Tumbling Down
Robert Lang and Elizabeth Valentine. The meek and mild clerk who spends his days stamping papers 'SEEN AND APPROVED' suddenly fulfils a wish, and applies the stamp to the pretty typist's knickers. (Robert Lang accidentally picked up the wrong stamp for the photo!)

There is a sensation in the mail order office when Harold Crombie (played by Robert Lang) decides to break the monotony. This quirky comedy introduced a new young director to the *Armchair Theatre* team.

The Walls Came Tumbling Down April 23, 1966 (10.15pm)

Teleplay by Nicholas Salaman
Cast included Ronald Fraser, Robert Lang, Norman Bird and William Mervyn – with Joan Newell, Rita Webb, Martin Friend, Anna Middleton and Elizabeth Valentine
Director Laurence Bourne
Designer David Marshall

Critic Kari Anderson (*Stage and Television Today,* 28/4/1966) didn't laugh—

> I'm prepared to believe that others watching it would find this essay on the turning worm amusing. ...
> [The characters] were all supremely silly.

This 'Season of Comedy' ended with a play described as "the story of a mixed-marriage controversy". *The Match* was specially written for us by one of our own story editors. Our policy was to avoid any possible conflict of interest in the relationships between our story editors and the writers we were commissioning. Our editors had to be the writers' friends, not their competitors. However, in this case the circumstances were different insofar that Norman Bogner was preparing to return to his native home in the USA, where he wrote the screenplay of a Harold Robbins novel, as well as writing many novels of his own.

The Match
Michael Cadman and Wanda Ventham in a story of a mixed-marriage controversy

The Match April 30, 1966 (10.0pm)

Teleplay by	Norman Bogner
Cast included	Lee Montague – with Nicola Pagett, John Franklin Robbins, Barbara Lott, Michael Cadman, Wanda Ventham, Arthur Pentelow, Ida Goldapple and Michael Robbins
Director	Don Leaver
Designer	Brian Eatwell

The tag 'specially written for *Armchair Theatre*' was extremely important for us. It was the very foundation of our enterprise. Sydney Newman's earlier emphasis on the writing was essentially the torch to carry. In spite of the irony of theatre being in the anthology title we were not aping stage, and certainly not cinema. Our audience was domestic.

I firmly believed that television drama must offer a style and content quite distinct from stage or cinema. Over thirty and more years later I am still of that opinion.

I have always used a basic rule of thumb to ensure an essential recognition of the differences between the media in which the drama is communicated: I believe that theatre is where the 'suspension of disbelief' comes naturally. Cinema is the medium of environment – D.W. Griffith/de Mille size and action. Television drama is essentially a matter of personality, of the close-up – even the big close-up.

The reviewer in *The Sunday Telegraph* (1/5/1966) saw *The Match* as a play—

> which cleverly exploited an embarrassing Jews and Gentiles situation. ... The young man blurts out, "She's not Jewish." The appalling 'inter-family' dinner party that ensued, and on which the play closes, made a scene to remember and possibly learn from.

So, true to comedy, a happy ending, and true to *Armchair Theatre* an ending to that season with entertainment and something to think about after the event.

Stars from *Armchair Theatre* — 1966
Charlie Drake
Alfie Bass and Sidney James

Stars from *Armchair Theatre*

Above: Britt Ekland makes her debut in *A Cold Peace* – December 1965

Below: A play with a north country setting – *The Pity of it All* – January 1966

Billie Whitelaw and Nigel Stock

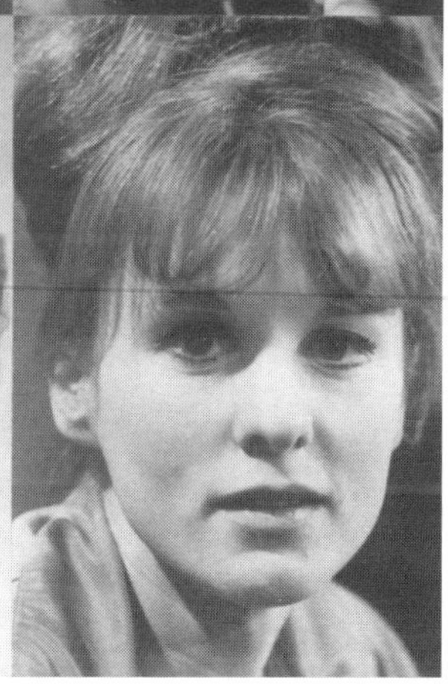

Ann Firbank **Patricia Shakesby**

CHAPTER 11

Armchair Theatre – 1966-67 – Eleventh Season

Victim of our own Success?

The new run opened with a first television adaptation of a Noel Coward short story and, unlike the normal one-hour slot, *Armchair Theatre* was given 90 minutes to do this romantic comedy justice.

Pretty Polly
The first Coward story to be dramatised for television
Lynn Redgrave and Donald Houston: she is a plain girl who undergoes a Cinderella transformation when the rich aunt with whom she is travelling dies in Singapore; he is the teaplanter uncle who takes a Cowardian pleasure in his niece's liberation from his disagreeable sister-in-law

Pretty Polly July 23, 1966 (10.05pm ABC) (10.15pm ATV)

Story by	Noel Coward
Teleplay by	William Marchant
Cast included	Lynn Redgrave, Donald Houston and Zia Mohyeddin – with Dandy Nichols – and Poulet Tu, Leon Sinden, Lillias Walker, Gwenda Wilson, Stuart Cooper
Director	Bill Bain
Designer	Patrick Downing

Despite the disadvantages, William Marchant's adaptation of Noel Coward's *Pretty Polly* held the viewers.

The Daily Telegraph (25/7/1966) reviewer saw it as—

> crisp, light, relaxed entertainment, a neat piece of theatre made vivid by notable acting.

At the beginning of this eleventh year of *Armchair Theatre* Marjorie Bilbow wrote an article in *The Stage and Television Today* (28/7/1966) headed—

> The single play is so vulnerable – it must be loved, guarded, and given every chance

Those words were something of a summary of what I had said to her in an interview. Reading that article again over thirty years later, the resonances are considerable. After three and a half years of my producing *Armchair Theatre*, she quoted me as saying—

> It's been suggested by one school of thought that if there were fewer single plays on television more time could be devoted to ensuring that they were better than they are now. I don't think this is a true argument at all.
>
> For one thing, it depends on a belief that if you had to choose say 30 plays instead of 50 you would inevitably select the ones which were better than the 20 you had to leave out. This doesn't follow at all because there is no way of knowing for certain that a play is going to turn out as you hope it will until it has been done.
>
> The only result of putting on fewer plays is that you cut down on opportunities and this immediately sets a limit on the commissioning of new plays – particularly plays from new writers. Only with the single play is the writer free to use his imagination to the full; fewer opportunities would inhibit them and frustrate the directors; and there would be a diminishing of standards and audiences would suffer in the long run.

Now, after ten years of a successful series, providing continuity throughout each season, we realised that the single play had the least captive audience of any form of entertainment programming. We had to fight even harder against the easier options of drama series and soap operas. Fortunately, with fine writing, fine performances and dedicated crews, we still made a strong impact. As well as losing the preferred Sunday evening slot, ATV was insisting on split transmission times. We at ABC, for the Midlands and the North, transmitted at 10.05pm, immediately after an episode of the successful series *Public Eye*, and ATV in the London area started ten minutes later, following the News. Thus, for some viewers the single 90-minute teleplay followed immediately after a drama series, and for others it was pushed to a 10.15pm start. The pressure was on.

A week later, we were back to the more usual style for *Armchair Theatre*.

The Wager
Peter Vaughan plays a government minister who bets against the chances of his own party in a general election

The Wager
Anthony Valentine and Caroline Mortimer play two young people caught up in the politics of a general election

The Wager	July 30, 1966 (10.45pm)
Teleplay by	Hugo Charteris
Cast included	Peter Vaughan, Caroline Mortimer, Rachel Kempson, Paul Stassino and Daphne Anderson – with Anthony Valentine, Nicole Shelby, Endre Muller, David David, Norman Scace, Edward Brayshaw, Frank Littlewood, Rex Garner and Mary Kay
Director	John Moxey
Designer	Michael Knight

In *The Stage and Television Today* (4/8/1966) Marjorie Norris headed her review—

> What a pity we can't see this ABC play again

It was the weekend of World Cup celebrations, and the schedule on that Saturday evening was altered to accommodate that rare event. *The Wager* did not start until 10.45pm, and therefore suffered in the ratings. The call for a second showing, however, indicated its success, but it didn't get another viewing. ITV in those days did not consider repeats.

Marjorie Norris referred to this play as—

> a production cast by ABC with the delicate exactness that in itself is a connnoisseur's delight...

Allan Prior, following the success of his Blackpool Trilogy, provided our next production. He adapted his own novel *The One-Eyed Monster*. Adapting a novel to a feature film is quite the norm, but reduction to a one-hour drama (actually 55 minutes with the commercials) is well nigh impossible. Thus, the story that became the teleplay was necessarily only part of the book – and featured a street market-trader who dispensed homely advice with each sale, and who went on to become a famous TV personality. Comedy and high tragedy.

The One-Eyed Monster August 11, 1966 (10.05pm ABC) (10.15pm ATV)

Teleplay by	Allan Prior (an adaptation from his own novel)
Cast included	Rupert Davies – with Rex Garner, Kathleen Breck, Ann Kennedy, John Cater and Alan Wheatley – also Edward Caddick, David Saire, Ken Parry and Totti Truman Taylor
Director	Robert Tronson
Designer	David Marshall

Rupert Davies played Miffin, the street-trader, who unfortunately thought that TV was "a high place to do good in". I had first met Rupert Davies in my early acting days, when he was playing Seyton (I was playing Malcolm) in Michael Redgrave's *Macbeth* at the Aldwych Theatre in London (1947/48); and then, later, when he starred in a television series in Canada, while I was beginning to learn of the "corrupting effects of mass popularity" (Marjorie Norris, *Stage and Television Today*) at CBC in Toronto.

In these later years of Network schedulers' fixation – 'soaps are everything' – that story might well get re-invented: a sort-of hybrid *Coronation Street* crossed with the Esther Rantzen show: everyday problems and lifestyle hung out to dry with TV's soap-powder, whiter than white, homespun philosophy. But Allan Prior's story was different. His intent was a keen look behind the scenes of the 'One-Eyed Monster' studios.

The *Daily Mirror* (8/8/1966) referred to John Cater as playing—

> A real tail-snapping rodent in the television rat-race.

The strong cast for this next play reads like a line-up of top Irish acting talent.

Great Big Blonde August 13, 1966 (10.05pm ABC) (10.15pm ATV)

Teleplay by	Hugh Leonard
Cast included	Maureen Toal, Joe Lynch, Patrick McAlinney, Gerry Sullivan and guest star Marie Kean – with David Kelly, Marie Hastings, John McKelvey, Howard Charlton, Adam Verney, Harry Hutchinson and John Keenan
Director	Guy Verney
Designer	Philip Harrison

The excellent writer, Hugh Leonard, was continuing his association with *Armchair Theatre,* and with Director Guy Verney who had built a strong rapport with the Irish writer and actors. Certainly, if there ever was a retrospective of Hugh Leonard's work, it must include the successful teleplays and Guy Verney's contribution.

Cyclops in 'Professional Eye on Programmes' (*Television Mail,* 19/8/1966) wrote—

> Its attitudes, its atmosphere, and its dialogue were artful distillations of middle-class Dublin by a master of the Dublin scene. ...played with deadly arid documentary precision ... The immense accomplishment of writing and playing...

Director, designer and writer were all new names for us in the following.

A Fair Swap August 20, 1966 (10.05pm ABC) (10.15pm ATV)

Teleplay by	Jeremy Paul
Cast included	Daniel Massey, David Hutcheson, Derrick Sherwin, Rosemary Martin – with Hilda Braid, Anthony Brown, Thelma Holt, Robert Hornery, Howard Taylor and John Burch
Director	Lionel Harris
Designer	Stephen Saxe

Thelma Holt later became renowned as a powerful impresario of theatre production.

Jeremy Paul's teleplay was described in one review as—

> ...a polished and entertaining play he pinpoints the pressures, the subtle shifting of conscience, and the coming to terms with moral attitudes at the higher executive levels.

This first teleplay by these co-writers inspired contrasting comparisons with the styles of N.F. Simpson and Ionesco, and was even described as 'Capraesque'. Certainly, the oddity of ordinary people reflecting private fantasies presented a difficult genre for TV drama, the comedy bordering on farce. The tightrope of eccentric behaviour was absurd and yet entirely sympathetic.

The Signal Box of Grandpa Hudson	August 27, 1966 (10.15pm)
Teleplay by	David Nobbs and Peter Tinniswood
Cast included	Ian McShane, Suzan Farmer and Billy Russell – with John Woodvine and Margery Withers – also Bill Shine, Barry Jackson and Michael Parker
Director	Basil Coleman
Designer	Philip Harrison

The veteran Billy Russell, fine exponent of character comedy, played Grandpa – a nonagenarian and obsessive train spotter.

Basil Coleman, the most caring and gentle of directors, handled this difficult genre finely.

David Hope (*Stage and Television Today,* 7/9/1966) was appreciative—

> Faultless acting ... Coleman's direction was—as it had to be—super-efficient, and designer Philip Harrison deserves special mention for the zany exuberance of his sets.

This zany story-telling was not everyone's 'Horlicks at bedtime'. The one-eyed Cyclops (*Television Mail,* 2/9/1966) wrote—

> There were some memorable moments in it; notably when Geoffrey eventually came to Wendy's home and became involved in some highly comical cross-talk. But these were infrequent plums in a sad, sad duff.

At this time, it was becoming evident that *Armchair Theatre* was in some ways the victim of its own success. Writers, directors and actors whom the series had nurtured were now providing competition from other companies using their talents. And rightly so. Nothing wrong with good healthy competition, of course, so long as the playing field is level.

I welcomed the wider competition, and that was never more so than when Sydney Newman asked me to join him at the BBC. I declined, and instead relished the opportunity to run *Armchair Theatre* in competition against my old congenial boss with all the weight of the BBC Television Drama empire behind him.

We still wanted to lead in breaking new ground. I had the great good fortune in that the best still wanted to work on *Armchair Theatre*, which meant that I was surrounded by continued energy and dedication from all in the Department at Teddington Studios. I could never get complacent with such as Howard Thomas, Brian Tesler, Lloyd Shirley – and not to forget George Kerr for the all-too-short time that he was there – to prod, provoke and support me.

In addition, of course, there were the unique 'story editor/writer' relationships, and also the directors and designers, all of whom were consistent in their high standards.

And the performers...

Co-star Gwen Watford – that very fine actress, twice the winner of 'Television Actress of the Year' – said she was glad to get "an attacking part".

The Noise Stopped September 3, 1966 (10.05pm ABC) (10.15pm ATV)

Teleplay by	John Hale
Cast included	John Nettleton, Gwen Watford, Leslie Sands and Clare Kelly – with Simon Gough, Sara Aimson, John Harvey and John Barcroft
Director	Charles Jarrott
Designer	Michael Hall

An accessible story dealing with a clash between career and marriage, both in crisis. It introduced another new talent to television drama: John Nettleton in the leading role. He, at the age of 37, was fresh from the Royal Shakespeare Company.

David Hope in *The Stage and Television Today* (8/9/1966) wrote—

> The play was altogether a bit thin on motivation – which was a pity because many of the individual scenes were beautifully written, and John Hale's command of conversational idiom is impressive. When this latter quality is matched by first-class acting it is always irresistibly watchable ... [John Nettleton] made an excellent first impression ... [He] made the transition into the new medium with accomplishment.

I received a letter (dated 4/9/1966) from one viewer—

> As a black man I was shocked at the use of the word "nigger" in your Armchair Theatre play last night. ... this six-letter word is more obscene and more of an insult than any of your four-letter ones.

The offensiveness of a character is sometimes assumed, regardless of context and outcome, to be supported by those involved in the creation of the play. In this case, the character who uttered the offensive word was indeed an offensive man and he got his just deserts in the old morality play manner – he was struck dead.

It is interesting to note that this production, even at the late hour of transmission, held its audience and even improved upon the rating for the preceding programme, the series *Public Eye*, in the ABC Television areas.

The next was more then just a whodunit, and had been specially written for our anthology.

Dead Silence	September 10, 1966 (10.05pm ABC) (10.15pm ATV)
Teleplay by	Monte Doyle
Cast included	Patrick Allen, Glynn Edwards and Ronald Lacey – with Anne Blake and Jeremy Longhurst – also Joanne Dainton, Michael Gaunt, Donald Layne-Smith and Hamilton Dyce
Director	John Moxey
Designer	David Marshall

Despite the changes in transmission times, Monte Doyle's *Dead Silence* bolstered the ratings, even beating the prime time Saturday evening light entertainment offering (*Mike & Bernie's Show*) with double the audience.

Sylvia Clayton (*Daily Telegraph*, 12/9/1966) wrote of *Dead Silence*—

> The orthodox Whodunit? in which the author is more conjuror than psychologist, is unfashionable on TV.

Margaret Campbell (*Stage and Television Today*) headlined our *ABC* production as a—

> Well constructed *ATV* thriller

She went on to say—

> Director John Moxey and the writer were grooved and tongued with nary a join to be seen. Every turn, polished and smooth.

It wasn't long after that Moxey departed for the 'LA gold rush'.

Barrett Keller—His Mark	September 17, 1966 (10.05pm ABC) (10.15pm ATV)
Teleplay by	Gerald Vaughan-Hughes
Cast included	Bernard Bresslaw, Petra Markham, Christopher Sandford, Shelagh Fraser – with Leslie Lawton, Denis Goacher, Simon Gough, Sheena Marsh, John Kidd, Edward Malin, Clive Colin-Bowler, Robert Booth and Gillian Way
Director	Guy Verney
Designer	Roy Stannard

The subject of the art and antique world pre-dated, by some years, the popular appeal that came much later in both drama series and factual programmes. All those involved earned the plaudits.

David Hope (*Stage and Television Today,* 22/9/1966) headlined his review—

> Good writing, right casting, witty direction, splendid design

Kenneth Easthaugh (*Daily Mirror,* 19/9/1966), although critical of its ending, opined that—

> it was so entertainingly written.

We continued with stronger stuff. It was a 'message play', which dealt with a matter of conscience: the conflict for an idealist CND worker when challenged by the opposing needs of her boy-friend seeking to work as a research scientist in chemical warfare.

Light the Blue Touch Paper September 24, 1966 (10.10pm ABC) (10.20pm ATV)

Teleplay by	John Hale
Cast included	Anna Massey, Ronald Hines, Neil Stacy – with Duncan Lamont and Winifred Dennis
Director	Charles Jarrott
Designer	Eileen Diss

The welcome and successful combination of writer and director provided what Alice Frick (*Stage and Television Today*) described as—

> Hale play one of the best in Armchair Theatre
> ... It's a joy to see a good well-constructed, well-presented teleplay

This production also included a rare visit to Teddington Studios by one of the best designers in the business: Eileen Diss.

Another work, for which I have warm and special memories, followed on – a lovely story:

The Tilted Screen October 1, 1966 (10.05pm ABC) (10.15pm ATV)

Teleplay by	Noel Robinson
Cast included	Yoko Tani and Fredric Abbott – with Brian Anderson, Reg Lye, Georgie Sterling and Nita Pannell – also Charles Stanley, Diane Elliot and Terence Donovan
Director	Bill Bain
Designer	Peter Le Page

This play called for a Japanese actress to play the leading role, and we had the good fortune to have Yoko Tani join us. Her playing of the character Michiko, a university graduate who arrives in Australia to marry, unprepared for the culture shock, was quite beautiful.

The strong Australian environment was built, not only from the writer – Noel Robinson, a journalist, who had only recently left her home country – but also, by co-star Fredric Abbott (originally from Sydney) and by 'down-under' Bill Bain who directed. Peter Le Page designed, and between them they gripped our audience.

It was another of the happy occasions when, in the new and unhelpful transmission slot, *Armchair Theatre* was able to build on the rating of the earlier, preceding show.

We followed with something of a zany thriller. The setting was not far short of being 'camp' – representing an apartment which had been re-decorated by a strange young man 'squatter'. This time the lead was played by a French actress who, at seventeen, had been the youngest ever prima ballerina in her own country.

The Three Barrelled Shotgun	October 8, 1966 (10.05pm ABC) (10.15pm ATV)
Teleplay by	Donald and Derek Ford
Cast included	Michael Crawford, Katherine Kath and June Barry – with Walter Gotell, Totti Truman Taylor, John Denison and Kenneth Colley
Director	Patrick Dromgoole
Designer	Stan Woodward

I well remember *The Three Barrelled Shotgun:* it involved me in a ticking off from boss Howard Thomas. My usual practice was to be on hand at all times during the two days of the studio camera rehearsal, and to watch the 'build' at all stages. However, on this occasion, I had been instructed to be away from Teddington to attend a meeting with Lloyd Shirley at our Hanover Square offices. My being away coincided with Howard Thomas hosting a visit to the Studios by a group of MPs. The run-up to the new franchises was beginning. Clearly, the intention was to impress the MPs. Howard Thomas would have been showing off this top-notch ABC Television programme, *Armchair Theatre*, with some pride. It didn't turn out that way, or so it was reported to me, when eventually I returned to the Studio. I was promptly summoned to the Managing Director's office. Apparently, the MP's had not found the rather bizarre 'camp' setting of the teleplay at all attractive. (Patrick Dromgoole had decorated one of the walls in the sitting room with a very large blow-up of a photograph of his own spectacled eyes, 'watching' what went on in the room.) Certainly nothing like the socially conscious, down-to-earth, kitchen-sink image of *Armchair Theatre* they had probably come to expect! Moreover, in particular, Howard Thomas pointed out that the nude statue of a woman – the centre-piece in the set – was offensive and "must not be photographed like that". If it remained, it had to have "some clothes on".

I made (probably quite ineffectual sounding) apologies, explaining that I had been away from the studio and had only just returned. I was most annoyed because I believed that had I been there when the MPs were making their tour, I could have dealt with any awkward moments. As it was, Howard Thomas himself had been taken aback. Privately I'm sure that he would have had no objections at all. However, what was meant to impress the MPs did not, and that was bad at this critical time.

The irony in all this is that the nude figure was duly clothed as ordered: Patrick Dromgoole added frilly bra and knickers – and in fact, it looked a great deal more offensive like that than just plain nude.

David Hope (*Stage and Television Today*) described Michael Crawford's performance as—

> electric ... this stinging portrait of a decadent youth

His review ended with—

> A special word of praise for Designer Stan Woodward, whose sets provided uninhibited fun in the modern baroque manner; they made a really creative contribution to the play.

A striking example of how wrong it can be to allow anyone uninitiated to 'see the works'. The only way to judge a meal is at the table, not in the kitchen.

That run ended with an opportunity for Patrick Macnee to be able to change his image and play a role unlike John Steed. This was still the age when having a lead in a successful television series was not as prestigious as playing a lead in a single play (even better if that was in theatre). In the world of the 'luvvies' and many of the class newspapers' drama critics, television did not rate. TV was tabloid stuff. But, a single play might just be acceptable and worthy.

The Long Nightmare	October 15, 1966 (10.10pm ABC) (10.20pm ATV)
Teleplay by	Michael Harald
Cast included	Patrick Macnee, Ursula Howells and Gerard Heinz – with Philip Bond, Geoffrey Sumner, Patrick Godfrey, Margot Thomas, John Quayle, Christopher Denham, David Hanson, Frances Pigeon, Elmer Soiron, Greville Steele, Ray Marioni, Katie Newman, Elaine Wells and Jacques Cey
Director	Joan Kemp-Welch
Designer	Stan Woodward

Michael Harald's teleplay, like the previously successful *The Gong Game*, concerned the long shadow of war stretching into later years. Patrick Macnee played a former officer who under torture had become a coward.

Famous TV director Joan Kemp-Welch had only recently become freelance and was much in demand. We were lucky to get her to join us for this production, the only time I worked with her.

During this challenging run, we had tried to extend the style, having produced plays as contrasting as, say, *Pretty Polly* on the one hand, and *Light the Blue Touch Paper* on the other. The story editors were, perhaps, the most challenged. Of those thirteen teleplays, ten were in the care of Terence Feely, with Norman Bogner and Robert Banks Stewart backing up the others.

January 28, 1967, began a run of twelve weekly productions. We continued to suffer the split timings of transmissions in London and elsewhere, and still on Saturday nights with the added problem of following immediately after an episode of a popular drama series. ATV ran *The Baron* immediately before, and our own ABC schedule led with *The Avengers*. To ask an audience to continue to watch a 'single drama' after such pre-conditioning is, at best, over-hopeful. Certainly nothing like the earlier and most successful programming of the play on the Sunday night following the variety show *Sunday Night at the London Palladium*. That had been the recipe for giving the play a real chance, and it had worked wonderfully. The test for survival was in earnest.

We launched this run with a new Donald Churchill script, relying on his past successes. "Starting with a winner" as *TV World* put it.

The Floating Population January 28, 1967 (10.05pm ABC) (10.30pm ATV)

Teleplay by	Donald Churchill
Cast included	Ian Bannen and Wendy Craig – with Noel Davis, Anthony Collin, Sheridan Grant, Leslie Dwyer, Derek Hunt, Louise Dunn, Robert Langley, Alan Helm, June Liversidge and George Day
Director	Jonathan Alwyn
Designer	Michael Knight

Brian Brooke had now joined the team – a talented story editor. (Sadly, he died all too young after being with us for only a short time.)

In spite of the odds against us, we got off to a good start. In London, even finishing as late as 11.30pm, the ratings held up, only being beaten that whole evening by such as *Life With Cooper* and *The Baron*.

Richard Sear in *The Stage and Television Today* (2/2/1967) made the trenchant point when he wrote—

> There are occasions when the pattern of independent television cries out for a second channel. Something that will lift it clear of the pig race of the ratings. The timing of ABC's Armchair Theatre, down among the late hours of Saturday night, is a mute plea for such a space. Drama, because it is the orphan of the family circle, stands in the background, half-ignored. A waif; erratic, brilliant, shocking, sometimes stupid but always original. ... Give it room to win the prizes it often deserves and certainly needs ... Since Sydney Newman first hacked his flamboyant way through the vegetable rubbish of week-end viewing to make Armchair Theatre lusty, live and intelligent, it has always earned from me affection and admiration. He has disappeared into the ionosphere of the BBC – the pattern remains. I was not disappointed with the first of the new season's run, Donald Churchill's *The Floating Population*. ... The result was a splendid, credible 1967 romance without sentimentality, without the clichés of writhing sex. Practical, well directed, produced with flair.

And the audience responded kindly.

Mrs Morris of Worcester wrote—

> Congratulations to Donald Churchill and actors Wendy Craig and Ian Bannen for the best ABC *Armchair Theatre* for a long time

Mrs Gale of Birmingham wrote—

> Thank you for The Floating Population. Really wonderful entertainment.

The exploratory nature of the single play – the test bed of new ideas and styles – was demonstrated again in our next production.

A Magnum for Schneider February 4, 1967 (10.05pm ABC) (10.30pm ATV)

Teleplay by	James Mitchell
Cast included	Edward Woodward, Joseph Furst, Ronald Radd and Peter Bowles – with Ivor Dean, Martin Wyldeck, John Scarborough, Helen Ford, Francesca Tu, Judy Champ and Russell Hunter
Director	Bill Bain
Designer	David Marshall

A Magnum for Schneider introduced the character Callan. The later series of that name led to Edward Woodward's success in America.

Russell Hunter played the memorable character, Lonely.

Critic Kenneth Easthaugh, in his review, foresaw the potential in James Mitchell's creation—

> William Shakespeare crossed swords with TV writer, James Mitchell this weekend and, in terms of sheer impact, Shakespeare lost ... For I spy a first-rate spy … His name is 'Callan' and his portrayal by Edward Woodward in the *Armchair Theatre* play, was the event of the weekend.

Some years later, the first series of *Callan* was repeated on Channel 4 but, unfortunately, the original episode, *A Magnum for Schneider*, from *Armchair Theatre*, was not shown. Jeremy Isaacs said he forgot to include it.

What's Wrong With Humpty Dumpty? Feb 11, 1967 (10.5pm ABC) (10.30pm ATV)

Teleplay by	Hugh Whitemore
Cast included	Lynn Redgrave, Katharine Blake and Donald Houston – and John Clark
Director	Charles Jarrott
Designer	Patrick Downing

Lynn Redgrave returned to us fresh from her success in the film *Georgy Girl* (her previous *Armchair Theatre* role in Noel Coward's *Pretty Polly* had led to the film casting). Lynn married John Clark not long after this meeting on the set at Teddington.

John Clark had recently returned from working in television for CBC in Toronto, where he hosted a continuing children's series, and where, when I had finished my training, I directed one of those episodes (*Summer Magazine*) – part of my baptism of multi-camera live production.

The following week we offered quite a change of comedy style with:

Never Mind the Quality, Feel the Width Feb 18, 1967 (10.05pm ABC) (10.30pm ATV)

Teleplay by	Vince Powell and Harry Driver
Cast included	Frank Finlay, John Bluthal and Dudley Foster – with Charles Lamb, Venetia Maxwell, Michael McKevitt, Christopher Benjamin and Denis Carey
Director	Patrick Dromgoole
Designer	Stan Woodward

Never Mind the Quality, Feel the Width was another *Armchair Theatre* play to develop into a series – the title becoming common parlance.

National Theatre player Frank Finlay switched from playing Iago to Sir Laurence Olivier's Othello on stage, to the role of an Irish trouser maker in London's East End – period high tragedy to modern broad comedy.

Cyclops in *Television Mail* (24/2/1967) described it as—

> a tiny gem in that long sequence which started way back with 'Abie's Irish Rose' ... Vince Powell and Harry Driver adorned the convention with some sharp observation of character and with warm bubbling fun that made it (to me, at least) irresistible viewing. The performances of Frank Finlay as Kelly and John Bluthal as Cohen ... were beyond praise. If this was dramatic journalism, with undertones of the 'Saturday Evening Post', it was journalism at a high level of achievement. ... A highly professional TV writing team ... That elusive combination of good writing, splendid acting, and attentive production which makes for good viewing.

Easier in the Dark by Robert Muller followed, but with quite a story before the story. Dodo Watts, the doyen of casting, informed us that Judy Garland was interested in doing a television play in England and for *Armchair Theatre*. At first I felt a degree of scepticism, but also considerable excitement and 'wouldn't it be wonderful...if only…' After much questioning, it was deemed a serious possibility, and an exploratory meeting was requested. Lloyd Shirley arranged for a meeting on the boat that ABC kept moored on the Thames at the Teddington Studios. This was the special venue for VIPs. If you were invited to lunch or to attend a reception "on the boat" – especially at the Captain's table – you were indeed honoured! (I have often thought how singular it was that ABC had this boat as part of their studio venue. Rediffusion, reputed as being run like a Navy Command, had to make do with city offices in Kingsway and the Aldwych.)

We knew that the choice of writer for this project was crucial, and we agreed to involve Robert Muller. We were absolutely delighted when Judy Garland duly arrived to meet us, and in the Captain's Quarters' we spent some time happily discussing the bones of the story, the star character and when she might see a draft of the script, and so on. It was entirely amiable, entirely stress free, and positive.

There was I, this news-boy from small-town Newhaven in Sussex, England, about to produce a vehicle for this worldwide super-star of the movies! Hollywood cinema has never been class conscious, and ITV in the UK tried not to be. The BBC was historically class ridden.

To say that I was excited at this prospect is the under-statement of all time. And this production was not to be some sort of hyped 'special', but to form part of our normal scheduling, which was a splendid indication of the high regard for *Armchair Theatre* and ABC Television far beyond the confines of the UK Network. The meeting ended with a contract for Robert Muller to write the script as he had outlined and we had discussed. Judy was happy. We, at Teddington, were very happy. The script was named *Easier in the Dark.*

All was on course until – very close to the time to go into active production – we were informed that Judy Garland had become ill again. It was the sad, sad beginning of the end for her. We were too late.

However, we had a show to keep on the road – and a script written with a leading character for a star American actress. After the great disappointment, we had extraordinarily good fortune. Dodo Watts sent the script to Shelley Winters, and she wanted to do it! Spirits were high again.

Shelley Winters had been acclaimed the fine actress that she was, for her work in theatre in the USA (notably the group that based their work on the Stanislavski Method) as well as for her excellent Oscar-winning film work. She was indeed ideal casting for the lead as "the wife of an American Embassy official in Britain, who has abandoned her husband out of unbearable boredom: who got tired of pretending to be alive".

Easier in the Dark was basically a two-hander. Two heavy leads with just three other small roles. Our good fortune continued in that the first-rate theatre actor, Michael Bryant, made up the very strong duo.

The coming together of these two fine talents evokes a special memory for me. It was the countdown to the start of the recording of the show: those final few minutes and then seconds of high tension. Remember this was when recording was 'as live' – editing and re-takes were taboo. (Our only small licence was in the form of inserts – usually short film sequences – but even these had to be 'played in' during the overall tape recording.)

The countdown to the start was always critical, and on this occasion dramatically so. Shelley Winters – full of nervous energy – paced about. Everyone else in the studio was still and quiet, with Michael Bryant the calmest, his composure notable.

"Ten seconds," the FM announced. "Nine, eight…" Shelley couldn't contain herself any longer. She belted out to Michael, "I don't know how you can be so calm!" Astonishingly, and quick as a flash – as "five, four..." was counted – he replied, "Haven't you read *An Actor Prepares?*"

Even the countdown seemed to hang-fire for a moment. How was she going to react? For it to be suggested to a dedicated, famous star-student of the Actors' Studio (the American home of 'The Method') that she might not have read the book upon which their theory was based, was audacious. However, it was also impressively apt, and halted Shelley's pacing. From that split second before the start, both actors were in tune, and they delivered fine performances.

Easier in the Dark February 25, 1967 (10.05pm ABC) (10.30pm ATV)

Teleplay by	Robert Muller
Cast included	Shelley Winters and Michael Bryant – with John Garrie, Neville Becker and Mollie Peters
Director	Don Leaver
Designer	Patrick Downing

In spite of the high marquee value of a USA star name, the ratings were only marginally higher than the previous week. After all our high hopes, the *Daily Mirror* described the play as "routine". At least the reviewer praised Michael Bryant, for his "fast expanding talent".

Easier in the Dark
Shelley Winters and Michael Bryant

We continued with “a thriller with a twist” – an uneasy move to try to make the late Saturday night transmission slot work – but it didn’t really fit the *Armchair Theatre* genre. However, whatever the style of play, we could still ensure top-flight performances, and with that, I had great satisfaction. Nadja Regin (from Yugoslavia) and Mia Nardi (from Hungary) brought glamour to this production.

Reason for Sale	March 4, 1967 (10.05pm ABC) (10.30pm ATV)
Teleplay by	Donald and Derek Ford
Cast included	Nadja Regin and Mia Nardi – with William Lucas, John Glyn Jones and Mark Dignam
Director	Patrick Dromgoole
Designer	Malcolm Goulding

From thriller-with-a-twist to comedy-with-a-twist, we moved into the dark undertones of a Donald Churchill look at ‘real life’.

The Happy Sacking	March 11, 1967 (10.05pm ABC) (10.30pm ATV)
Teleplay by	Donald Churchill
Cast included	Peter Vaughan, Jim Norton, Carole Mowlam, Mona Bruce, Frederick Piper and Barry Letts – with Roger Avon, Christine Rodgers, Anthony Barton and Richard Young
Director	Guy Verney
Designer	David Marshall

Barry Letts went on to become the producer of successful BBC Sunday classics.

I was often suggesting to Donald that he should concentrate on writing for theatre (as well as television). Had he done so, I believe that he would have had the kind of success that Alan Ayckbourn had later. Although he did eventually write some stage plays, he kept TV as his main aim (and indeed his acting was always to be enjoyed). Fortunately for us, he continued to write for *Armchair Theatre.*

The press had reservations about *The Happy Sacking. The Sunday Times* (19/3/1967) reviewer wrote—

> ABC’s property warehouse in [Sydney Newman’s] day must have been stocked with more kitchen sinks than a builder’s merchant’s. Under the current impresario, Mr Leonard White, Armchair Theatre has become less didactic and more entertaining: currently it is a reasonably fair bet for a more or less beguiling hour on Saturday night. Of the last half dozen or so plays, I found Donald Churchill’s too twee and Robert Muller’s too portentous, but the rest have been so agreeable that nowadays I tend to make this a date even at the cost of some football, which is often good for a laugh...

Armchair Theatre at 10.30pm on a Saturday night, taking viewers away from football!

Stars from *Armchair Theatre*

Britt Ekland, Maureen Davis, Caroline Mortimer, Shelley Winters, Neil Stacy, Pauline Yates

The following production – *The Exploding Azalea* – was written by John Mortimer, but I didn't produce it. Unlike the large majority of our scripts, this one was not commissioned. The extant script was submitted to Lloyd Shirley, and considering John Mortimer's great reputation, we decided that, naturally, we must do it.

Unfortunately, I did not like the play. More to the point, I did not think that it was right for our anthology. It was set in an "upper room in a Balkan capital" and the outside world "never impinged on this interior". It felt to me more like a one-act play for theatre. On television, such a restricted location is often interpreted as a contrivance for the sake of economy ("cheaply closeted", *Sunday Telegraph*) whereas in theatre such limitations are perfectly acceptable.

But who was I to deny the talent of such a writer – or indeed the wishes of my enthusiastic boss? *Armchair Theatre* was a broad church, and although I had no desire to produce this script, I certainly did not want to stop it. Thus, I stood aside for this one production, and Lloyd Shirley produced it himself.

The Exploding Azalea March 18, 1967 (10.05pm ABC) (10.30pm ATV)

Teleplay by	John Mortimer
Cast included	Kenneth Haigh, James Maxwell, George Murcell and Tessa Wyatt
Director	Jonathan Alwyn
Designer	Peter Le Page (Produced by Lloyd Shirley)

Tessa Wyatt played the mute girl who delivers the deadly flowers – we never saw that, of course.

Unlike my own reservations, and those of *The Sunday Telegraph* and others, the critic of *The Guardian* (20/3/1967) took an opposing view and liked it for those very same reasons—

> John Mortimer gave us an unusual chance to enjoy craftsmanship … he put the onus on his own dialogue and on to the actors. In consequence, we had the chance of hearing some "talk" and seeing three fine performances.

I certainly would not argue about the fine performances.

John Harrison, who wrote the next teleplay, renewed an association that we'd had some twenty years before. In 1946, we were both actors at the Stratford-upon-Avon Memorial Theatre (before it became the Royal Shakespeare). It was my first job after being demobbed from the Army. John was the Good Angel and I, the Bad Angel in Marlowe's *Dr Faustus*.

John had become a very successful theatre director (notably at Leeds before the creation of the West Yorkshire Playhouse) and he had also taken on the role of dramatist.

In line with the true style of *Armchair Theatre*, John Harrison's play posed some pertinent questions. The setting was in the not too distant future – in a world of more leisure than work – and the question was posed as to whether this might lead to more love than hate?

Any Number Can Play	March 25, 1967 (10.05pm ABC) (10.30pm ATV)
Teleplay by	John Harrison
Cast included	Adrienne Corri, Donald Houston, Alex Davion, John Paul and Philip Madoc – with Bernard Horsfall, Kenneth Watson, Annette Robertson, Peter Mason, Martin Sterndale, Sally Alexander, Shrivendra Sinha, Alan Brown, Anthony Chinn, John Trenaman, David David, Iain Sinclair, Robert Lee, Horace James, Robert Crewdson, Jane Jordan Rogers, Tracy Connell and Calvin Butler
Director	Don Leaver
Designer	David Marshall

Any Number Can Play was described in the *Sunday Times* (2/4/1967) as—

> An unusually vivid and lively play of ideas ... a thought-provoking play of some dramatic power and not inconsiderable psychological penetration.

A quirk in the scheduling meant that Don Leaver was director of two plays in a row. The second was another teleplay for us:

A World of Time	April 1, 1967 (10.05pm ABC) (10.30pm ATV)
Teleplay by	Robert Muller
Cast included	Billie Whitelaw – with Betty Baskcomb, Donald Hewlett, Sheila Fern, Walter Sparrow, Bernard Gallagher and Charles Thomas
Director	Don Leaver
Designer	Stan Woodward

Billie Whitelaw played the lead in a play that might have been written for her. *The Times* (2/4/1967) reviewer saw her as having "virtually carried the play", which he described as—

> a rather weird but effective study of kleptomania specially written by that talented author, Robert Muller.

In terms of attracting an audience, our next production presented *Armchair Theatre* with one of its toughest tests ever. *Call Me Daddy* played on the Saturday night opposite *The Eurovision Song Contest* (BBC) which was live and indeed a year when the UK won. Needless to say, our drama suffered to the degree of getting less than half of the usual rating. A great pity.

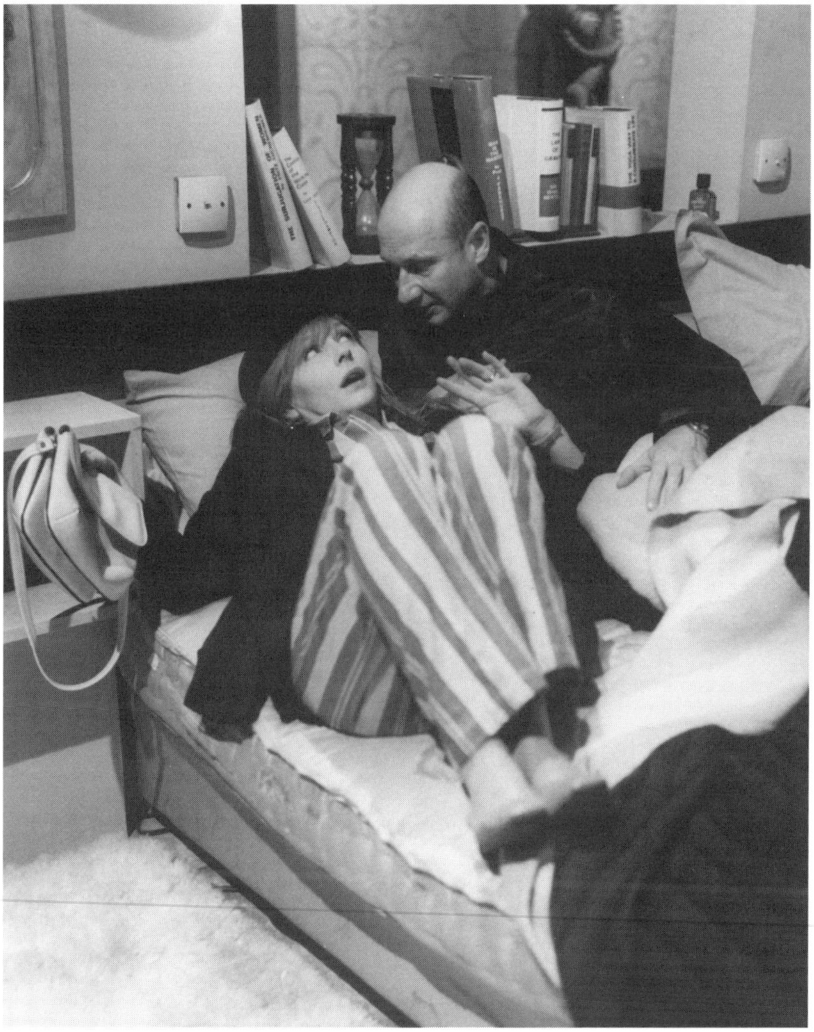

Call Me Daddy
Judy Cornwell and Donald Pleasance

Call Me Daddy April 8, 1967 (10.05pm ABC) (10.30pm ATV)

Teleplay by	Ernie Gebler
Cast included	Donald Pleasance and Judy Cornwell
Director	Alvin Rakoff
Designer	David Marshall

Ernie Gebler was 'Ernest' when he wrote serious novels, but now enjoying and succeeding with a trip into romantic comedy, he called himself 'Ernie'.

A rare two-hander for us. Donald Pleasance playing a romantic role was rarer still. The work of Rakoff, Pleasance and Cornwell wrought a gem.

TV Times (6/4/1967)—

> Pleasance plays a love scene and comes into his own as a television screen lover.
>
> For Miss Smith, typist second-class, it looks like a choice of bread-and-butter pudding or oysters with champagne; between a peasant lover or a feudal baron. Can she aquire a taste for eating snails with Hoffman?

The bad luck of clashing with *Eurovision* would be more than redressed when, some months later, the production of *Call Me Daddy* won a top honour in the USA.

This run of twelve weekly transmissions finished with the final teleplay:

I am Osango	April 15, 1967 (10.05pm ABC) (10.30pm ATV)
Teleplay by	Giles Cooper
Cast included	Roy Dotrice and Lynn Redgrave – with Kathleen Michael, Ken Jones, Leon Sinden, Mollie Sugden, Frank Gatliff, Stafford Byrne, Dan Jackson and Judy Champ
Director	Bill Bain
Designer	Peter Le Page

For *Armchair Theatre* – the anthology that was so richly based on the talents of writers for television – it was a significant honour to produce and present this work by Giles Cooper, whose very sad and tragic death meant that he never saw the play screened.

Philip Purser (*Sunday Telegraph,* 16/4/1967)—

> never had Cooper strolled so coolly into the twilit zone between the explicable and the inexplicable. ... [and] aptly concluded the contribution of an imperfect, unique, undervalued, peculiarly televisual talent.

Marjorie Bilbow (*Stage and Television Today,* 20/4/1967)—

> Bill Bain's punctiliously matter of fact direction was exactly what was needed to counterbalance the story's tendency to wander into the realms of science fiction. The moments when Aaron Toft's bedroom became a prison cell were handled with discretion and an absence of theatricality which demands the highest praise … [This play] was a potent reminder of the magnitude of our loss.

And with that, we went off the air for a couple of months.

We resumed in July 1967, with a run of thirteen weekly productions. Apart from the obvious competition with summer occupations, we continued to be on-air late on Saturdays. Transmissions were now less split on the network. London at 10.10pm was only slightly behind the Midlands and the North (our own franchise regions) at 10.05pm.

Our first still had *Armchair Theatre* scheduled to follow immediately after *The Avengers* in our own regions. For us the pressure was on to hold the after-10pm audience. We opened with a new comedy – not your sit-com variety, but richer with Jack Rosenthal's "accurately observed characters, and the frivolity rooted in pathos" (Marjorie Bilbow, *Stage and Television Today*).

Compensation Alice July 1, 1967 (10.05pm ABC) (10.10pm ATV)

Teleplay by	Jack Rosenthal
Cast included	Sheila Hancock and Robert Lang – with Adrienne Poster, Susan George, Pamela Miles, Joan Benham, Margaret Nolan, William Ellis, John Savident, Catherine Kessler, Janet Bruce, Billy Milton, Donna Reading
Director	Patrick Dromgoole
Designer	Brian Graves

Marjorie Bilbow (*Stage and Television Today,* 6/7/1967) in her review – headed "Bright, happy ABC comedy" – highlighted the problem of late scheduling—

> If ever there was an example of the waste of tucking single plays away in the dark corners of the evening, it was ABC's "Compensation Alice" by Jack Rosenthal ... It's natural home was the peak-hour family audience. ... If this play had turned up in a selection of pilot comedies I should be loud in my demands for a series. ... "Compensation Alice" was that rarity, a comedy about women that is founded in reality and does not rely on silliness, bitchiness or nagging to make us laugh.

It certainly was rewarding that our forays into comedy were still seen to deliver the cutting edge for which *Armchair Theatre* was renowned.

Finely played by a star trio, *Slight Formality* addressed issues around adoption and race.

Slight Formality July 8, 1967 (10.05pm ABC) (10.10pm ATV)

Teleplay by	Richard Harris
Cast included	Michael Craig, Virginia Stride and Errol John
Director	Kim Mills
Designer	Peter Le Page

The Times (10/7/1967)—

> A childless couple, passionately eager to adopt a child, were interviewed by a gentle and considerate official from the Adoption Society who happened to be coloured. The result was a cleverly and deliberately inconclusive study of social uneasiness nicely played...

Then the Saturday evening schedule changed. The current run of *The Avengers* had ended, and *Armchair Theatre* now followed both *Callan* and the News.

From an English social problem, we moved into a suspense thriller, set in Milan.

Quite an Ordinary Knife July 15, 1967 (10.05pm ABC) (10.10pm ATV)

Teleplay by	Jordan Lawrence
Cast included	Judy Parfitt, William Squire, Jeremy Brett, T.P. McKenna – with Renato Roman and Marie Makino
Director	Alan Cooke
Designer	Eddie Wolfram

This play was not in our usual style. Ann Purser (*Stage and Television Today*) found it "contrived and too melodramatic". Nevertheless, it did nudge *Armchair Theatre* back into the TAM Top Twenty ratings – just – with over 10 million viewers. *Summer Playhouse* (Rediffusion) and *Love Story* (ATV) – transmitted in primetime – were dominating the ratings at this time.

Another Branch of the Family July 22, 1967 (10.05pm ABC) (10.10pm ATV)

Teleplay by	Emanuel Litvinoff
Cast included	Bernard Cribbins, Margery Mason, Ewan Hooper and Freddie Jones – with Lulu (a chimpanzee, not the singer)
Director	Kim Mills
Designer	Michael Hall

The cast met the challenge of the old adage, 'never act with animals or children' – and Bernard Cribbins probably wished he hadn't when during rehearsals he felt the sharpness of Lulu's teeth. She bit him on the hand. From then on Bernard wore gloves, which, amusingly, Peter Black (*Daily Mail*, 24/7/1967) picked out in his review as "a clever touch… lending his hands the suggestion of paws".

This one-off play achieved the highest rating of any programme on that Saturday night in London, Midlands and the North. We were back in the Top Ten programmes that week – beating by a considerable margin the episode of the successful *Callan* series.

Television Audience Measurement (TAM)
Week ending Sunday July 23, 1967
Top Twenty Programmes – Homes in Millions

1	Coronation Street (Mon 17th)	Granada	7.40
2	Coronation Street (Wed 19th)	Granada	7.15
3	Summer Playhouse	Rediffusion	7.05
4	World in Action	Granada	6.55
5	Love Story	ATV	5.85
6	News at Ten (Wed 19th)	ITN	5.75
7	Cinema	Granada	5.70
8	News at Ten (Mon 17th)	ITN	5.65
9	Another Branch of the Family (AT)	ABC	5.55
9=	The Blackpool Show	ABC	5.55
11	News at Ten (Thur 20th)	ITN	5.50
12	News at Ten (Tue 18th)	ITN	5.45
13	The Love Affair	BBC1	4.90
13=	Half Hour Story	Rediffusion	4.90
15	This Week	Rediffusion	4.85
16	Till Death Us Do Part	BBC1	4.75
17	The Golden Shot	ATV	4.65
18	Opportunity Knocks!	ABC	4.60
18=	Black & White Minstrel Show	BBC1	4.60
20	Steptoe and Son	BBC1	4.45
20=	Relatively Speaking	BBC1	4.45

***Another Branch of the Family* at No.9**

Love Life July 29, 1967 (10.05pm ABC) (10.10pm ATV)

Teleplay by	Hugh Leonard
Cast included	George Baker, Diana Coupland, Pauline Delaney – with Pauline Collins and Martin Dempsey – also Carmen Munroe, Bill Golding, Evelyn Lund, Gabrielle Walsh, Liz Davis, Maurice Good and John Kay
Director	Guy Verney
Designer	Stan Woodward

Cyclops in the *Television Mail* (4/8/1967) wrote—

> an example of contemporary stage and TV drama in one of its better moods. It cast a dazzling light on ordinary life...

On August 5, 1967, *Armchair Theatre* was transmitted simultaneously on all regions. That week we presented a tougher story from an expert on Army drama: the plight of a boy soldier trapped for six years within the Queen's Regulations.

The Education of Corporal Halliday August 5 1967 (10.10pm)

Teleplay by	Robert Holles
Cast included	Gary Bond, George Sewell, Peter Williams, John Keightley, Peter Mason, John Nettleton, Bernard Archard, Anita Prynne, Ron Daniels, Arthur Griffiths, John Tate, Helen Ford, Brian Harrison and Richard Steele
Director	Bill Bain
Designer	Michael Hall

Alice Frick (*Stage and Television Today*, 10/8/1967) wrote—

> Gary Bond was first-rate … George Sewell was equally fine … [an] efficient production team responsible for this summer bonus...

Alas, the simultaneous broadcast time – 10.10pm – vanished! The very next week we were back to split transmissions, with a commissioned play from another new writer for television – a former Fleet Street columnist and critic. Described as a "psychological thriller" by *Television Mail* (18/8/1967), it was possibly the nearest we got to presenting a tragedy.

Nursery Tale August 12, 1967 (10.05pm ABC) (10.10pm ATV)

Teleplay by	Derek Monsey
Cast included	Katharine Blake, Jean Anderson, Powys Thomas, Fiona Walker, Charlotte Selwyn, Nellie Hanham and Olwen Brookes
Director	Charles Jarrott
Designer	Terry Pritchard

Critic Cyclops (*Television Mail,* 18/8/1967) wrote—

> 'Nursery Tale' succeeded in screwing up tension to an almost unbearable degree without raising its voice and without any violence other than a token slap on the face. ...

> Performances were outstanding ... Katharine Blake was to perfection the handsome, talented, neurotic wife, atracting our sympathy and admiration as well as our anxiety. But Jean Anderson reached a lofty stature as an actress with her portrayal of Nanny…

Ann Purser (*Stage and Television Today,* 17/8/1967)—

> Brilliant acting...
> I found it an absolutely riveting play...

An individual viewer wrote—

> Be thankful for a writer who can stimulate thought and provoke a family discussion.

On those occasions when the performances achieved such acclaim, it gave me a great deal of personal satisfaction. If there had been any change of emphasis in the style of *Armchair Theatre* since Sydney Newman's days in the chair it was demonstrated, I believe, in the high standard of performance. The concentration on the importance of commissioning new writing and writers for television that I inherited was our bedrock.

We continued this summer run with another commissioned teleplay – light-hearted yet rich in character. Our strength in casting under the remarkable and fine judgment of Dodo Watts continued with:

Marriage and Henry Sunday	August 19, 1967 (10.05pm ABC) (10.10pm ATV)
Teleplay by	Emanuel Litvinoff
Cast included	Warren Mitchell, Gwen Watford and Donald Morley – with Lynda Marchal, Michelle Ser, Talya Vashti, Shirley Patterson and Eve Gross
Director	Kim Mills
Designer	Stan Woodward

This play provided Warren Mitchell with an opportunity to escape his role as Alf Garnett (*Till Death Us Do Part*) and change the pace and style of his acting to portray a very different character. Henry Sunday is a bachelor, past the first flush of youth – eager to get married, but nervous of women. He resorts to handing the job of finding 'Miss Right' over to science. He is sure that the computer can select his 'mate to measure'.

Cyclops in *Television Mail* (25/8/1967) described it as—

> a production with abundant warm humour and with its own congruent and appealing style. ... excellent performances from the four principals ... Warren Mitchell, whose public *persona* is that of the unspeakable Alf Garnett, was almost unrecognisable as Henry Sunday, whose simplicity and uncertainties contributed to a very entertaining and enjoyable play.

Alice Frick (*Stage and Television Today,* 24/8/1967) thought it—

> a rather old fashioned play ... [but] a pleasure to see Warren Mitchell being somebody else besides Alf Garnett, and with equal sureness and conviction.

The Times (21/8/1967)—

> Warren Mitchell escaped from the notoriety of Alf Garnett to a very precisely judged piece of comic pathos...

Lynda Marchal is now of course well known in a very different and successful way as Lynda La Plante, writer and producer.

Our next presentation – a teleplay by an excellent novelist – was one of those stories that the audience either strongly dislikes or enthusiastically applauds.

The Girl	August 26, 1967 (10.05pm ABC) (10.10pm ATV)
Teleplay by	William Trevor
Cast included	Joss Ackland, Brenda Bruce, Shelagh Fraser, Janina Faye, Philip Locke, Dennis Waterman, Stephen Whittaker, Rodney Archer, Kaplan Kaye, Anthony Villaroel, Carol James, Siobhan Taylor and Christine Cauldrey
Director	Alvin Rakoff
Designer	Eddie Wolfram

William Trevor's play was tough stuff (at least for the sixties) and we knew it would be a tough assignment to make the story palatable and hold our audience throughout.

George Melly in *The Observer* (3/9/1967) described it as Pinteresque—

> ...real avant-garde territory ... the invasion of an ordered suburban household by prole menace and violence ... Trevor's idiosyncrasy of language and attitude did succeed in holding the cry of *'déjà vu'* at bay ... [the plot] had more logic than is usual on these occasions.

Michael Billington in *The Times* (28/8/1967) wrote—

> Armchair Theatre presented an extremely enjoyable and typically stylish play ... What made the play so good was the quality of Mr. Trevor's dialogue, which always avoided the obvious and expected.

Later, Michael Billington apologised for having credited this production to ATV instead of ABC Television (due to "a faulty telephone line") and added—

> I should like to say again that I thought it was a splendidly taut piece of writing. I was only sorry to see that it triggered off a slightly hysterical reaction in some quarters – one lady wrote to me attacking me strongly for praising it...

And certainly some of our audience were moved to write their objections in *TV Times*. One viewer, aged 13, declared that the production—

> portrayed young people as destructive, abusive layabouts. It is through such plays as this that today's young gets such a bad reputation.

Three other viewers expressed similar views—

> Nobody, except morons, derives satisfaction from such a play. It was revolting.
>
> In writing this drivel, William Trevor has assisted in glorifying thuggery.
>
> If TV continues to show this type of play we can only expect young hoodlums to resort to similar tactics.

Even so, it held its inherited audience on this unlikely Bank Holiday weekend. In ATV's London region, it fared even better than the feature film and the popular light entertainment show earlier in the evening.

With an *Armchair Theatre* debut for the story editor, John Kershaw, we returned to something rather more accessible.

Split Level	September 2, 1967 (10.05pm ABC) (10.10pm ATV)
Teleplay by	Stewart Farrar
Cast included	Robin Bailey, Sally Bazely, Richard Leech and William Fox – with Roderick Jones, Maurice Jones and Martha Gibson
Director	Guy Verney
Designer	Kenneth Mellor

Reading (*TV Times*) now, over thirty years later, *Split Level* has remarkable resonances with real life situations that have come about since—

> It is about a woman civil servant, in love with a man in a foreign embassy, who has shown him confidential documents and wound up in the dock with her life in ruins. ... [She] has agreed to "tell all" to a newspaper, and the Fleet Street man ... has taken her away secretly to a remote Welsh fishing inn to "ghost" her story ... The hard and shabby truth, of course, is that espionage is the dirtiest game of all ... Stewart Farrar's "Split Level" ... is a rare, brave and shocking play, because it squares up to the brutal facts without flinching.

Elizabeth Goodman wrote in *The Stage and Television Today* (7/9/1967)—

> it was a neatly thought out, well constructed play about the oil and water nature of love and espionage ... the relationship between Penfold, the pleasant, well-meaning outsider, and the girl, deeply enmeshed in the frightening tangle of espionage, was absorbing and sad. ... Robin Bailey's performance gave the play depth and reality

Though accessible, *Split Level* did not hold its audience as well as might have been expected. The vagaries of show biz.

Another good catch for us: a teleplay by Fay Weldon, billed as "love in the local election". Again, for just one week, *Armchair Theatre* was transmitted in all areas at the same time.

Poor Cherry		September 9, 1967 (10.10pm)
Teleplay by	Fay Weldon	
Cast included	Dilys Laye, Judy Cornwell, Gwen Nelson, Jane Birkin, John Wood, Peter Arne and John Glyn-Jones	
Director	Piers Haggard	
Designer	Darrell Lass	

Fay Weldon had written seven or eight plays during that year: her reputation attracted a splendid cast. It was refreshing and stimulating to have the woman's voice – something that was still rare among the many writers who contributed to *Armchair Theatre*. Edna O'Brien, Gwen Cherrell, Mary Hocking, Elaine Morgan were among the few to represent the distaff side until then.

Poor Cherry also introduced George Markstein to *Armchair Theatre* as a story editor. George was an escapee from the stresses of making *The Prisoner* at Elstree Studios. I gather that our 'family' at Teddington – despite the inevitable pressures – offered a more 'human' environment.

Poor Cherry attracted good critical response.

Cyclops ('Professional Eye' *TV Mail,* 15/9/1967) gave it a full column review—

> ...a brief adventure among fascinating people and their problems, pleasing both to eye and ear, 'Poor Cherry' must rank high even among the excellent productions of Armchair Theatre. Look for the Weldon label next time.
> Dilys Laye—too often seen in parts beneath her capacity—drew in a hard line the character of a contemporary (but subtler!) Mrs Jellyby ... Abbie was beautifully played by the luscious Miss Cornwell ... All [various actors and production staff] are mentioned because all deserve it.
> It is, like other of Fay Weldon's plays that I have seen, unemotional and unsentimental ... we await the unravelling of knots as an intellectual exercise—with our minds, not our hearts.

The Sunday Telegraph (23/9/1967) reviewer opined—

> I was afraid that [Fay Weldon's] invention was showing signs of tiring, but Poor Cherry for ABC proved to be a sweet and kindly comedy not of disillusion, but of acceptance.

Henry Raynor in *The Times* (11/9/1967)—

> Fay Weldon's tale of a wife's compensating for a drab marriage by involvement in political causes and adultery obviously offered rewarding acting parts and dialogue both neatly stylized and articulately educated.

This excellent play did not achieve the rating figures I had anticipated.

With our following production, I certainly was straining our audience's loyalty. Religion with a touch of satire on a Saturday night is not exactly your pint and fish'n'chips fare. I guess that I only got this one past Programme Controller Brian Tesler because *Don't Forget the Basics* was written by the very good comedy writer, Terence Frisby, and because the cast was led by Leo McKern (a rare occasion during this time that we put the star credit above the title of the play). Designer Eddie Wolfram, had the monumental task of creating the front elevation of St Paul's Cathedral in the studio.

Don't Forget the Basics took a comic look at a mass sit-in on the steps of St Paul's. The demonstration has been triggered by Henry Thomas, a lathe operator – played by Henry Woolf – who is converted to religion by a stranger in a pub. He promptly goes to St Paul's and, quite simply, begins to sit. The Archbishop (Leo McKern) is intrigued by Henry's approach to Christianity. He decides to join him. National crises follow. There are resonances in Henry of the Chaplinesque, or perhaps of Jacques Tatti. Is he revolutionary or just another crank? Whatever, his antics and those of the Archbishop attract full media coverage.

Don't Forget the Basics	September 16, 1967 (10.5pm ABC) (10.10pm ATV)
Teleplay by	Terence Frisby
Cast included	Leo McKern – with Robert Eddison, Henry Woolf and Tom Criddle – and Arthur Pentelow, Dan Meaden, Robert Gillespie, Frederick Danner, Rex Robinson, Tommy Godfrey and Henry Knowles
Director	Alan Cooke
Designer	Eddie Wolfram

We had attempted a difficult play, and the ratings took a dive.

Michael Billington in *The Times* (18/9/1967) described it as—

> a rather damp satyrical squib

I think the above comment might have been evoked by Frisby's use of a "crowd-dispersing thunderstorm" to resolve the situation. Not unrealistic: many a time police work in breaking up a demonstration has been helped considerably by a stroke of bad weather. But I guess 'reality' in fiction doesn't always work. Michael Billington went on to write—

> Mr Frisby's mistake was that he tried to make a perfectly serious point while resorting to a whimsical sub-Shavian jokiness ... However, there was a very good performance from Henry Woolfe as the zealous convert and Robert Gillespie caught brilliantly the quirky, jerky intonations of many a television news-reader.

Cyclops (*Television Mail*) thought that—

> It probably read quite well; indeed, there is a good play somewhere in it, but just didn't come off.

The next transmission was indeed an aberration for *Armchair Theatre*. Under the guidance of Lloyd Shirley, we elected to take a theatre production from the Victoria Theatre Company at Stoke-on-Trent and present it as a 'special'. The situation was that this Company, under its artistic director, Peter Cheeseman, had been exiled from their theatre building in Stoke after a 'difference of opinion' with the management. Help was needed to keep Cheeseman's company together. ABC Television stepped in to support them and decided to present their production – *The Heroism of Thomas Chadwick* – written by Peter Terson, and based on two stories from the Potteries author, Arnold Bennett. Terson was one of the many excellent writing talents given early opportunities by Cheeseman, and became the resident playwright of the 'Vic'. Cheeseman and Terson: the 'Two Peters'. The theatre play was adapted for television.

For this show there had to be a re-arrangement of credits and responsibility. We presented it as *The Story Teller* rather than the familiar *Armchair Theatre*.

The Heroism of Thomas Chadwick September 23, 1967 *The Story Teller*

Teleplay by	Peter Terson	
Stories by	Arnold Bennett	
Cast included	Ken Campbell, Anne Raitt, Gillian Brown, Ellis Dale, Susan Glanville, Christopher Martin, Edward Clayton, Terence Davies, James Hayes, David Hill, Harry Jones, Diana McMahon, Anton Vogel, Jane Wood	
Director	Mike Vardy	
Designer	James Weatherup	(Produced by Peter Cheeseman)
Special music	Jeff Parton	

It was necessary to give Peter Cheeseman his full dues. He was given the Producer credit while I became Executive Producer. It also provided an opportunity for a new young director, Mike Vardy, to begin to get experience in television drama. He was responsible for the camera work and transferring the whole into the television environment. We did not simply want a photographed 'theatre' production. James Weatherup's design helped to make the transformation.

ABC always maintained a strong interest and support for the theatres in their franchise regions, the Midlands and the North. So, the ill wind that had driven this Company into exile for some six months did blow some good. Indeed, soon after this gesture, Peter Cheeseman and his Company were reinstated at the Victoria Theatre, Stoke, under a new independent trust formed of the Arts Council and the local authorities. For many years, Cheeseman remained a leading light – if not leading Artistic Director – in regional theatre in England.

J.D.S. Haworth, in *The Stage and Television Today* (28/9/1967) commented—

> It is such an admirable gesture for television to sponsor a production by an established theatre group ... Whether it was entirely successful ... is a rather different matter.

Not entirely successful? Well, I guess he was about right. We started with a production set up for theatre presentation in the very strong style that Peter Cheeseman had evolved. To translate it into a very different format as demanded by the camera was somewhat ambitious.

The *Sunday Times* (24/9/1967)—

> ABC's Leonard White, who revitalised the Saturday play, employed Peter Terson of "Zigger Zagger" to adapt [for television] Bennett's stories, as The Heroism of Thomas Chadwick, and a very workmanlike job he made of it.

The eleventh season of *Armchair Theatre* ended, having still attracted an average of over 10 million viewers late on a Saturday night.

Anthony Davis, writing in his 'ad lib' column (*Television Mail*) under the heading CAN THE TV PLAY SURVIVE? took—

> a long look at the record-breaking Armchair Theatre … the longest-running series of one-shot plays ever produced here by a single company.

In his summary, covering *Armchair Theatre* up to the end of the eleventh season, Davis described the changing phases through the years, starting in 1956 under Dennis Vance who (despite having secured J.B. Priestley's first television play) concentrated "on revivals of stage plays and adaptations of novels". After Sydney Newman took over, things changed. Although out of his first thirteen productions, ten were still adaptations, he thereafter got into his stride, focussing on "specially written plays about contemporary life". And the label 'kitchen sink' was applied (a convenient tag for much publicity, which Sydney would not deny, but in my opinion not a true generalisation). However, this ethos gained considerable attention, which Sydney enjoyed. The plays were "talked about and audiences rose".

It is ironic that the production that gained a record high audience during this period – *The Cupboard* (a comedy thriller by Ray Rigby, starring Donald Pleasance) – was attributed to Sydney Newman but had in fact been produced by me as one of the *Armchair Mystery Theatre* series.

Anthony Davis continued his review by considering that—

> By 1963 the pendulum had swung, the public were growing tired of slices from real life. The cry from the suburbs was for stories with a beginning, a middle and an ending.

He then stated that when I took over from Newman, I set out to provide such stories. He quotes me as saying, "The story comes first." Not by any means an entirely original idea but maybe a timely reminder.

Davis explained that—

> in the past five years there have been fewer first plays

In that part of his analysis, he was wrong. I produced more scripts specially written for *Armchair Theatre* than were made while Sydney Newman was in charge. And that is not including others, which, while not 'special for us', were nevertheless written for television.

The question remained, however: "Can the TV play survive?"

Twelve Years of ABC's *Armchair Theatre*
Front: Dodo Watts — Managing Director Howard Thomas — Marie Donaldson
Back row: George Kerr, Dennis Vance, Lloyd Shirley, Sydney Newman, Leonard White

CHAPTER 12
Armchair Theatre – 1968 – Twelfth Season
"A Sense of Occasion"

Armchair Theatre's twelfth season was launched at a press reception at the Café Royal in London on January 29, 1968. Unlike today, when critics and reviewers are sent video cassettes of productions for them to view at their individual convenience, the press reception launch of a new season was the recognized means of attracting pre-publicity. The separate productions, in general, were then viewed off-air. In that way, both the launch and the transmission had more of an 'occasion' about them.

The critics and previewers greatly enjoyed the hospitality at these affairs and usually turned up in numbers to meet representatives of the authors: William Marchant, Roger Woddis, William Corlett, Donald Churchill, Scott Forbes and Derek Bond. Also, the actors: Dinah Sheridan, Judy Cornwell, Frances White, Joanne Dainton, Ilona Rodgers, Jane Murdoch, Jenny White, Penny Brahms, James Villiers, Leslie Phillips, Michael Craig, Malcolm Armstrong, Bernard Cribbins and Donald Sinden. All involved in upcoming productions.

Apart from the usual launch of this season, a special luncheon, hosted by Howard Thomas, was given at the Cheshire Cheese in Fleet Street on January 23, 1968. Invited to join us for this celebration were Dennis Vance, the original Drama Supervisor, and director of the first production in 1956; Sydney Newman, producer from 1958-62; George Kerr, who had been in the original team with Dennis Vance and later returned as Drama Executive for a short period in 1963-64.

The press were represented by Julian Critchley (*Times*), Stanley Reynolds (*Guardian*), Leonard Marsland Gander (*Daily Telegraph*), Michael Donne (*Financial Times*), Philip Purser (*Sunday Telegraph*), John Whitley (*Sunday Times*), Edward Mace (*Observer*), Brian Mulligan (*Variety*), Tony Gruner (*Kine Weekly*) and Edward Durham Taylor (*Stage and Television Today*).

The rest of the party was made up of the then current team on *Armchair Theatre*: Lloyd Shirley (Drama Supervisor), George Markstein and Brian Brooke (Story Editors), Dodo Watts (Head of Casting), Marie Donaldson and George Spackman (Press Officers) and myself (Producer).

The celebration of the past eleven years of ABC's domination of the weekend play slot on television, with fine achievements, culminating in winning the International Emmy award in the USA, was also, alas, something of a wake. The new company, Thames Television (engineered out of the merger of ABC Television with Associated Rediffusion) meant that ABC was to lose its unique power in weekend scheduling. The cosy, but very effective, love-hate arrangement between ABC (weekend contractors for the Midlands and the North) and ATV (weekend contractors for London) where these two companies ran the primetime Network at weekends, was finished.

Although ABC still had half a year to run before the new franchises started in July, the change of influence and scheduling started immediately. *Armchair Theatre* was moved to a weekday transmission in London: Wednesday, starting at 10.30pm. Fortunately, within our own regions ABC stuck to its guns and continued to transmit at the weekend.

So, London viewers during this new interim period saw the first *Armchair Theatre* production of the twelfth season on Wednesday January 31, 1968 and ABC transmitted to their viewers on Saturday February 3. This was probably the beginning of the new ways, where boardroom strategy took over from programme makers.

In 1966, we had had the good fortune to become the first TV company to obtain the rights of a short story by Noel Coward – *Pretty Polly*. Coward had been so pleased with the result that he sold ABC Television the rights to adapt and produce six more of his short stories. Not perhaps in the perceived usual style of *Armchair Theatre* to be doing a run of Coward, but for all his theatricality he did demonstrate a finely observed and deep understanding of social problems – as in such plays as *Vortex* and *This Happy Breed.*

Starring Beryl Reid as the eponymous London charlady, this play got the season off to a good start.

Mrs Capper's Birthday January 31, 1968 (ATV)
February 3, 1968 (ABC)

Story by	Noel Coward
Teleplay by	William Marchant
Cast included	Beryl Reid, Arthur Lowe, Sylvia Coleridge, Jill Dixon, Pauline Yates and George Baker – with Denis Goacher, John Humphry, Penny Brahms, Maudie Edwards, Richard Coleman, Richard Curnock, John Keenan, Christopher Sandford, Christian Fletcher, Jessie Robins, Eunice Black, Jacqueline Ingles, Roderick Jones and Tom McLaren
Director	Guy Verney
Designer	Eddie Wolfram

Mrs Capper's Birthday
Beryl Reid and Arthur Lowe

Despite the break-up of the networking and the late-night scheduling *Mrs Capper's Birthday* (showing at the weekend in the Midlands and the North) built on its inherited rating, beating *Man in a Suitcase* and *Public Eye*, which were being transmitted in London that evening.

Next came more usual fare for us, in that George Markstein, our Story Supervisor (a new role under the aegis of Lloyd Shirley) introduced the next writer with "a play about the spies that spy on spies... a black spy story".

The Wind in a Tall Paper Chimney February 7, 1968 (ATV)
February 10, 1968 (ABC)

Teleplay by	Robert Holles
Cast included	Donald Sinden, Bernard Cribbins, Judy Cornwell and John Steiner – with Anthony Marlowe, David Stoll, Alan Lawrence, Jenny White, John Channel Mills and Billy Cornelius
Director	Peter Sasdy
Designer	Robert Macgowan

This one dropped a few points in the ratings as compared with *Mrs Capper's Birthday* the week before.

The Scallop Shell
Frances White

A week later, we were up against considerable competition from the Winter Olympics.

The Scallop Shell		February 14, 1968 (ATV) February 17, 1968 (ABC)
Teleplay by	William Corlett	
Cast included	Gwen Watford, Stephen Murray, Dorothy Alison – with Frances White, Robert Cartland and Eric Woofe	
Director	Bill Bain	
Designer	Eddie Wolfram	

The performances inspired many inches of newsprint, garnering valuable critical plaudits.

Angela Moreton (*Stage and Television Today,* 22/2/1968) described this play as having—

> a carefully tuned Chekhovian aimlessness about it.

Virginia Ironside (*Daily Mail,* 15/2/1968) despite reservations, found it—

> immensely watchable and Gwen Watford played the pathetically emotional mother really excellently

Rosemary Say (*Sunday Telegraph,* 18/2/1968)—

> Gwen Watford's performance in William Corlett's The Scallop Shell (ABC's Armchair Theatre) stood out head and shoulders in a week that showed some first-class acting elsewhere.

Although we put great emphasis on our new writers, I was always very pleased when the performances were so successful. It enhanced my belief that television is the medium of personality.

Thence, after the touch of very English "Chekhovian", we moved to Donald Churchill's accessible comedy about a despatch-clerk who suddenly has the chance to assume the role of a tycoon and decides to take a second look at a former girl friend. The clerk was played by Harry H. Corbett, and his 'former' by Nyree Dawn Porter.

A Second Look — February 21, 1968 (10.30pm (ATV))
February 24, 1968 (10.15pm ABC)

Teleplay by	Donald Churchill
Cast included	Harry H. Corbett and Nyree Dawn Porter – with Richard Vernon, Toke Townley, Joan Hickson, Anthony Dawes, Anthony Collin and Julia Jones
Director	Jonathan Alwyn
Designer	Roy Stannard

Barry Norman (*Daily Mail,* 22/2/1968) described it as a—

> charming but lightweight fable ... and much the better for Miss Porter as a delicious gold-digger...

He spent half the review in eulogising her talents (and why not indeed?) and wondering why she had not been promoted to "star status in the cinema" Well, in television drama at that time in the UK, we were very happy to be ahead of the cinema.

With the popularity of those two leads – Nyree Dawn Porter and Harry H. Corbett – the ratings held up well, even building after the late News.

The next play was transmitted at 11pm in London – two hours later than the ideal time from which it had once benefited.

This was a drama firmly in the style of our remit: "here and now and socially conscious and compelling". An English suburban family home is thrust into contact with the moral dilemma of the Vietnam war, dividing family and friends.

The Contact		February 28, 1968 (11.00pm ATV) March 2, 1968 (10.15pm ABC)
Teleplay by	Roger Woddis	
Cast included	Dinah Sheridan, Sara Aimson, Malcolm Armstrong, Peter McCann, Jessica Dunning and Basil Henson	
Director	Jonathan Alwyn	
Designer	Neville Green	

Dinah Sheridan had performed in one of the early television plays to be broadcast from Alexandra Palace, thirty years before, and this was her first television role since then. All her professional work had been in cinema and theatre.

Roger Woddis, the author, afterwards wrote to me—

> I'm lucky to have had such a first-rate director and cast for my first Armchair Theatre.

Peter Black (*Daily Mail*, 29/2/1968) wrote—

> Inter-company squabbling between ABC and Rediffusion still works its mischief. *Armchair Theatre,* a major ITV drama series, went out at 11 p.m. in the London area again last night.
> It is a definitive sign of Lord Aylestone's capability as the new Chairman of ITA that this in-fighting between companies should have been allowed to continue for five weeks.
> Isn't he supposed to run the thing in the interests of us, the audience? Why doesn't he do it?

I like to think that Peter Black did the trick: Rediffusion in London scheduled our next transmission for 9pm! They also changed the day from Wednesday to Friday. Of course, it was all tempered by the fact that this could only be an interim arrangement, as both Rediffusion and ABC were shortly to be merged.

At ABC in the Midlands and the North, transmission remained at 10.15pm on the Saturday.

The following week we were back with a play described as "a suspenseful teaser" – a story about a reported confession of murder, but without a body. Probably more suitable for *Armchair Mystery Theatre* than *Armchair* 'proper': *A Very Fine Line.*

A Very Fine Line — March 8, 1968 (9.00pm ATV); March 9, 1968 (10.15pm ABC)

Teleplay by	C. Scott Forbes
Cast included	Michael Craig and Leslie Phillips – with Gerald Sim, Stephanie Cole, Lillias Walker, Joanne Dainton, Louis Negin, Ron Daniels, Jacki Newman, Alec Ross, Pam Ruddock, Frank Seton, Peter Flannery, Jane Murdoch and Ian Ainsley
Director	Don Leaver
Designer	Patrick Downing

Last in this run was a play not specially written for *Armchair Theatre* – described as "a dramatic investigation of the gulf between public image and private view, with the reputation of a 'great man' at issue".

Unscheduled Stop — March 15, 1968 (ATV); March 16, 1968 (ABC)

Teleplay by	Derek Bond
Cast included	James Villiers, Helen Cherry, Guy Rolfe, Gerald Harper, Caroline Blakiston, Ernest Milton, Ilona Rodgers, Hugh Latimer, Michael Smee, Barry Warren, Jan Carey and Shusha Assar
Director	Toby Robertson
Designer	Malcolm Goulding

Unscheduled Stop was the first work that the actor Derek Bond had written for television, and it also introduced director, Toby Robertson, to our team.

Alice Frick (*Stage and Television Today,* 21/3/1968) called it—

> this melodrama

Sylvia Clayton (*Daily Telegraph,* 16/3/1968) could only find entertainment in James Villier's performance of—

> a memorably amusing drunk

It was just too theatrical at a time when television drama was aiming for close-up reality.

As this part of the season ended, newspaper reports carried the news that our next run was to "return two weeks earlier". Welcome indeed for *Armchair Theatre*. Oddly, it was at the expense of ABC Television's other drama skein, *Mystery and Imagination*, which would now have a run of only four productions instead of the six planned.

At this time, *Armchair Theatre* had been announced as a finalist for an Emmy International Award (Entertainment Division) in America for that year. In those finals, ITV had two drama productions competing. ABC's *Call Me Daddy* (by Ernest Gebler) and Rediffusion's *The Good and Faithful Servant* (by Joe Orton). It must have been the year for Donald Pleasance: he played a lead in both finalist productions!

Armchair Theatre won the Award – a unique achievement at that time for ITV and the UK.

Unfortunately it was at a time when franchises were being changed and therefore *Armchair Theatre* was inevitably going to lose it's caring home at ABC Television.

The work of Gebler, Rakoff, Pleasance and Cornwell had wrought a gem for *Armchair Theatre* – yet ABC did not rejoice or show any great enthusiasm for this accolade. I was, at short notice, delegated to go alone to the States to receive the Award. There was no invitation to the director, Alvin Rakoff, to go with me. Had it been just a year earlier the achievement would have been proclaimed from the mastheads (print and transmitter).

As it was, I got back from the ceremony-that-never-was in the USA* and merely handed over the Award to Howard Thomas in his office in Hanover Square – with just he and I present. There was no party for the cast and crew. No celebration at all. Not even a glass of anything, thank you.

There was still some distance between the cinema moguls of Elstree at Associated British Picture Corporation and their television enterprise at Teddington studios. Those at ABPC seemed still to dismiss TV as relatively unimportant – "it won't last". Even the winning of this Emmy in the USA did not rate in the world of cinema production.

It was with great reluctance, I'm sure, that at one time the 'brass' at Elstree were driven to beg us at Teddington to use their contract actors in our casting, as they had no work for them in the film studios. Very little came of that – we at Teddington were making our own stars.

Remembering ABC Television's lack of enthusiasm for the winning of the Emmy, calls to mind another incident. I had been reading a book of short stories by Peter Ustinov, and one of them in particular struck me as being very attractive for a teleplay. I made advances to try to get the rights. Ustinov was playing at the Chichester Festival Theatre at the time, and he invited me to meet him there for lunch and talk about it. Regardless of outcome, I greatly looked forward to that delight. And a delight it certainly was, though not in respect of my request to get the rights for the story. It transpired that he wanted to hold on to them for a proposed film and so they were not at that time available. Towards the end of our conversation, I suggested that, as Associated British Cinemas was our parent company, there might be some interest in making the film. Peter Ustinov replied, "Oh, you mean that Company of Scottish Accountants!" What could I say to that?

*See Prologue: Stranger than Fiction

However, I had dramas of fiction to continue to produce, and they were more important than dwelling on the past. Indeed, this next section of our twelfth season launched two weeks earlier than originally scheduled, and started with four first plays for television.

We kicked off with a teleplay written by Kenneth Burley, the Wanstead newspaper sub-editor. The female lead character attracted Honor Blackman back to ABC Television for the first time since she had left *The Avengers*, and after her role in the Bond film as Pussy Galore. In *Recount*, she played the middle-aged wife of a parliamentary candidate in a by-election, who discovers she is pregnant after twenty-two years and just before her daughter is to get married. Jane Birkin played the nineteen-year-old daughter.

Recount	April 18, 1968
Teleplay by	Kenneth Burley
Cast included	Honor Blackman – with Jack Watling, John Turner, Richard Warwick, Richard Hurndall, Gillian Raine and Jane Birkin
Director	Bill Bain
Designer	Eileen Diss

Transmission of *Armchair Theatre* remained split between two different nights. Following the Saturday late night News it built on its inherited rating and held up well against the successful series *The Avengers* (which felt rather like competing with my own offspring).

Viewer-critic Mrs R. Chave of Winchester wrote—

> It had everything, perfect casting, sensible human story, lovely Honor Blackman, plus a happy ending. No violence or loud background music. One could relax whilst being completely enthralled. May we have more plays like this?

Having won the International Emmy Award, *Call Me Daddy* was repeated (April 25, 1968 in London; April 27 in our areas) a year after its first showing.

James Thomas (*Daily Express*) wrote—

> Sometimes the prize is worth the giving and the winner deserving of the award. Such is the case with Ernie Gebler's play Call Me Daddy which won the "American Emmy" for the best international TV programme of the year.

Donald Pleasance and Judy Cornwell in *Call Me Daddy* – repeated

James Pettigrew (*Sunday Mirror,* 28/4/1968) described it as—

> one of the best plays in a series of consistently high quality

Stanley Reynolds of *The Guardian* (29/4/1968), writing about the young actresses of that time, centred on salutations to Judy Cornwell—

> Has there ever been a decade before when pretty girls looked like so many peas in a pod? ... Miss Judy Cornwell, who is a rose among daisies. This last week saw her in two varying rôles, as bosum buddy to a beatnik in BBC-2's "Theatre 625" play, "The Fall of Kelvin Walker" ... and in a grateful repeat of a thoroughly amusing comedy duet [Call Me Daddy] ... She has an innocence that is not synthetic, a prettiness that is not porcelain, and a subtle way of being sexy or vampish which is comic and therefore not garish. ... Where other young actresses act like rather plain and immodest whores when called upon to do a comic send-up of the swinging dolly, Miss Cornwell glows into action. She also has the ability to use her voice in a way which extends the characterisation beyond the physical. ... She is the wisp of a girl, the little melting secretary, the failed art student, the passing figure in the typing pool or bus queue. Her talent is the illumination of the ordinary and the everyday, and it is a rare talent.

That rare talent then went off to Malta to join Anthony Newley in the film, *Can Heironymous Merkin Ever Forget Mercy Humppe and Find True Happiness?*

And I got on with the next *Armchair Theatre* production.

A complete contrast: the environment was South Africa and the firsthand experience of the writer.

No Easy Walk	May 2, 1968 (ATV) May 4, 1968 (ABC)
Teleplay by	Guy Slater
Cast included	Michael Pennington, Arne Gordon, Hazel Penwarden, Michael Turner, Christopher Sandford, Michael McGovern, Erica Rogers – with Zaikes Mokae, John Berrymann, Delores Mantez, Carl Badenhorst, Jack Morrell, Constantin de Coguel and Billy Cornelius
Director	Guy Verney
Designer	David Marshall

George Melly in his *Observer* review (5/5/1968) wrote—

> Finally, and far too briefly, No Easy Walk, an under-publicised first play by Guy Slater set in South Africa. On one level, as a documentary on what life is like in that tragic country, it was admirable. But, in its second theme, the destruction of several liberal lives and hopes by the selfish revolutionary exhibitionism of a young English visitor, it went beyond propaganda and became ... a work of art.

James Thomas (*Daily Express,* 2/5/1968) highlighted his review, "Tucked away: the drama of the odd corner . . ." and went on to say—

> I am continually baffled that ITV tucks away one of its top dramas of the week, ARMCHAIR THEATRE, at 10.30 on Thursday evenings. For this series was from the start a landmark in TV theatre, and still turns up playwrights and artists who deserve a better deal.
>
> Tonight this crusading drama series tackles, in the midst of Britain's row over racialism, the problem of colour prejudice in South Africa. It is a first TV play by Guy Slater, 26-year-old son of our Ambassador to Havana. He wrote his play "No Easy Walk" after a three-month visit to South Africa when he came down from Cambridge.

Divided screenings, varying late-night transmissions, and the shock of the franchise changes all continued to add problems for the existence of *Armchair Theatre* and the single play. Nevertheless, a breakdown of the ratings for the Top Five Single Plays for March of that year showed that *Armchair Theatre* topped 12 million viewers per show.

The twelfth season continued with another first play for television, and another written by a journalist:

The Escape Club	May 9, 1968 (ATV) May 11, 1968 (ABC)
Teleplay by	James Gibbons
Cast included	Stephen Murray, Rosemary Leach, Avice Landon and Michael Bates – with Duncan Lamont, Michael Robbins, Henry Manning, Michael Nightingale and Gareth Thomas
Director	Charles Jarrott
Designer	Michael Hall

The Escape Club was inspired by Sir Francis Chichester's lone yachtsman achievement – how the ambition to emulate that must have glowed in thousands of starry-eyed dreamers the world over. Gibbons wrote of one such dreamer, James Wharton, middle-aged and doomed to garden pottering, planning his adventure to get away from it all. Unknown to his wife he would "buy a ketch and do a mini-Chichester to the West Indies". But a sea of red tape, and a sea-crazy young woman who wants to join the adventure, cause complications unforeseen in the dream. Stephen Murray played the man wanting to escape the commuter's straight-jacket.

This play competed with some important soccer on that Saturday night: one of the hazards of Saturday scheduling. The ideal Sunday spot had been hi-jacked by American cinema.

Another 'first for television' was written by the then theatre critic for the *Daily Mail*. Escape from the domestic humdrum featured again, but in a very different way.

Home Movies May 16, 1968
May 18, 1968

Teleplay by	Peter Lewis
Cast included	Glenda Jackson, Ray McAnally, Grant Taylor, Viola Keats, John Hallam and Jesmine Dee
Director	Robert Tronson
Designer	Kenneth Mellor

Peter Black (*Daily Mail,* 17/5/1968)—

> Moving out of the dining-room into the kitchen, as all critics should from time to time, my colleague Peter Lewis has cooked up in Home Movies ... a sad and absorbing story of a haunting.
> … as an imaginative look at an unimaginable grief, it was a perceptive and sensitive piece of writing, to which the playing of Glenda Jackson and Ray McAnally added a painful integrity.

Sylvia Clayton (*Daily Telegraph,* 17/5/1968)—

> The domestic in-fighting became terse, tense, even macabre. Its tone, with its occasional echo of Edward Albee, suggested a playwright of power and promise.

In *The Sunday Telegraph* (19/5/1968) the reviewer wrote—

> We seemed to be plunged into Artificiality Week in the TV ... Peter Lewis's artifice drew closest to life. The full secret was very skilfully and graphically revealed ... Old recriminations were rawly exposed before the comforting make-believe closed once more over the wounds. With a performance by Ray McAnally in striking contrast to his Spindoe characterisation, a matching one by Glenda Jackson and Robert Tronson as director, it was easily the best thing in a bleak batch.

This next teleplay provided a cast list of ten – entirely for women.

You and Me May 23, 1968
May 25, 1968

Teleplay by	Robert Muller
Cast included	Yvonne Mitchell and Billie Whitelaw – with Tessa Wyatt, Mercia Mansfield, Sally Alford, Janet Hannington, Angela Galbraith, Aimee Delamain, Brenda Cowling and Damaris Hayman
Director	Kim Mills
Designer	Darrell Lass

Sarah Snow (*TV Times*) described it as—

> a strong story of love, with revenge one of its underlying emotions. Two women's conflict over the affections of a girl.

Peter Black (*Daily Mail,* 24/5/1968) thought that Robert Muller's—

> imagination is more intellectual than dramatic

Sylvia Clayton (*Daily Telegraph,* 24/5/1968) wrote—

> The play was designed as a vehicle for two star players, Yvonne Mitchell and Billie Whitelaw. ... But I have seldom seen a more lethal piece of miscasting than the warmly friendly Billie Whitelaw...

An interesting comment in view of the fact that the part had been specially written for Billie Whitelaw, who later became Robert Muller's partner. (Lew Grade may have had his fictional *Love Story*, but we had the real thing – several times – behind the scenes on *Armchair Theatre*.)

The critics may not have liked it but the audience must have been of a different opinion. The rating held up better than the two previous shows, holding the inherited figure from the News, and actually building in our region.

Marcus's "modern look at love" starred Richard Pasco playing a schoolmaster as a confused hero – "love need only be true and perfect for as long as it lasts".

The Glove Puppet May 30, 1968 June 1, 1968

Teleplay by	Frank Marcus
Cast included	Richard Pasco, Jacqueline Pearce, Ronald Lacey and Vickery Turner – with Julian Herrington, Pam Ruddock, Mark Elwes and Olga Linden
Director	Patrick Dromgoole
Designer	Stan Woodward

Jacqueline Pearce in *The Glove Puppet*

Peter Black (*Daily Mail,* 31/5/1968) in his review, headed, "Thank goodness for plays that don't need rescuing", wrote—

> The collection of writers ABC TV is finding for *Armchair Theatre* is giving the series a fine run into the end of its season. They create a sense of occasion which lasts through the play ... and you can't ask for more of TV drama.

"A sense of occasion". That, I believe, was what the whole drama team at ABC Television aimed at. We were so aware of the very ephemeral nature of the medium that we strived to make the *Armchair Theatre* part of it as special as possible. We didn't always satisfy our intentions, of course, and the single play was having a rough ride, but generally, I do believe that we stuck to our dedication.

Specifically, about Frank Marcus's *The Glove Puppet*, Peter Black wrote—

> [It] is a very good one; a funny and accomplished comedy about the fate that gapes for the male who is romantically chivalrous and idealistic about women, but does not see them very clearly. ... Another pleasure of this play is how firmly the characters exist, not just as attitudes but in their own right. ... Director (Patrick Dromgoole) and designer (Stan Woodward) fell eagerly upon a script that they could enhance and did not need to rescue.

A few weeks before *The Glove Puppet* was transmitted, Frank Marcus became Drama Critic of *The Sunday Telegraph*. In an interview, he is quoted as saying—

> Playwriting and criticism I see as parallel activities, not overlapping. In each I try to do the same thing, but using different methods. In both spheres, originality and concern with modern ideas are what I go for.

The following week's production brought together six splendid actresses.

The Three Wives of Felix Hull		June 6, 1968 June 8, 1968
Teleplay by	Fay Weldon	
Cast included	Dilys Laye, Elvi Hale, Patricia Lawrence, Clare Sutcliffe, Sally James and Felicity Gibson – with Charles Gray, Fulton Mackay, Stanley Meadows and Billy Cornelius	
Director	Alan Cooke	
Designer	Eddie Wolfram	

Sylvia Clayton (*Daily Telegraph,* 7/6/1968) described it as a—

> comedy of manners ... Miss Weldon writes clever, bitchy often funny dialogue. Her characters do not so much meet as collide.

Elizabeth Goodman (*Stage and Television Today,* 13/6/1968) opined that—

> her perception of the emotions and longings of real people has been so exact and familiar that watching her plays has been positively cathartic. ... Behind the sharp and usually entertaining front of Fay Weldon's writing there has always been a hard truth lurking, and often an unpleasant one.

But, summarising this play, Elizabeth Goodman thought it—

> a glossy and ingenious piece of writing leading from nowhere to nowhere.

These short plays were required to deliver – in less than an hour – a promising beginning, a compelling middle and a satisfying ending. Success varied, and in the case of *The Three Wives of Felix Hull* the viewing figures slipped. Nevertheless, we were very pleased to have Fay Weldon contributing her special qualities to *Armchair Theatre*'s writing galaxy.

That galaxy was further enhanced in our next. Ken Campbell was at that time an actor at the Victoria Theatre Stoke-on-Trent, working with Director Peter Cheeseman in that very special and successful environment, encouraging and launching new writers. In this, his first play for television, unlike more recent creations, he wrote for a cast of twenty-four characters.

One Night I Danced With Mr Dalton June 13, 1968 (10.30pm ATV)
June 15, 1968 (9.05pm ABC)

Teleplay by	Ken Campbell
Cast included	Donald Churchill, Richard Leech and John Alderton – with Pauline Collins, Christine Rodgers, Beatrix Mackey, Kathleen St John, Evelyn Lund, Walter Sparrow, Susan Tracy, Guy Ross, Malcolm Howard,Tania Trude, Martha Gibson, Billy Hamon, Julian Barnes, Sally Gosselin, Catherine Howe, Bonita Shawe, Ania Marson, Olive Milbourne, Joan Cooper, Adam Verney and Ken Campbell
Director	Guy Verney
Designer	Peter Le Page

Donald Churchill, one of the top comedy writers of *Armchair Theatre* played the lead in *One Night I Danced With Mr Dalton*, and the cast included the writer, Ken Campbell, playing a small part. John Alderton and Pauline Collins afterwards went on to be a team domestically as well as professionally.

Ken Campbell's bizarre story rated as well as the very popular *Opportunity Knocks!*, *The Invaders*, and the feature film showing to London viewers on that night.

Martin Jackson (*Daily Express,* 13/6/1968) wrote—

> Rarely does television unearth a new writing talent with a gift for comedy. But Ken Campbell is a name, I wager, you will be seeing on many more screen credits after his first TV play, One Night I Danced With Mr Dalton.

Martin Jackson's prediction was right, and Ken Campbell went on uniting his performance and writing skills, developing his own unique style.

Sylvia Clayton in her review in *The Daily Telegraph* wrote—

> There was a confident lunatic logic ... that made it the right light comedy for a hot summer evening. ... Mr Campbell writes fresh, funny dialogue but is never facetious because it is based on genuine observation.

Mr Campbell has certainly made quite a name for himself with his "lunatic logic" since then.

Further, the difficult running-down period of the end of ABC Television's franchise confused the focus considerably, and certainly didn't help us to maintain the excellent brand-image built over many years. From the ITA headquarters downstream, the chill wind of uncertainty blew up the Thames to Teddington.

And so, we came to the last production of *Armchair Theatre* made by ABC Television – the four hundredth since the anthology started in 1956. For this, and to mark the occasion, we changed style to something of a celebratory piece – with a running time extended to ninety minutes.

Robin Turner headlined it in the *Daily Express* (25/7/1968)—

> The old show goes out . . . in a blaze of allegory

Alfred Lynch at the wheel

Valerie French and Alfred Lynch

The Paper Dolls with Stanley Holloway

Stanley Holloway, Alfred Lynch, Valerie French and The Paper Dolls

The Ballad of the Artificial Mash

Unlike the first show twelve years earlier (*The Outsider*, adapted by George Kerr from the famous stage play by Dorothy Brandon, which was deeply rooted in the proscenium format) we now looked at the freer opportunities of 'in the round'.

I had long been a frequent visitor to the original Victoria Theatre in Stoke-on-Trent, where Peter Cheeseman was cleverly pioneering new writing and new forms. There I had seen a production of Peter Terson's *The Ballad of the Artificial Mash*, and enjoyed it thoroughly.

Peter Cheeseman, who had directed the theatre version, adapted the script for television. Its mixture of docu-drama story with music gave it an unusual edge as a teleplay of today and tomorrow, while the elements of musical interpretation provided a different style from the general run of *Armchair Theatre*. Sydney Newman had tried something similar with *His Polyvinyl Girl*.

To provide a direct link with the start of the series, we invited Dennis Vance, who had directed the first production, to return to us and direct *The Ballad of the Artificial Mash*. Flamboyant Dennis – who had earlier pioneered a one-camera follow-the-action style of studio drama – welcomed the challenge.

Actress Gillian Brown – who composed and arranged the music – was also in our cast.

A considerable novelty for *Armchair Theatre* was the inclusion of the then popular all-girl group 'The Paper Dolls' who had soared up the musical charts with their first recording.

The Ballad of the Artificial Mash July 25, 1968 (10.30pm ATV)
July 27, 1968 (10.15pm ABC)

Play by	Peter Terson
Teleplay by	Peter Cheeseman
Cast included	Stanley Holloway, Alfred Lynch, Valerie French, Mark Dignam, Derek Francis and Aubrey Richards – with The Paper Dolls – and Dawn Beret, Felix Felton, Dennis Shaw, John Malcolm, Desmond Stokes, Billy Milton, Peter Miles, Peter Badger and Gillian Brown
Director	Dennis Vance
Designer	David Marshall
Music by	Gillian Brown

Armchair Theatre Number 400 was an "Agricultural Satire". Dealing as it did with the problems of the health, sexwise, of an agricultural travelling salesman peddling artificial mash, it was perhaps a harbinger of troubles nowadays – over thirty years later – when genetically modified produce is highly controversial.

TV Times (7/1968)—

> What bothers Terson is the thought of the unknown side-effects that the artificial foodstuffs of today might have upon the men and women of tomorrow.

Perhaps we ought to have stuck to a safer show for the 400th, although I am glad we didn't – even though some of the critics did not like it.

Stanley Reynolds (*Guardian*) wrote of *The Ballad of the Artificial Mash*—

> which ended 12 years of ABC's *Armchair Theatre* – ITV's most distinguished television playhouse … A brave attempt ... Terson on television is like a fish out of water ... There were scenes in "The Ballad" that were begging for a live audience...

Angela Moreton (*Stage and Television Today,* 1/8/1968) headed her review—

> Too much fantasy and too long

Armchair Theatre, throughout the years, gave strong support to the unique realism of teleplays, with considerable success, but we always believed in experimenting with different styles. We could allow poetic vision some opportunity alongside 'kitchen sink' and suchlike.

Peter Black (*Daily Mail,* 26/7/1968)—

> Peter Terson's Ballad of the Artificial Mash dramatised the problem [factory farming] in a funny and lusty parable ... Terson's technique of blending popular song idiom with broad, poster-type dialogue and characterisation gave the play great energy. But as a parable it was too funny to be effective.

Michael Billington in *The Times* (26/7/1968) gave it more credit—

> Terson's Musical Morality
> ABC's Armchair Theatre certainly ended its career last night with a bang rather than a whimper. It's 400th and final production was *The Ballad of the Artificial Mash* by Peter Terson, an invigorating musical morality tale about the dangers of modern scientific farming methods. ... With a narrator clad like a circus ringmaster, the Paper Dolls acting as a glamorous singing chorus and characters given names like Major Fatstock-Gadget and Old Manure, it was clear from the start that the play was anything but realistic. The method chosen, however, was in perfect harmony with the theme and the central message emerged with a forceful simplicity. ... In all, the play seemed to me lively, pungent, comparable to *Zigger Zagger* in its use of a provocative cartoon style and comparable to the rest of Mr. Terson's work in its feeling for country life.

George Melly, writing in *The Observer*, described *The Ballad of the Artificial Mash* as "the most ambitious play" he reviewed that week—

> ...it was good that this long-lived series should have shown the courage to go out, if not with a totally satisfactory and resounding bang, at least with a show of squibs and rip-raps...

Maurice Wiggin (*Sunday Times,* 28/7/1968) also raised the pertinent question of expected style in television drama at that time—

> We are always expecting a masterpiece from Mr Terson, but though his style has considerable and welcome vivacity, and is entirely his own, his fondness for fantasy works against him in this most literal of all media.

Angela Moreton (*Stage and Television Today,* 1/8/1968) ended her review with—

> So we say goodbye to Armchair Theatre. Let's hope what follows, whatever form it takes, chalks up to its credit as many successes as its fore-runner.

Was it the end?

As Harry Secombe said, "You can't rest on your laurels – they turn into wreaths".

It was Goodbye, ABC Television, but Hello, Thames Television

Playhouse

It wasn't the end, but it certainly was different and, without doubt, this franchise round marked the start of a total change of philosophy so far as regional ITV was concerned.

At Teddington Studios, we were moving from a company that was seriously concerned with its regional identity, and which concentrated on its strength as a producer of drama, supplying week-end programmes only – to a completely new company responsible for London weekday programming. Thames Television opted for a wider remit: it had to do so. The old ABC characteristics were gone.

Howard Thomas remained at the helm as Managing Director, and Brian Tesler as Director of Programmes. Lloyd Shirley was Controller of Drama. Thames Television now produced contributions to the *Playhouse* anthology, and followed those with a short run of live dramas called *Premiere*. Several other new series were announced. *Armchair Theatre* didn't return until the beginning of 1969, and had by then lost its place as a habit forming date with the box.

Thus, Thames Televison launched its drama schedule under the *Playhouse* banner with three 90-minute plays adapted from stories by Noel Coward. The adaptations were all by William Marchant, who had previously made such a success of Coward's *Pretty Polly* for *Armchair Theatre*.

The first was duly cast to match the title with the leading lady making a most welcome visit from her Hollywood home:

Star Quality
Glynis Johns

Star Quality	August 5, 1968 (8.30pm) *Playhouse*
Story by	Noel Coward
Teleplay by	William Marchant
Cast included	Glynis Johns and Robert Hardy – with Barry Justice and Jim Norton – also Mona Bruce, Anne Gordon, Joyce Barbour, Tandy Cronin, Roy Maxwell, Elizabeth Knight, Simon Gough, Anthony Dawes, John Keenan and Marika Rivera
Director	Guy Verney
Designer	David Marshall

The reviews for *Star Quality* were generally favourable.

Peter Black (*Daily Mail,* 6/8/1968)—

> *Star Quality* gave me 90 minutes of unalloyed pleasure.

James Thomas (*Daily Express,* 6/8/1968)—

> a production far removed from the television play of 1968.

Mary Malone (*Daily Mirror,* 6/8/1968)—

> when Miss Johns was on you couldn't take your eyes off her. That was star quality.

Tom Stoppard, writing in *The Observer* (11/8/1968) – the playwright as critic—

> I was so riveted by this ... that I missed more than half of 'Theatre 625' [BBC2] ... a terrific opportunity for Glynis Johns, fully realised, and for Robert Hardy whose brilliantly observed performance as the feline director was actually frightening. But perhaps most of the credit should go to their director, Guy Verney. One got an idea of what good TV directors are all about by comparing this production with BBC-1's Hay Fever (Play of the Month) which came an awful cropper.

But Nancy Banks-Smith, in her inimitable style, wrote in *The Sun* (6/8/1968)—

> Do tell me if I am being silly, but perhaps it could be cut by half an hour ... perhaps a complete change of cast might be an improvement. Except for Bobby Hardy.
> 'Star Quality' is a second-rate play...

Star Quality also provoked a memo from Lloyd Shirley. He wrote—

> I am sure you will be as delighted as I was to learn the <u>only</u> production that swam against the tide in the struggle for the audience with the BBC was STAR QUALITY. I am very pleased that the viewers gave their endorsement to this production which I thought was handled not only with artistry, but with an enormous degree of professional skill.

And the viewers wrote as well. Often those viewers who take the trouble to write are those uncomplimentary, and so it was good to have the happy missives on this occasion.

Mrs Taylor of Wednesbury, Staffs—

> Star Quality had exactly that, provided in a sparkling performance from Glynis Johns … a joy to behold in this ITV play.

Mrs W. Norton of Kingston-upon-Thames—

> I can hardly find the words to express my admiration of your superb production "Star Quality". ... How shattering to think that such a gem should now be gone for ever, and that all that sheer perfection and shining talent was for one performance only!
> However, thank you, THANK YOU, for such memorable viewing (and that includes everybody concerned)

Well, alas, the gem has seemingly gone forever, Mrs Norton. It was nominated for an Emmy Award, yet I cannot find any copy of it in existence in the archives. Long gone, together with all the other worthies – the tape presumably wiped and re-used, as was the practice.

Glynis Johns telephoned me some time later saying how much she would like to find a copy of the production, but, unless someone has one hidden at the back of a cupboard or under the bed, I fear that none exists.

Well, television is essentially ephemeral.

The second, a very different story, introduced American actor Shelley Burton (*The Boston Strangler*).

Bon Voyage
Shelley Burton and Constance Cummings

Bon Voyage	August 12, 1968 (8.30pm) *Playhouse*
Story by	Noel Coward
Teleplay by	William Marchant
Cast included	Constance Cummings, Rachel Kempson, Richard Vernon, Libby Morris and Meir Tzelniker – with Shelley Burton, Bessie Love, Maurice Good, Denis Goacher, Stephanie Beacham, Mark Edwards, David Toguri, David Spenser, Tommy Yapp, Reg Peters, Angie Grant and Alan Lawrence
Director	Guy Verney
Designer	David Marshall

Set on a luxury liner on a Pacific cruise, it called for excellent design from David Marshall, which again provoked a rare internal memo (13/8/1968), this time from Sir Philip Warter, Chairman of Thames Television—

> Just to let you know how much I enjoyed "Bon Voyage" last evening. Everything about it well done and for once I appreciated the value of the sets. Congratulations to all concerned.

Reference to the "value of the sets" echoed the running battle we had over the costs of elaborate sets which were often thought to be unnecessary. But we had one of the best, if not *the* best, design departments in the business and we fought to keep those standards high. We couldn't always match the movie studio or location level, but we were dedicated to avoiding theatrical unreality. Our design team was first-rate.

Sylvia Clayton (*Daily Telegraph,* 13/8/1968) described it as—

> A highly theatrical romance

Perhaps – but in design terms it was not 'theatrical'.

Mary Malone's verdict (*Daily Mirror,* 13/8/1968)—

> agreeably done and splendidly acted

But again some critics were not impressed with the adaptation:

Robert Ottaway (*Daily Sketch,* 13/8/1968)—

> a slice of whimsy, and gushed with sentiment like a damp spinster.

Michael Walsh (*Daily Express,* 13/8/1968) headed his review—

> Where was the Coward wit and sparkle?

The critics did not necessarily reflect the reception of viewers, who wrote congratulatory letters:

Miss Heathcote (London SW12)—

> Thank you for Monday night's wonderful play! I can't tell you how very much I and all my friends enjoyed it. ...
> Please, please let us have more plays of this type.

Mrs Allen (Bath)—

> Thank you for your wonderful production of "Bon Voyage" ...
> Class producers are rare these days...

Not too rare, I hoped!

At No.3 the series *Never Mind the Quality, Feel the Width* – originally an *Armchair Theatre* teleplay screened on February 18, 1967, and written by Vince Powell and Harry Driver

Television Audience Measurement (TAM)
September 22, 1968

Top Twenty Programmes –		Homes in	Millions
1	Coronation Street (Mon 16th)	Granada	6.80
2	Coronation Street (Wed 18th)	Granada	6.60
3	Never Mind the Quality [series]	Thames	6.40
3=	The Most Beautiful Hotel in the World	YTV	6.40
5	News At Ten (Tue 17th)	ITN	6.15
6	Five Miles to Midnight	BBC	5.95
7	The Black & White Minstrels	BBC	5.80
8	Sherlock Holmes	BBC	5.65
9	Marty	BBC	5.50
9=	World in Action	Granada	5.50
11	Nearest and Dearest	Granada	5.40
12	Sportsnight With Coleman	BBC	5.30
12=	The Forsyte Saga	BBC	5.30
14	Oh Brother!	BBC	5.15
14=	Opportunity Knocks!	Thames	5.15
14=	Saratoga Trunk	BBC	5.15
17	Softly, Softly	BBC	5.00
18	News At Ten (Wed 18th)	ITN	4.90
19	Dixon of Dock Green	BBC	4.85
19=	Run For Your Life	BBC	4.85
19=	Top of the Pops	BBC	4.85

Technical disputes caused a delay, and the last of the *Playhouse* trilogy had to wait over a month for transmission. *The Kindness of Mrs Radcliffe* had to stand alone in the ninety-minute *Playhouse* slot. An attempt was made to regain continuity by prefacing the play with a series of short clips from the previous two productions.

The Kindness of Mrs Radcliffe September 23, 1968 (8.30pm) *Playhouse*

Story by	Noel Coward
Teleplay by	William Marchant
Cast included	Phyllis Calvert – with Anthony Nicholls, Joan Hickson, Frances White, Kathleen Michael, Rachel Gurney, Sarah-Jane Gwillim, Rachel Thomas, Miriam Mann, Frank Barrie, Sheila Keith, Eileen Way, Rose Hiller and Martin Johnson
Director	Bill Bain
Designer	Fred Pusey

This 'teaser' offended Robert Ottaway (*Daily Sketch,* 24/9/1968) who apparently thought it was—

> trailers for programmes long gone. As padding it was fine but as TV drama it stank.

As to the show itself, he thought that Coward had written a—

> horse opera … a suburban cowboy saga.

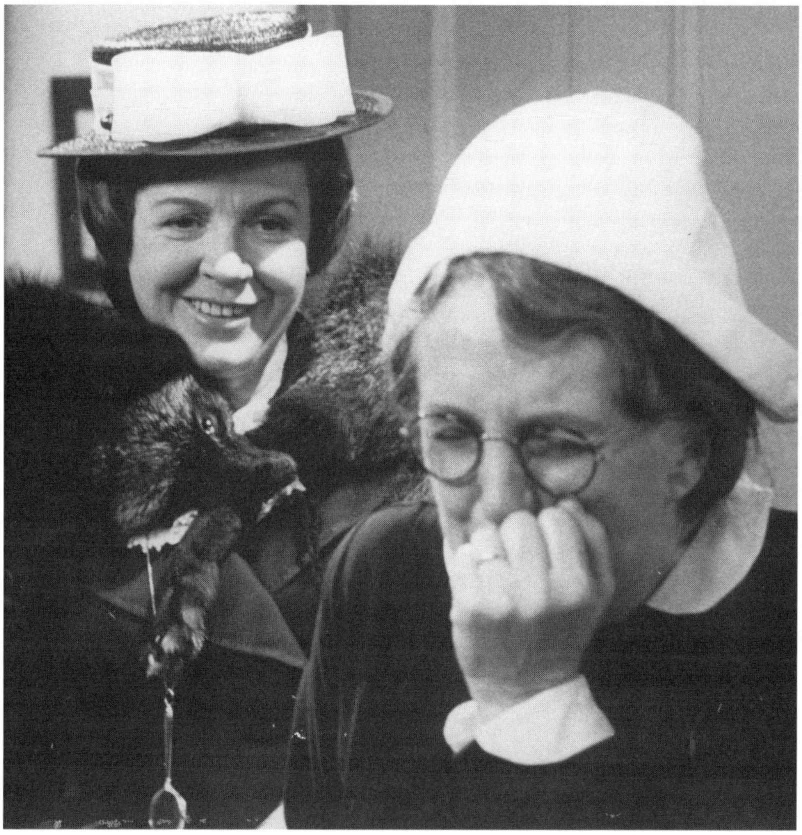

The Kindness of Mrs Radcliffe **Phyllis Calvert and Joan Hickson**

Nevertheless, *The Kindness of Mrs Radcliffe* stood up very well in the ratings, with some 12 million viewers, just short of the BBC's ever-popular *Forsyte Saga*, and in a week when *The Avengers* did not even appear in the Top Twenty.

Stanley Reynolds (*Guardian,* 24/9/1968) wrote—

> This was a brilliant character study of the nasty, unfeeling woman, stepping though life in hobnail boots, and sincere in her belief that she is wearing velvet slippers … a rare comedy, a study of the sincere monster, and it worked superbly.

James Thomas (*Daily Express,* 24/9/1968) disagreed, describing it as—

> a play which simply was not worth the main viewing time on the commercial channel.

He clearly hadn't seen the viewing figures.

Michael Billington, in *The Times* (24/9/1968) summed up—

> Last night, Thames Television brought us the last in a very successful series of adaptations of Noel Coward stories … Phyllis Calvert was admirable as Mrs Radcliffe...

Premiere

Following *Playhouse* came *Premiere* – something of an experiment, and certainly not playing safe. We elected to run a short series of five live teleplays – a sort of re-inventing *Armchair Theatre*, not recorded 'as live' but honestly live, the performances transmitted directly as happening in the studio. No opportunities for editing, no pre-recording, no re-takes.

It was thought that perhaps we were losing something of the 'event'– the immediacy and sharing the experience of creating the performance. In a full-page advertisement in the evening newspapers, it was described thus—

> Tonight at 9.00 the first in Thames Television's 'Premiere' series begins. And at that time precisely the actors, cameramen and technicians in Thames' Studio One will step out on to the thin ice of a live TV drama production. ... Nothing but the tension of a first-night, heightened by the split-second timing of television and an unseen audience of millions.
> Nobody, not even the critics, has ever seen 'Flower Dew' before. They will join tonight in watching the play as it happens.

Members of the audience were also invited to be a 'Critic for a night' and submit a review of each play in the series. A money-prize was offered the best in each case and they would be printed in *TV Times*.

At that time, *TV Times* had gone into a new format, which set out details of programmes in insultingly small print and without any showbiz flair. Often important credits were omitted, all on the pretext of making room for more features.

The first teleplay, specially written for this live transmission, was a story about a Porton Down type of research centre where a scientist had died after an accident with 'Flower Dew', a nerve gas that kills at a touch. Roy Clarke's theme was that the obscene and blasphemous work dehumanises the staff. A subject certainly of the time – if not timeless – and pertinent to live television drama.

Flower Dew October 2, 1968 (9pm—live) *Premiere*

Teleplay by	Roy Clarke
Cast included	Janet Munro, Edward Fox, Anthony Booth, Terry Scully, Barbara Lott and John Welsh
Director	Dennis Vance
Designer	David Marshall

Peter Black of the *Daily Mail* (3/10/1968) took a constructive view of the project, insofar that he recognized that being live, inevitably it would be—

> old fashioned and stagey …
> Dennis Vance, dusting off his years of experience as pioneer of live drama in the days when it was the only way, successfully accepted the challenge to do it again …
> Roy Clarke very nearly brought it off.

Joan Kemp-Welch, one of the most respected and experienced TV directors, wrote an article reviewing the argument: "LIVE DRAMA. Is it turning back the clock?"—

> Producing recorded television drama is here to stay. It would be foolish to pretend otherwise. …
> Authors are no longer writing for "television", but for "films".

Thereby diminishing the existence of television drama as a separate and different genre from cinema drama. She pointed out that from the actors' point of view—

> Live television ... does make sustained portrayals possible.

From the point of view of the audience she wrote—

> I believe the nervous tension a live play imparts does communicate itself to a great degree …
> The sense of electricity and urgency, vitality and freshness, that live performances impose upon the actor and the whole studio, more than justify the grave risks that a producer takes when he considers putting live drama on the screen.
> It becomes the art-form that television so often denies itself. If a certain amount of live drama were to be produced each year, the discipline that must result would not only be a tremendous boost of efficiency to the individual television studios but would give us some exciting times.

"Grave risks" indeed!

Our second transmission of *Premiere* was a story set in the enclosed world and the ready-made tensions of the army. Two strands of the plot concern a Commanding Officer who is trying to save his regiment from Whitehall manoeuvres to 'phase it out' and at the same time dealing with a young card-carrying Communist sergeant.

The Night of Talavera October 9, 1968 (9pm—live) *Premiere*

Teleplay by	Robert Holles
Cast included	Edward Woodward, Ray Brooks, Bernard Archard, David Glover, Peter Copley, John Nettleton, David Garth, George Waring, Clifford Cox, Michael Elwyn, Anthony Langdon, Lindsay Campbell and John Devaut
Director	Mike Vardy
Designer	Peter Le Page

In this one, the critics found the live production more to their liking.

The *Sunday Times* (13/10/1968) review declared that it was—

> vastly more entertaining, far better done, than the first ... Whether "The Night of Talavera" was genuinely a play, a work of art, or a clever and resourceful "dramatised documentary" lash-up knitting together several topical themes, is a matter for academic discussion. But it was all watchable, even compulsive, entertainment.

I had a problem in the selection of directors to deal with these live productions. Who, after all this time of video tape recording, would want to go live? Who, in fact, could deal with it? I felt that I had to go back to those who had done it before, for safety. But, it didn't turn out like that.

As it happened, the old-timers were, in fact, more nervous of the process than those with little or no experience of live drama. Clearly, those that *knew*, remembered too well all the possibilities of what could go wrong: they knew too much! Whereas, the uninitiated proceeded blindly on the strength of their enthusiasm.

Mary Malone (*Daily Mirror,* 10/10/1968) wrote—

> The Wednesday war for audiences is hotting up and best value came from ITV with their well-written (by Robert Holles), well-acted story of a regimental CO fighting on two fronts at once. ... splendidly worked out ... and it was a play which for once gained by being acted live.

Peter Black (*Daily Mail,* 10/10/1968) summed up *The Night of Talavera*—

> Edward Woodward as the C.O., Bernard Archard as the sergeant major, David Glover as the adjutant and Ray Brooks as the sergeant topped a cast which demonstrated once again that though the case for live drama is by no means proved there's no doubt it does something for actors.

For the third of the five live teleplays, we produced an American story, but set in London.

My Country 'Tis of Thee October 16, 1968 (9pm—live) *Premiere*

Teleplay by	Don Cornelius
Cast included	Barry Morse, Jan Sterling, Linda Liles, Anna Cameron, Derek Waring, Margaret Robertson, Sarah Marshall, Danny Daniels, Bruce Boa, Gretchen Franklin and Etain O'Dell
Director	Henry Kaplan
Designer	Stan Woodward

The writer was Don Cornelius, and this was his first for UK television. He had worked before with Henry Kaplan, the director, in the USA, and I had known Henry's work in Canada while we were both at CBC in Toronto, some ten years before.

My Country 'Tis of Thee concerned London's little colony of expatriate Americans at that time: why they were here and what they thought, mainly through the eyes of a young woman seeking freedom denied her in the United States.

Mary Malone (*Daily Mirror*, 17/10/1968) who had been so glowing in her praise of *The Night of Talavera* the week before watched only the first fifteen minutes of this ninety-minute production and then judged it to be—

> comic strip words that did for Americans played by British actors.

In an attempt put the record straight for the archives, I informed her that 'comic strip' or not, the words were written by an American (not anything phoney by a non-American) and further that leading and feature roles had been played by Americans. Barry Morse, although originally English, had been playing American parts in the US for some twenty years and was certainly acceptable as such; even playing an American role in a long-running series there. I took issue in that the criticism was based on watching for only fifteen minutes. Surely, the readers deserved something more responsible than that. If she had watched all, but declared that she wanted to switch off after fifteen minutes – that would be fair enough.

The revamped *TV Times* on this occasion gave only the cast list. No other production credits were given.

We followed up with another story applicable to the time, and therefore especially apt for live TV drama – so much so that the largest anti-Vietnam demonstration to date was expected that same weekend. The play was about the clash between two demonstrators of former years, one who had become a bank clerk, and the other who remained an anarchist. A serious subject, but the author was quoted at the time as saying "I think the students' ideas are interesting but their behaviour is highly send-upable". So, in *Foxhole in Bayswater* he sent it up.

Foxhole in Bayswater October 23, 1968 (9pm—live) *Premiere*

Teleplay by	Emanuel Litvinoff
Cast included	Donal Donnelly, Mark James, Ilona Rodgers, Nerys Hughes, Rosalind Speight, Peter King, Bert Allison and Arnold Peters
Director	Peter Duguid
Designer	Eileen Diss

Stanley Reynolds in *The Guardian* (24/10/1968) liked it—

> Donnelly was playing an American neo-Trotskyite rebel leader who has sneaked into England illegally for Sunday's anti-Vietnam demonstration. ... [He] was brilliant in the role of Marlon ...
> In a wild swirl of stage movements (extremely impressive in a live television play) the police break in, fighting off Marlon's hippy defenders, only to have the arrest halted by a call from the Home Secretary who says Marlon is wanted on "Panorama" ... and the "David Frost Show" as well. The hungry media will obviously make his stay indefinite.

Henry Raynor (*Times,* 24/10/1968) described it as a—

> Comedy of unrest ... admirably topical...

Peter Black's review (*Daily Mail,* 24/10/1968) almost entirely concerned the 'new' *TV Times'* decision to scrap the old format that had given due credits, especially to the writers—

> It is utterly contemptible that it should help to under-rate artists who are already lower-rated than they ought to be.

And so say I. He went on to generalise—

> Another strange policy of this magazine is to pretend that all the programmes come from some unnamed source. The great asset of ITV is its regionalisation, which provides 15 different outlets of varying size and personality. It is very important that the regional flavour should be identifiable and thereby encouraged. TV Times ignores it.

I agree that regional identity should be given due credit. I always wanted our productions to start with 'An ABC Television Production', but I never succeeded in that. As it was, the general 'ident' only signified the franchise holder. Now, alas, it is getting well-nigh impossible to achieve, with the moves towards monopoly in the new millennium.

Peter Black did get around to reviewing Emanuel Litvinoff's *Foxhole in Bayswater*—

> it was a funny, observant and literate comedy about the decline of an old student revolutionary into a husband and TV personality.

Angela Moreton (*Stage and Television Today,* 31/10/1968) found the play "boring" but said of live presentation—

> The advantage of presenting Emanuel Litvinoff's play live was that it was allowed to be bang up-to-date, with plenty of references to Sunday's march. This sort of topicality has disappeared in the immediate sense from the taped play, almost without one noticing. There was a skilful use of an attractive set and the play ... showed no signs of cramping or restriction. The crowd scenes, both of young revolutionaries, and at the end, of police, were exceptionally well-handled.

A plus in the live genre extending the style beyond the narrative.

The last of this *Premiere* short run of live productions won over those critics who had been sceptical of the live experiment. Margery Baker joined us from the Features department to direct this production. She had been a winner of the Guild of Television Producers and Directors Award.

No Reflection on You	October 30, 1968 (9pm—live) *Premiere*
Teleplay by	C. Scott Forbes
Cast included	David Buck, Anna Cropper, Hugh Manning, Helen Christie, Phyllida Law, Michael Graham Cox, John Stone, Leslie Schofield, Gary Burfield and Michael Howarth
Director	Margery Baker
Designer	Tony Borer

Sean Day-Lewis (*Daily Telegraph,* 31/10/1968)—

> [This] series of new plays played live, which started so badly, ended last night on a high level ...
> Mr Scott Forbes has a considerable gift for realistic dialogue and characterisation and the exchanges between the bored husband and anxious wife had a marvellously effective economy.
> The play also had dramatic tautness and, with the aid of an expertly underplayed production by Margery Baker, it maintained its tension without any kind of red-herring trickery.
> The eccentric new order at the *TV Times* ensured that David Buck, who took the leading part as the husband, was not even mentioned in the cast list. Both he and Anna Cropper as his wife deserved every credit.

Nancy Banks-Smith (*Sun,* 31/10/1968) wrote—

> 'No Reflection' was extremely effective dramatically. ...
> I have not been over kind to 'Premiere', but I enjoyed this effectively unfinished whodunit by C. Scott Forbes.

The 'Be a Critic Contest' that *TV Times* ran with this series was judged by Philip Purser (*Sunday Telegraph*); Peter Jackson (Editor, *TV Times*); and Brian Tesler (one-time theatre critic for the student newspaper, *Isis at Oxford*, and now Director of Programmes, Thames Television).

The first of the five winners, Mr Hugh Rorrison of Leeds, summed up Roy Clarke's *Flower Dew*—

> ...the dramatic situation could not be taken seriously and the intended black comedy became farce with a flabby ending.

Mrs Clegg (Ealing) liked Robert Holles' *The Night of Talavera*—

> This was a good play, well conceived, well directed and thoroughly well played.

For Jack Verdin (London SW4) Don Cornelius's *My Country 'Tis Of Thee*—

> came as a disappointment after the fine entertainment of the previous week. ... shallow material.

Beryl Leatham Thomas (Oswestry) reviewing Emanuel Litvinoff's *Foxhole in Bayswater* didn't agree with some of the professional critics who liked it. She did not appreciate this "literate comedy" and seemed to think that it hadn't been rehearsed!

The last prize-winner (and what mean prizes they were, with *TV Times* forking out all of five pounds to each) a Mr Campion (of Plymouth) reviewed C. Scott Forbes' *No Reflection on You*, writing that—

> it is a bit of a shock to realise that [the police] still have powers to invade our homes at any hour, rummage though our possessions and seize "for analysis" anything that takes their fancy. ...
> Anna Cropper and David Buck are convincing victims of this nightmare visitation. ... skeletons are dragged from cupboards ... a promising career is wrecked ...
> The inspector's breezy, "No harm done" when withdrawing from this irreparable ruin stresses the need for a drastic change in a curiously undemocratic law.

Only one in five of the 'viewer critics' winners in this competition wrote of enjoying the teleplay. I didn't have the chance to read any of the others submitted and so I have no idea how the 'losers' reacted.

CHAPTER 13

Armchair Theatre – 1969 – Thirteenth Season

A Touch of Bathos

Armchair Theatre did eventually get back on-air at the beginning of 1969. Some papers had forecast that it was over forever. Certainly, the break and changes in scheduling just about scuttled the continuity that the anthology had enjoyed for so long.

T.S. Ferguson in *The Sunday Telegraph* (5/1/1969) who had predicted that it would return, headed his preview, "The Happy Return" and wrote—

> It's therefore with some relief that I can tell you that it starts again tomorrow. ... Leonard White has been producer of the series for six years, and it's been developing the whole time.

It was the start of the thirteenth season, and due to be the last in black-and-white. We had become very used to monochrome by that time and the thought of 'going colour' was almost melodramatic. 'Electric Theatre'.

T.S. Ferguson quoted me at that time as saying—

> In this new series there's a movement towards asking the audience to suspend their disbelief a bit more and not to be bogged down by 'television reality' … in the series as a whole there's a definite flavour of the unusual.

We had certainly moved on from the earlier 'kitchen sink' tag.

A run of ten productions began on Twelfth Night with a David Perry teleplay, which followed the News Headlines on the Monday night. David had been one of the early writers for *Armchair Theatre*, notable for *The Trouble With Our Ivy*, a macabre comedy which Sydney Newman had produced in 1961. This one I described as an "unlikely game of make-believe. Not exactly Postman's Knock but more like a charade that gets a little rough".

The Frobisher Game	January 6, 1969 (8.30pm)
Teleplay by	David Perry
Cast included	Dandy Nichols, Bill Fraser, Avice Landon, Richard Pearson, Vanessa Lee and Peter Graves – with Alan Haines, Edward Sinclair and Clive Marshall
Director	Patrick Dromgoole
Designer	Eddie Wolfram

Sylvia Clayton (*Daily Telegraph,* 7/1/1969) described it as an—

> ingenious comedy of errors ... Watching this play was like seeing an elaborate piece of conjuring, cleverly sustained until the ending, which tried one trick too many ...
> [the play had] considerable originality and intelligence.

Martin Jackson (*Daily Express,* 7/1/1969) headlined, "It's fun spotting the TV trends", and wrote—

> Watching *Armchair Theatre*, which returned to ITV last night, is always good for trend-spotting the passing fashions of TV drama. This season the flavour is comedy with kinky black edges. ...
> Dandy Nichols playing a part far removed from Alf Garnett's Silly Old Moo turned in a marvellous performance...

But, like Sylvia Clayton, he thought that by the final twist—

> the joke had been whittled away in the mechanics of the plot.

TVRatings produced for JICTAR
Week ending Sunday January 12, 1969
Top Twenty Programmes – Homes in Millions

	Programme	Company	Homes
1	Coronation Street (Mon 6th)	Granada	7.55
1=	Till Death Us Do Part	BBC	7.55
3	Max	Thames	7.50
4	Coronation Street (Wed 8th)	Granada	7.25
5	The Frobisher Game (AT)	Thames	6.95
6	Mr Digby, Darling	Yorkshire	6.90
6=	The Forsyte Saga	BBC	6.90
8	The Avengers	Thames	6.80
9	Two Way Stretch	BBC	6.75
10	Opportunity Knocks!	Thames	6.70
11	The Power Game	ATV	6.65
12	World In Action	Granada	6.60
13	The Rolf Harris Show	BBC	6.55
14	The Reporters	Yorkshire	6.50
15	The Morecambe & Wise Show	BBC	6.30
16	News At Ten (Thurs 9th)	ITN	6.25
17	News At Ten (Mon 6th)	ITN	6.20
17=	So Evil My Love	BBC	6.20
19	The Dick Emery Show	BBC	6.05
20	The Fossett Saga	Lon.wk/end	6.00

Armchair Theatre
***The Frobisher Game* at No.5**

Stanley Reynolds (*Guardian,* 7/1/1969) was appreciative—

> David Perry's "Frobisher Game", so excellently acted and superbly directed by Patrick Dromgoole.

Julian Critchley (*Times,* 7/1/1969) didn't like it—

> a play which told us nothing and failed to make us laugh.

Nancy Banks-Smith (*Sun,* 7/1/1969) wrote of *The Frobisher Game*—

> The game was played savagely. And the most memorable thing about the play (it has disturbed me all night like biscuit crumbs in bed) was the menace generated by Bill Fraser and Avice Landon. Dressed in a little brief authority they revelled and rolled in it.

Next in this run of ten came another from Emanuel Litvinoff who described it as "the first play I have conceived for television".

A Foot in the Door January 13, 1969

Teleplay by	Emanuel Litvinoff
Cast included	Frank Finlay, Joe Melia and Margery Mason – with Jacqueline Maude, John Rye, Peter Cartwright, Bryan Robson, Ray Browne, Brenda Lawrence, Lesley Nunnerley, Frances Cohen, Margaret Courtenay, Pam Ruddock and Jack Wild
Director	Kim Mills
Designer	Tony Borer

Sylvia Clayton (*Daily Telegraph,* 14/1/1969) described it as being—

> like an hour-long commercial on how to become a successful personality. It over-simplified both problem and solution.

Stanley Reynolds (*Guardian,* 14/1/1969) picked up on the news that it was a first teleplay, calling it—

> rather old-fashioned ... [yet] somehow refreshing.
> Frank Finlay played [the] failed salesman, David. And a marvellous job he did of it. ... The good thing about Litvinoff's play, apart from the highly credible characterisation, cast with a fine sensibility, was that it dealt with a genuine fact: the better you know yourself, the better you can do your job, whatever that job might be.

James Thomas (*Daily Express,* 14/1/1969), referring to *Armchair Theatre*, declared—

> the fire has gone out of it. Whatever campaigning the series used to have has been dampened presumably in an effort to court an audience which no longer wishes to be disturbed.

Yes, we lost about three-quarters of a million homes viewing on this one, but even so, over 12 million viewers did watch it.

Quite a change of mood next with the casting of pop singer Joe Brown in a straight acting role in another first play for television.

What*'s *a Mother For? January 20, 1969

Teleplay by	Charles Laurence
Cast included	Joe Brown, June Whitfield and Mona Washbourne – with Arnold Yarrow, Claire Davenport, Christopher Webb, Kenneth Waller and John Steiner
Director	Charles Jarrott
Designer	Stan Woodward

Director Charles Jarrott returned to us for this production after directing Sean Connery and Michael Caine in *The Male of the Species* for NBC, and before starting work on *Anne of a Thousand Days* with Richard Burton. I was very happy to have my old colleague, Charles Jarrott, back with us.

TVRatings produced for JICTAR – Week ending Sunday January 26, 1969 Top Twenty Programmes – Homes in Millions							
1	Coronation Street (Mon 20th)	Granada	7.70	11	The Rolf Harris Show	BBC	6.50
2	Max	Thames	7.60	11=	The Story of Dr Wassall	BBC	6.50
3	Coronation Street (Wed 22nd)	Granada	7.50	13	World in Action	Granada	6.45
4	Till Death Us Do Part	BBC	7.45	14	The Morecambe & Wise Show	BBC	6.40
5	Opportunity Knocks!	Thames	7.15	15	The Avengers	Thames	6.35
6	Nurse on Wheels	BBC	6.90	16	News at Ten (Tue 21st)	ITN	6.20
7	What's a Mother For? (AT)	Thames	6.85	16=	This Week	Thames	6.20
8	Mr Digby, Darling	Yorkshire	6.80	18	The Dick Emery Show	BBC	6.15
8=	The Forsyte Saga	BBC	6.80	18=	Shields for Murder	BBC	6.15
10	The Power Game	ATV	6.55	20	News at Ten (Mon 20th)	ITN	6.05

***Armchair Theatre* – *What's a Mother For?* at No.7**

Variously described as a farce or as a black comedy, *What's a Mother For?* found little favour with the reviewers. However, it pushed *Armchair Theatre* back up the Top Twenty ratings again, being the top-rated single play of that week, beaten only by popular long-runners such as *Coronation Street* and *Till Death Us Do Part*.

Again a change of style to something more serious: the story of two men of vastly different backgrounds, struggling for power, running neck-and-neck for a top job in Whitehall. This author, having been a civil servant for twenty years, knew what he was writing about. At pains to explain that the situation and characters were entirely imaginary, it nevertheless certainly had the ring of authenticity about it.

The Mandarins January 27, 1969

Teleplay by	E.Y. Bannard
Cast included	Peter Jeffrey, Peter Blythe, Ann Castle, Veronica Strong and Ronald Lewis – with Patrick Waddington, George Woodbridge, Judy Champ, Edward Evans, Roger Hammond and David Garfield
Director	Bill Bain
Designer	Tony Borer

Despite E.Y. Bannard's life experience, he didn't seem to convince the reviewers.

Marjorie Bilbow (*Stage and Television Today,* 30/1/1969) wrote—

> The in-fighting, back-biting, gossip-mongering and strategical manoeuvering held an acceptable degree of suspense. ... An adequately entertaining suspense drama ... mutated into a creaking tumbril for tired causes.

Other critics ignored it, and the viewers were not well impressed. It didn't get into the Top Twenty.

We switched to comedy with a serious undertow – "Comedy with black edges" as the writer described it. In this play his sense of humour was more akin to the 'drowning not waving' variety.

Go On—It'll Do You Good was the result of Michael Chapman's declared ambition "to write a play". He had only written a short story before. Michael had been a successful administrator, serving the top brass at ABC Television's Headquarters in Hanover Square. He then transferred to our Teddington Studios to work in the Drama Department doing the same sort of job, but being nearer the creativity. He kept a beady eye on us all. Clearly, there was a writer trying to get out.

Go On—It'll Do You Good
Barbara Couper and Jack Woolgar

I commissioned the teleplay, and Michael took some of his annual leave to write it. It told the imagined story in which the Ministry of Social Welfare is so interested in the well-being of senior citizens that it arranges their demise. Taking over from natural causes, you might say – 'The Farewell State'? It certainly was ahead of its time. I believe it was the first time that the problems of the ever-increasing numbers of older people in society had been tackled in television drama. Director Mike Vardy, following his success in the *Premiere* series, made his debut on *Armchair Theatre* 'proper'.

Go On—It'll Do You Good	February 3, 1969
Teleplay by	Michael Chapman
Cast included	Ronald Fraser, Jack Woolgar, Barbara Couper, Pauline Yates, Yootha Joyce and Michael Robbins – with Doris Rogers, Margaret Boyd, Nicholas Courtney, Stephen Follett, Gaynor Hodgson, Milton Johns, Seymour Green, Anthony Dawes, Damaris Hayman, Dennis Richards, Amy Dalby and Tom Georgeson
Director	Mike Vardy
Designer	Fred Pusey

Angela Moreton (*Stage and Television Today,* 6/2/1969) dubbed the play—

> Sinister but good fun
> One of the best black comedies or, should it be white satires, that I have seen for a long time ... The play parodied the heartlessness of bureaucracy and the whole edifice of State interference in people's lives. It was salutary—and fun.

Barry Norman (*Daily Mail,* 4/2/1969) saw—

> Plenty of black edges there, but very little sign of comedy...

On the contrary, Nancy Banks-Smith (*Sun,* 4/2/1969), found it—

> Funny? Yes. Frightening? No.

Sylvia Clayton (*Daily Telegraph,* 4/2/1969) headlined it as a—

> DISTASTEFUL SATIRE

Mary Malone's view (*Daily Mirror,* 4/2/1969) was—

> There was so much useful spirit and fight in this play about old age, usually a soppy and sentimental affair, that we may well look forward to a few more antique heroes. Why not? Exuberant and intelligent old people are well worth celebrating.

Two viewers wrote to us, objecting.

Mrs MacLean of Sutton Coldfield (a retired matron of a County Welfare Home) stated—

> I wish to protest in the very strongest terms … The play is in the worst possible taste and should never have been screened.

P.F. Lipton of Swaythling declared—

> I have never seen such an offensive play.

Another viewer, Mrs Burgess of Rotherfield, wrote to the *Sunday Mirror*—

> The Armchair Theatre play on euthanasia was a real treat.

Stanley Reynolds (*Guardian,* 4/2/1969)—

> "Go On—It'll Do You Good" might perhaps do more to point a social evil than the hard-hitting straightforward documentary. ... When done well, like Michael Chapman's play last night, a well-observed social comedy will make the audience start thinking as soon as they stop laughing. ... The plot was ingenious, the characterisation acute, the dialogue funny, and the moral sense, as in all superior comedy, impeccable.

Robert Ottaway (*Daily Sketch,* 4/2/1969) summed it up—

> it struck a neat blow for the sanctity of human life, and I enjoyed both its ingenuity and its message.

This particular teleplay, probably more than any other that I have produced, clearly demonstrated just how comedy can be so divisive.

Next something less provocative perhaps. Canadian writer, Ted Allan's play is a story about a favourite son working abroad, who is made out to be the 'wealthy big shot', but when he returns home to his family he is seen for what he really is. The author owned that the play was based on his own life.

The Good Son February 10, 1969

Teleplay by	Ted Allan
Cast included	Lee Montague, Ruth Dunning, John Glyn-Jones, Doreen Aris, Helen Cotterill, Zuleika Robson, Roger Morris, Frank Coda, Andrew Downie and Roy Murray
Director	Piers Haggard
Designer	Peter Le Page

Sylvia Clayton (*Daily Telegraph,* 11/2/1969) thought that—

> Ted Allan's play, which dealt honestly with a recognisable human situation, somehow seemed more like a dramatised letter to a problem page than real life.

Henry Raynor (*Times,* 11/2/1969) wrote—

> Probably it takes a good deal of courage these days to offer everybody a plain, straightforward, unsophisticated domestic drama. This is what Thames Television did with ... last night's Armchair Theatre play.

Barry Norman (*Daily Mail,* 11/2/1969) didn't intend to watch *The Good Son*, but—

> Anyway, I did watch [it] ... and very glad I am, too. A splendid, bitter-sweet little fable, written with a nice sense of irony and beautifully acted by all concerned, in particular by Lee Montague who seems incapable of giving a bad performance.

Then came *The Brophy Story* – the second teleplay from Guy Slater for *Armchair Theatre*. Guy, the son of an Ambassador to Cuba, wrote with first-hand knowledge of his strong narrative. Here he depicted "a defector to Communism" who is the subject

TVRatings produced for JICTAR
Week ending Saturday February 22, 1969

Top Twenty Programmes		Homes in	Millions
1	The Power Game	ATV	8.20
2	Coronation Street (Mon 17th)	Granada	7.75
2=	Two in Clover	Thames	7.75
2=	Coronation Street (Wed 19th)	Granada	7.75
5	News at Ten (Mon 17th)	ITN	7.65
6	News at Ten (Tue 18th)	ITN	7.50
7	News at Ten (Wed 19th)	ITN	7.35
8	World in Action	Granada	7.15
8=	The Best of Morecambe & Wise	BBC	7.15
10	Opportunity Knocks!	Thames	7.05
10=	The Roy Hudd Show	Yorkshire	7.05
10=	The Forsyte Saga	BBC	7.05
13	The Rolf Harris Show	BBC	7.00
14	The Brophy Story (AT)	Thames	6.90
14=	Dad's Army	BBC	6.90
14=	Run for your Life	BBC	6.90
17	The Dick Emery Show	BBC	6.85
18	Her Majesty's Pleasure	Granada	6.80
19	Nightmare Alley	BBC	6.55
20	The Avengers	Thames	6.40

Armchair Theatre
***The Brophy Story* at equal No.14**

of investigation by a TV journalist. Is Brophy "a maligned public servant or just an unpleasant character not worth bothering about"? That which set out to vindicate the actions of Brophy, in the end exposed the fallibility of the TV investigation. Guy Slater was still an actor at that time and wrote himself a small role in the play – one way for the author to keep an eye on his work!

The Brophy Story	February 17, 1969
Teleplay by	Guy Slater
Cast included	Neil Stacy, Ian Ogilvy, William Fox and Martin Dempsey – with Luanshya Greer, May Ollis, Walter McMonagle, Ann Marson, Jenny Oulton, Morris Perry, Haydn Jones, Robert James, John Kidd, Emily Richard and Guy Slater
Director	Guy Verney
Designer	Michael Hall

Ann Purser (*Stage and Television Today,* 20/2/1969) described it as a—

> Good strong story tightly produced

Overall, this politically orientated production was another that was under-reviewed.

We followed on with another comedy with a sinister edge. Leigh Vance said that he had written it for his own pleasure because he was tired of watching plays without an ending.

Edward the Confessor	February 24, 1969
Teleplay by	Leigh Vance
Cast included	Beryl Reid, Ian Holm and Alfred Burke – with William Abney, Parnell McGarry, Michael Dawson, Murray Noble, Miranda Marshall, Angela Rooks, Barbara New and Douglas Blackwell
Director	Henry Kaplan
Designer	Tony Borer

Beryl Reid, who had just returned from Hollywood where she had a triumph in the film of *The Killing of Sister George*, said of her role in this *Armchair Theatre* production, "It's nice to be playing a 'normal' part again." Beryl had just bought a Lancia Fulvia and was also learning to fly, and so it was hardly expected that we would get a 'normal' performance from this unique actress.

The story editor, Monica Menell, was new to the team. Canadian director, Henry Kaplan, was making a second visit to us.

George Melly (*Observer,* 2/3/1969) described this as—

> one of the worst plays that I've ever seen on TV

Nevertheless, it achieved a higher viewer-rating than our two previous productions.

A year after his debut for us with *The Scallop Shell*, William Corlett said of this next play, "I've tried to point out that people should sometimes stop and take stock of themselves. I've known quite a few people like the characters I've written about, girls who worry about their right to bring children into the world, and young men who search for the truth."

The Story-Teller March 3, 1969

Teleplay by William Corlett
Cast included James Villiers, Frances White, Michael Gothard and Phyllida Law – with Anna Wing, George Moon, Cyd Hayman and John Line
Director Piers Haggard
Designer David Marshall

The ratings for that particular week were interesting, showing that ATV's series *The Power Game* came top of the Top Twenty, beating even *Coronation Street*. Our own 'difficult' production, *The Story-Teller*, slipped somewhat, but still did better than *The Avengers* and *Softly, Softly*.

TVRatings produced for JICTAR
Week ending Saturday March 8, 1969

Top Twenty Programmes – Homes in Millions			
1	The Power Game	ATV	7.85
2	Coronation Street (Mon 3rd)	Granada	7.80
3	Coronation Street (Wed 5th)	Granada	7.60
4	Opportunity Knocks!	Thames	7.25
5	Two in Clover	Thames	7.20
6	News at Ten (Tue 4th)	ITN	6.95
7	World in Action	Granada	6.60
7=	Her Majesty's Pleasure	Granada	6.60
9	The Unguarded Moment (Film)	BBC	6.55
10	The Rolf Harris Show	BBC	6.50
11	The Dick Emery Show	BBC	6.45
11=	Dr Finlay's Casebook	BBC	6.45
13	The Story-Teller (AT)	Thames	6.40
14	The Roy Hudd Show	Yorkshire	6.30
15	The Avengers	Thames	6.25
15=	News at Ten (Wed 5th)	ITN	6.25
17	Softly, Softly	BBC	6.20
18	On the Buses	Lon.Wk/end	6.15
19	This is Tom Jones	ATV	6.05
20	News at Ten (Mon 3rd)	ITN	6.00
20=	Dad's Army	BBC	6.00

Armchair Theatre
***The Story-Teller* at No.13**

This particular production illustrated sharply the differing reception reported by the critics on the one hand and the viewers on the other.

The critics were at best luke-warm or 'kind':

Sylvia Clayton (*Daily Telegraph*, 4/3/1969)—

> Dramatically it was wooden...

Michael Billington (*The Times*)—

> A fairly elaborate contrivance to make a simple point.

And Mary Malone (*Daily Mirror*) tore it to pieces with her review concentrating on—

> The Night They Called for the Extras
> Reacting extras have even been known to contribute gestures if the director is feeling generous. When plot and dialogue are so racy that even the stars cannot muster enthusiasm what is a director to do but throw it to the extras – and like trained seals they reacted, a dozen glances to the left, a dozen to the right, as well trained as a chorus (or should it be a choir?) as the play ascended in a cloud of mist on to some plane beyond mortal ken.

Well, I'm sure that raised a laugh for the editor.

But strangely, *The Story-Teller* provoked more viewer correspondence in admiration than very many other productions:

K. Rogers of Trowbridge—

> An excellent play. I was particularly moved by the "Words of Wisdom"

F. Dury of Bristol—

> The quality of this play makes television worthwhile

R. Wean of Chislehurst—

> It meant something to me, even though it was a story. I would very much appreciate if you could send me a copy of the script

C.A. Ransom of Reading—

> The play enthralled me. I would like to congratulate those concerned in the production...

A. Markham of Maidenhead—

> Congratulations on the superb production. I was spellbound by the fascinating tale...

R.J. White of Luton—

> I really enjoyed...

W. Ealing of Eastleigh—

> I have been haunted by this play...Thank you. I've written to the Playwright. I shall remember it because it said something real.

Most unusually, viewers wrote wanting to buy a copy of the script.

The gap between critical appraisal and viewer appreciation yawned!

It was about this time that I made up my mind to leave Teddington Studios. After producing some 270 drama plays, I needed new stimuli. I wanted to get back to directing and perhaps to mix the media with my grass roots in theatre. But there were several productions still to be made.

Leonard White – 1969

Stars from *Armchair Theatre*

Britt Ekland, Ian Hendry, Michael Bryant, Caroline Mortimer & Leslie Phillips, Colin Blakely, Tessa Wyatt
Leslie Phillips, George Baker & Pauline Yates, Britt Ekland, Kathleen Breck, Shelley Winters, Kenneth More,
Norman Rossington, Kenneth More, Ian Hendry, Kenneth More, Neil Stacy, Isabel Dean

For our next teleplay, I made a case for it to be transmitted without a commercial break – a unique event in the ITV schedules for drama at that time. This was in the days when the rule of the commercial break was that it had to be 'natural'. In other words, the script had to be structured to make the break occur at a change of place or time. However, in respect of this play I considered that any break in the action would destroy the atmosphere. It was transmitted as an unbroken experience: no commercials!

German author Gert Hofman – at that time a lecturer in German literature at Edinburgh University – had many theatre credits in Europe. Also, this particular play had originally been a one-act version performed in New York. Hofman described it as "a parable personifying his feelings about American business life".

Set in Miami, *On Vacation* dealt with an over-the-top business executive who, while living it up in the flesh-pots of Florida, is the victim of a macabre endeavour to oust him. What looks like a bad practical joke at first, turns into his suicide.

On Vacation	March 10, 1969
Teleplay by	Gert Hofman
Cast included	Lionel Stander, Al Mancini, Mavis Villiers, Stephanie Beacham and Dawn Beret – with Edward Bishop, Clive Endersby, David Cargill, Tom Busby, Karl Held, John Bloomfield and Penelope Parry
Director by	Peter Duguid
Designer	Peter Le Page

Mavis Villiers had just come from a success on the American stage in *Philadelphia Here I Come*.

Angela Moreton (*Stage and Television Today,* 13/3/1969) found it obscure—

> It was, I suppose, another of those fashionable black comedies which can seem significant or utter twaddle according to one's outlook. Its chief merit was a solo performance of great vitality by Lionel Stander. ... Whatever it was, this peculiar mixture of the macabre and the obscure left a nasty taste in the mouth.

George Melly (*Observer,* 16/3/1969) viewed it as—

> a very poor play

One viewer who wrote in to me, a B. Johnson of Cheshire, was—

> thoroughly disgusted!
> If you consider yourself to be artistic and that this is your idea of family entertainment, then might I suggest that you had better check where the line between genius and insanity lies, because in my opinion you have crossed it.

"Artistic ... genius ... insanity"? Who, me?

On Vacation was the last of this first season of *Armchair Theatre* under the Thames Television franchise. The series was described as "particularly successful" with all but one of the plays featuring in the Top Twenty charts.

So, after ten years at what was probably the most congenial of all the television production houses, I was leaving Teddington Studios.

That weekend, in *The Times Saturday Review* (8/3/1969) Michael Billington wrote the following article—

> **On vacating the armchair**
> The single play is television's problem child. Cosseted by anxious critics, viewed with suspicion by ratings-conscious programme bosses and self-appointed guardians of morality and yet still loyally watched by the general public, it has shown a remarkable capacity for survival. For this, much of the credit belongs to the standards achieved over a long period by two particular series: B.B.C. 1's *Wednesday Play* and Thames Television's (formerly A.B.C.'s) *Armchair Theatre*. Now both are undergoing certain changes. The former is losing much of what Sydney Newman once called its "agitational contemporaneity": the latter is losing Leonard White, who has been its producer since 1963. Mr. White has resigned.
>
> His reasons for doing so are mainly personal: he would like to get back to directing again, either in the theatre or television. At the same time he admits to finding the producer's role less creatively satisfying than when he first started. "The main difference between *Armchair Theatre* now and then is that today one is dealing with a freelance market. When I began, the producer, story editor, and staff directors, were all working together as a team, all searching for new material and achieving some continuity. In a freelance world, however, the producer has to make do with the market as it is. Theoretically, of course, a much wider range of talent is now open to one, but one can't always wait for the right person to become available. I have to start by putting the On-Air necessity first. I begin with a production date and I've then got to find the right director."
>
> Glancing back over the *Armchair Theatre* files for the past six years, one is struck by the fact that so many of the best writers for television have contributed to the series: David Mercer, John Hopkins, Giles Cooper, Robert Muller, Hugh Leonard, Ken Taylor, John Hale, William Trevor, Peter Terson, are all names that leap out at one from the page. How does one ensure that a long-running play series, achieves high standards? "Our readiness to commission", says Mr. White, "has always been one of the great strengths. We have over-commissioned considerably but we prefer to have a write-off rather than miss the boat. The company – whether it knows it or not and one assumes it does – has in effect been subsidizing new writing. In a single season of plays it is possible you might not use as much as a third of the material commissioned. But this is exploration-money or development money and the system pays off when a single play develops into a series: this happened both with *Callan* and *Never Mind the Quality, Feel the Width*."

> How fares the single play as such? Has it been affected by last year's Independent television shake-up? "The fact that there are now more companies may make things more difficult in that they're all fighting for network time for their own drama. I wish the I.T.A. would solve this by acknowledging that there is an Inner Ring and an Outer Ring of companies and encouraging the Outer Ring to provide truly local drama for their own regions. In the same way that a local rep exists to serve a local audience, why should not the smaller companies provide plays that reflect the history and tastes of their own area? That at least is a positive approach and much better than companies using the complexities of the network system as an excuse for not doing any drama at all."

Having thought it appropriate to say that in 1969, how much more it applies in the present day. Except of course nowadays the smaller companies have been taken over by the big fat ones, and so hardly exist as independent companies.

John Willis declared in his lecture at BAFTA (1999) that inevitably ITV would some day become just one company. His father, Lord Ted, must have turned in his grave! If future franchise allocations do not stop this monopoly trend, viewers will have seen the last of any continuing regional drama. New writing diminished and talent damned.

In the 'Londoner's Diary' in the *Evening Standard* (17/3/1969) my departure was simply headlined—

> White leaves quietly

And I did. With nothing planned. But that's another story. The piece went on to say—

> After producing 185 programmes for Armchair Theatre and the first 40 episodes of the Avengers, Leonard White quietly left Thames Television at the weekend for good, with little more in mind than getting his early potatoes planted at his home in Newhaven.
>
> His reason for leaving does not come as a result of any row, or even clash of personalities.
>
> "I just found I was not getting enough out of it. It seems rather selfish, but I was just not giving myself any personal satisfaction, so I decided the time had come to leave and that is what I have done," said Mr. White.
>
> He produced the very first of the Avengers, and it was he who was responsible for introducing Honor Blackman as the first female lead in the series.
>
> "I don't think she has ever been equalled in the part," says White.
>
> He started producing Armchairs, as he calls them, in 1962, and for several years the programme was one of the star turns of ABC television. "We were a team of professionals who enjoyed turning out a good product."

Although I had left the Thamesside studios, there were still a few more of my *Armchair Theatre* productions to be transmitted. They were seen starting under the *Playhouse* presentation.

Romans and Friends	Sept 29, 1969	*Playhouse*
Story by	Leonore Coffee	
Teleplay by	William Marchant	
Cast included	Sylvia Sims and Dawn Adams – with Miranda Connell, Nicholas Selby – also Nike Arrighi, Guy Slater, Leonardo Pieroni, Niki Iveria and Simon Gough	
Director	Guy Verney	
Designer	David Marshall	

That week, Thames' new series, *Special Branch,* was third in the Top Twenty ratings, beating *Coronation Street*. *Romans and Friends* came in at No.13 (with about 12 million viewers). This marked the strong move away from the single play by the Controllers, in order to focus on the series. But, with our next production things turned around. We accepted the challenge.

Like Puppies in a Basket	October 20, 1969	*Playhouse*
Teleplay by	Kenneth Burley	
Cast included	Zena Walker, William Squire, Angela Down, Barry Evans – with Jerry Verno, Michael Gleave, Neil Bennett, Emmett Hennessy, Helana Ross, Paddy Stephenson and Reg Peters	
Director	Mike Vardy	
Designer	Stan Woodward	

James Thomas (*Daily Express,* 21/10/1969) declared that—

> The piece was nicely written, well acted, but in the end a very limited exercise.

Ann Purser (*Stage and Television Today,* 23/10/1969) "couldn't believe in them" and wrote—

> The girl is on The Pill and the boy has unintentionally switched them with the aspirins. So it is a terrible, cheating kind of happy ending with the girl wondering whether she may not have a bun, and a solution to her problem, in her oven.

Like Puppies in a Basket zoomed up the ratings to No.3 in London's Top Ten, and overall No.6 in the Network's Top Twenty of all programmes. The Wednesday edition of *Coronation Street* and *Special Branch* were over ten places lower. Not bad for my final plays with *Armchair Theatre.*

We continued this run of comedies with a commission with an unlikely title:

The Swan Won't Go In The Fridge October 27, 1969 *Playhouse*

Teleplay by	Charles Laurence
Cast included	Rosemary Leach, Peter Cellier and Monica Vassiliou – with Edward Atienza, Andrew Lane, Steve Plytas, Anna Burden, Eric Elliott, Edward Gardener and Michael Zorba
Director	Peter Duguid
Designer	Peter Le Page

Monica Vassiliou

Under the heading "Au pair girl farce brings laughs", Sylvia Clayton (*Daily Telegraph,* 28/10/1969) described this play as—

the tallest of tales …

An example probably as far removed as possible from the 'agitational contemporaneity' that Sydney Newman had coined for TV drama years before. This one achieved the highest number of viewers of this short run season.

The change from black-and-white to colour had been on and off for some time, but for 'technical reasons' (mostly Union adjustments) the start date of this expected 'revolution' was delayed. However, we were told that finally the date was set.

Wanting to mark the occasion, I made special efforts to get a script that depended upon colour for its dramatic impact. American writer Janet Burroway, then living in England (her husband, Walter Eysselinck, was the Artistic Director of the new Gardner Centre at the University of Sussex) provided us with a teleplay that demanded colour changes to make the dramatic point. Alas, when the transmission was due – again, and at the last moment – the 'colour agreement' was not in place. The production was seen in black-and-white and the whole point of the show was lost. A great disappointment, especially for Voytek (one of our fine designers) who was now making his debut as director for *Armchair Theatre.*

Cicely Courtneidge and Anna Quayle were on the front cover of *TV Times* that week in the salon of *The Beauty Operators* – the "Bizarre temple of Venus" as Sylvia Clayton described it. Joe Melia was the only man in the cast, and playing a ladies' hairdresser.

The Beauty Operators November 3, 1969 *Playhouse*

Teleplay by	Janet Burroway
Cast included	Cicely Courtneidge and Anna Quayle – with Joe Melia, Vivienne Martin, Janina Faye and Myvanwy Jenn
Director	Voytek
Designer	Patrick Downing

Henry Raynor in *The Times* (4/11/1969) thought it—

> Clever and honest
> … Voytek's direction was neatly varied in pace and admirably unemphatic.

If only the screening had been in colour!

Thus, my almost seven years of producing *Armchair Theatre* came to its last transmission with a touch of bathos.

James Thomas (*Daily Express*) once wrote of *Armchair Theatre* as being—

> A landmark in TV Theatre

Stanley Reynolds (*Guardian*)—

> ITV's most distinguished television 'playhouse' ... this crusading drama series...

"This crusading drama series" has been lost.

Today, the forever-ringing complaint is that television drama is expensive, yet there have been examples of independent producers proving that drama can be made at a reasonable cost and without losing any quality. But they have never been allowed to let anything rock the boat. The fat cats gather to protect their interests and proceed to blur the issues by buying up (no, sorry, merging with) other companies: "Don't send me the script – I'm only interested in the deal."

I believe that viewers are now denied the choice and experience they had in the sixties. With the invention and development of television came an opportunity for an entirely new form of drama, unlike anything before. That opportunity was grasped very quickly by the then drama programme-makers (notably so by the ITV practitioners who teased the BBC into following). It was different from theatre, different from cinema. Now the differences are at best blurred, but more commonly lost entirely. That, I believe, does matter.

However, I can only hope that this chronicle of my years when I had the great privilege of producing *Armchair Theatre* succeeds in honouring all those fine talents (not forgetting the splendid production asssistants, the first-rate technicians, the supporting staffs and essentially the, then, management who cared about the art of the business) who made it all possible. I hope that this record helps to redress the balance of their unsung praises. A forlorn hope? "The deed is all – the glory nothing"

C'est la vie. Or, as I say – C'est la TVie!

APPENDIX I

They Didn't Make It

My years as producer of *Armchair Theatre* cannot be truthfully recorded without mentioning that I had some failures and disappointments.

The Blood Knot

The first, and perhaps my most disappointing, was in 1963 when we made a television version of Atholl Fugard's *The Blood Knot* – a fine play set in South Africa. Charles Jarrott had seen it in London's West End and, like many others, was very impressed. I went to see it, and was equally impressed. Indeed, we secured the rights to do it in *Armchair Theatre*. It was an important play from a fine South African writer, and surely right for our anthology. Although written for theatre and set in one room with just two characters, it was for me certainly a play for today at that time. Charles Jarrott directed it with his usual love and care, and we were enormously pleased to have the original London cast giving fine performances. We recorded it on May 18, 1963, but it was never screened.

The Blood Knot	Recorded May 18, 1963
Written by	Athol Fugard
Cast	Ian Bannen and the Bantu actor, Zaikes Mokae
Directed by	Charles Jarrott
Designed by	James Goddard

I do not know to this day just why this production never got into the transmission schedules. Okay, so it wasn't an obvious ratings winner. Only a two-hander and a single set, being essentially a theatre piece – not the way that TV drama was moving in its style and form. And it was about South Africa. But it was a close-up of a very human predicament, avoiding any obvious head-on political involvement, and beautifully written. Yet Brian Tesler never agreed a transmission date for it in *Armchair Theatre* at that time or later – although it was considered several times. Repeatedly it would be pencilled into the schedule – and repeatedly it would be eased out. In some desperation (and because it had a moral message)

I even suggested that it might find a place in a religious drama series. It was considered by the Religious Department (frankly I'd have been happy for it to have a screening under any banner, just so that it would be seen) but they didn't screen it. Very disappointing. Sydney Newman, during his term in charge, had one or two similar disappointments, and so there were precedents for this. But that didn't relieve my feelings at the time.

Our rights ran out on this script and were smartly picked up by the BBC, which made its own production. And, of course, it was broadcast. Alas, *Armchair Theatre* in this case missed a notable 'first', and I believe that the our production was superior. There is some consolation: the original was saved, and remains in the BFI film and television archives.

The next year there was another loss. *The Bandstand* was a story of old age and loneliness – again, perhaps not compelling for all. It, too, was saved in the BFI archives.

The Bandstand Recorded April 16, 1964
Written by Guy Compton
Cast included Donald Pleasance, Norah Blaney, Margaret Vines, Alethea Charlton, Stanley Meadows, Carmel McSharry and Howard Charlton
Directed by Philip Saville

Retained in the BFI archives, yet not transmitted:

Unexpected Summer Recorded December 10, 1964
Written by Gwendolyn Gazeley

Another, recorded on New Year's Eve 1964, was also never transmitted.

Old Man's Fancy Recorded December 31, 1964
Written by Evan Jones
Directed by Toby Robertson
Designed by Voytek

These untransmitted tapes have remained, yet many others truly worthy of being kept never made their way into the archives.

There was one production that we failed to complete in the allotted time. It had to be abandoned and written-off. I have forgotten the title, but not my frustration. It was not possible to make an expensive decision to re-call the cast and production team to finish it the next day, or the next... The whole studio schedule was tightly geared to all the other programmes waiting, and of those there would be at least two other *Armchair Theatre* productions on the conveyor belt. The knock-on effect would have created more problems than it solved. That experience shook me considerably and was the stuff of nightmares. I'm thankful to say that that write-off was a one-off.

In our script department, the write-off option was a necessary and accepted part of our commissioning. Always a reluctant step to take and certainly not a common action. If inevitable, it was a decision taken at second or third draft stage. Usually amicably.

We may have had to write-off a commissioned script occasionally, but we never wrote-off the writer. Another commission was usually soon in place. The writers provided our very life-blood. Our fundamental strength was in our commissioning.

There was one notable example of an extant play script being bought but, alas, not going into production. It was at the time when Alan Ayckbourn was working in his early days with Artistic Director Peter Cheeseman at the 'Vic' Theatre in Stoke-on-Trent. On one of many visits there, I saw Ayckbourn's play, *Standing Room Only*, which I very much enjoyed. It was a comedic look at a future on the roads when the land would be gridlocked. A forecast then, and as I thought just right for *Armchair Theatre*. With great pleasure, I instigated the purchase of the rights of that play for our TV production.

But pleasure turned into deep disappointment. It seemed I was a lone voice in the department. None of the directors responded positively to it, but, more significantly, Programme Controller Brian Tesler did not see it being successful unless we cast a well-known comedian in the lead. Hancock was mentioned, but I thought otherwise. Excellent though Hancock was I felt that such casting or similar would unbalance Ayckbourn's intentions. The script remained unproduced while I still hoped very much that it would be done. My hopes were not realised, and eventually our rights ran out.

It hurts even more today, something like forty years later. How marvellous it would have been to have launched on TV and in *Armchair Theatre* a play by the now foremost and most successful playwright. What a miss! Prestige lost.

Another 'miss', not perhaps so crucial, but one that lingers in my 'might-have-been' memory. It concerns a crazy idea I had to make a TV version of *He Who Gets Slapped* (Andreyev/Guthrie) and I very much wanted Paul Scofield to play 'He'. I asked him and he was certainly interested.

It so happened that Jane Fonda was visiting London at that time, and I thought that she would make a very interesting Consuella. I managed to get a meeting with her at the Savoy

Hotel, and explained the project, including Paul Scofield's interest. She found the prospect attractive. I was elated. Those distinctive leading stars together in a 'special' for us – the story set in the highly visual environment of circus life. Exciting.

I put the idea to our Programme Controller. Quickly, his response came: he thought there were "too many circus films already". The balloon burst – I couldn't send in the clowns. Stop dreaming. No time for that. On with the next. But, now, as I write this all these years later, the memory provokes nostalgia.

APPENDIX II

*The Avengers**

The First 40 Episodes

Produced by Leonard White

First Season – with Ian Hendry and Patrick Macnee – 26 episodes

Running characters:
Keel – played by Ian Hendrey
Steed – played by Patrick Macnee

Story Editor – Patrick Brawn

1. ***Hot Snow*** Jan 7, 1961 (Midlands & North)
Teleplay by Ray Rigby Based on a story by Patrick Brawn
Cast included Moira Redmond, Catherine Woodville
Directed by Don Leaver Designed by Alpho O'Reilly

2. ***Brought to Book*** Jan 14, 1961
Teleplay by Brian Clemens
Cast included Ingrid Hafner, Carol White, Philip Stone
Directed by Peter Hammond Designed by Robert Fuest

3. ***Square Root of Evil*** Jan 21, 1961
Teleplay by Richard Harris
Cast included Ingrid Hafner, George Murcell, Delphi Lawrence
Directed by Don Leaver Designed by Patrick Downing

4. ***Nightmare*** Jan 28, 1961
Teleplay by Terence Feely
Cast included Ingrid Hafner, Robert Sansom, Helen Lindsay
Directed by Peter Hammond Designed by Robert Fuest

5. ***Crescent Moon*** Feb 4, 1961
Teleplay by Geoffrey Bellman & John Whitney
Cast included Patience Collier, Bandana Das Gupta, Eric Thompson, Roger Delgado, Harold Kasket
Directed by John Knight Designed by Alpho O'Reilly

6. ***Girl On The Trapeze*** Feb 11, 1961
Teleplay by Dennis Spooner
Cast included Ingrid Hafner, Delana Kidd, Nadja Regin, Edwin Richfield
Directed by Don Leaver Designed by Paul Bernard

**The Avengers* theme tune composed and played by Johnny Dankworth

7. ***Diamond Cut Diamond*** Feb 18, 1961
Teleplay by Max Marquis
Cast included Ingrid Hafner, Douglas Muir, Sandra Dorne
Directed by Peter Hammond Designed by Robert Fuest

8. ***The Radioactive Man*** Feb 25, 1961
Teleplay by Fred Edge
Cast included George Pravda, Christine Pollen, Ingrid Hafner
Directed by Robert Tronson Designed by Alpho O'Reilly

9. ***Ashes of Roses*** Mar 4, 1961
Teleplay by Peter Ling & Sheilah Ward
Cast included Ingrid Hafner, Olga Lowe, Peter Zander, Hedi Erich
Directed by Don Leaver Designed by Patrick Downing

10. ***Hunt the Man Down*** Mar 18, 1961 (London starts Ep.1)
Teleplay by Richard Harris
Cast included Ingrid Hafner, Melissa Stribling, Maurice Good
Directed by Peter Hammond Designed by Robert Fuest

11. ***Please Don't Feed the Animals*** April 1, 1961 (London takes Ep.2)
Teleplay by Dennis Spooner
Cast included Ingrid Hafner, Tenniel Evans, Carole Boyer
Directed by Dennis Vance Designed by Patrick Downing

12. ***Dance with Death*** Apr 15, 1961 (London catches up/ takes as Ep.3)
Teleplay by Peter Ling & Sheilah Ward
Cast included Ingrid Hafner, Caroline Blakiston, Angela Douglas, Geoffrey Palmer, Diana King, Ewan Roberts
Directed by Don Leaver Designed by James Goddard

13. ***One for the Mortuary*** Apr 29, 1961
Teleplay by Brian Clemens
Cast included Peter Madden, Frank Gatliff, Toke Townley
Directed by Peter Hammond Designed by Robert Fuest

14.***The Springers*** May 13, 1961
Teleplay by John Whitney & Geoffrey Bellman
Cast included Douglas Muir, Charles Farrell, Brian Murphy, Margo Andrew, Donald Morley, Arthur Howard
Directed by Don Leaver Designed by Alpho O'Reilly

15. ***The Frighteners*** May 27, 1961
Teleplay by Berkely Mather
Cast included Ingrid Hafner, Philip Locke, Willoughby Goddard, Dawn Beret, Stratford Johns, David Andrews, Doris Hare, Philip Gilbert
Directed by Peter Hammond Designed by Robert Fuest

16. ***The Yellow Needle*** June 10, 1961
Teleplay by Patrick Campbell
Cast included Ingrid Hafner, Wolfe Morris, Margaret Whiting
Directed by Don Leaver Designed by Alpho O'Reilly

17. ***Death on the Slipway*** Jun 24, 1961
Teleplay by James Mitchell
Cast included Nyree Dawn Porter, Frank Thornton, Peter Arne, Billy Milton, Sean Sullivan, Douglas Muir, Gary Watson, Hamilton Dyce
Directed by Peter Hammond Designed by Robert Fuest

18. ***Double Danger*** July 8, 1961
Teleplay by Gerald Verner
Cast included Ingrid Hafner, Vanda Hudson, Peter Reynolds
Directed by Roger Jenkins Designed by James Goddard

19. ***Toy Trap*** July 22, 1961
Teleplay by Bill Strutton
Cast included Tony Van Bridge, Sally Smith, Brian Jackson, Mitzi Rogers, Brandon Brady, Nina Marriott
Directed by Don Leaver Designed by Douglas James

20. ***The Tunnel of Fear*** Aug 5, 1961
Teleplay by John Kruse
Cast included Ingrid Hafner, John Salew, Murray Hayne, Doris Rogers, Miranda Connell, Douglas Rye, Morris Perry, Douglas Perry
Directed by Guy Verney Designed by James Goddard

21. ***The Far Distant Dead*** Aug 19, 1961
Teleplay by John Lucarotti
Cast included Katharine Blake, Tom Adams, Francis de Wolff, Guy Degy, Andreas Mulandrinos, Michael Mellinger, Reed de Rouen
Directed by Peter Hammond Designed by Robert Fuest

22. ***Kill the King*** Sept 2, 1961
Teleplay by James Mitchell
Cast included Ingrid Hafner, Moira Redmond, Carole Shelley, Andy Ho, Patrick Allen, Lisa Peake, Peter Barkworth, Ian Colin
Directed by Roger Jenkins Designed by Paul Bernard

23. ***Dead of Winter*** Dec 9, 1961
Teleplay by Eric Paice
Cast included Ingrid Hafner, John Woodvine, Carl Duering, David Hart, Michael Sarne, Zorenah Osborne, Neil Hallett, Sheila Robbins, Arnold Marle, Norman Chappell, Blaise Wyndham
Directed by Don Leaver Designed by Robert Fuest

24. ***The Deadly Air*** Dec 16, 1961

Teleplay by Lester Powell
Cast included Ingrid Hafner, Ann Bell, Keith Anderson, John Stratton, Michael Hawkins, Richard Butler, Allan Cuthbertson, Geoffrey Bayldon, Doouglasa Muir
Directed by John Knight Designed by Robert Macgowan

25. ***A Change of Bait*** Dec 23, 1961

Teleplay by Lewis Davidson
Cast included Ingrid Hafner, Gary Hope, Gillian McCutcheon, John Bailey, Victor Platt, Henry Soskin, Robert Desmond, Harry Shacklock
Directed by Don Leaver Designed by James Goddard

26. ***Dragonsfield*** Dec 30, 1961

Teleplay by Terence Feely
Cast included Sylvia Langova, Alfred Burke, Barbara Shelley, Morris Perry, Keith Barron, Ronald Leigh-Hunt, Eric Dodson, Michael Robbins
Directed by Peter Hammond Designed by Voytek

Second Season – with Patrick Macnee and Honor Blackman

Steed – played by Patrick Macnee – continues with new running characters:
Cathy Gale – played by Honor Blackman
Venus Smith – played by Julie Stevens
Dr Martin King – played by Jon Rollason

Story Editor – John Bryce

27. ***Mr Teddy Bear*** Sept 29, 1962

Teleplay by Martin Woodhouse
Cast included Honor Blackman, Douglas Muir, Tim Brinton, John Horsley, Michael Robbins, Bernard Goldman, John Ruddock
Directed by Richmond Harding Designed by Terry Green

28. ***Propellant 23*** Oct 6, 1962

Teleplay by Jon Manchip White
Cast included Honor Blackman, Justine Lord, Frederick Schiller, Geoffrey Palmer, Catherine Woodville, Trader Faulkner, Ralph Nossek, John Dearth, Nicholas Courtney
Directed by Jonathan Alwyn Designed by Paul Bernard

29. ***The Decapod*** Oct 13, 1962

Teleplay by Eric Paice
Cast included Julie Stevens, Lynne Furlong, Wolfe Morris, Philip Madoc, Douglas Robinson and The Dave Lee Trio
Directed by Don Leaver Designed by Terry Green

30. ***Bullseye*** Oct 20, 1962
Teleplay by Eric Paice
Cast included Honor Blackman, Mitzi Rogers, Judy Parfitt, Bernard Kay, Laurie Leigh, Charles Carson
Directed by Peter Hammond Designed by Robert Macgowan

31. ***Mission to Montreal*** Oct 27, 1962
Teleplay by Lester Powell
Cast included Jon Rollason, Patricia English, Angela Thorne, Harold Berens, Mark Eden, Gerald Sim, Malcolm Taylor, Iris Russell, Pamela Ann Davey, Alan Curtis
Directed by Don Leaver Designed by Terry Green

32. ***The Removal Men*** Nov 3, 1962
Teleplay by Roger Marshall & Jeremy Scott
Cast included Julie Stevens, Edina Ronay, Reed de Rouen, Patricia Denys
Directed by Don Leaver Designed by Patrick Downing

33. ***The Mauritius Penny*** Nov 10, 1962
Teleplay by Malcolm Hulke & Terrance Dicks
Cast included Honor Blackman, Philip Guard, David Langton, Alfred Burke, Edward Jewsbury, Richard Vernon, Sylvia Langova
Directed by Richmond Harding Designed by Philip Harrison

34. ***Death of a Great Dane*** Nov 17, 1962
Teleplay by Roger Marshall & Jeremy Scott
Cast included Honor Blackman, Billy Milton, Leslie French, Clare Kelly, Frederick Jaeger, John Laurie
Directed by Peter Hammond Designed by Patrick Downing

35. ***The Sell-Out*** Nov 24, 1962
Teleplay by Anthony Terpiloff & Brandon Brady
Cast included Jon Rollason, Carleton Hobbs, Arthur Hewlett, Frank Gatliff, Anne Godley, Michael Mellinger
Directed by Don Leaver Designed by Terry Green

36. ***Death on the Rocks*** Dec 1, 1962
Teleplay by Eric Paice
Cast included Honor Blackman, Ellen McIntosh, Hamilton Dyce, Naomi Chance, Meier Tzelniker, Gerald Cross
Directed by Jonathan Alwyn Designed by James Goddard

37. ***Traitor in Zebra*** Dec 8, 1962
Teleplay by John Gilbert
Cast included Honor Blackman, William Gaunt, Danvers Walker, Noel Coleman, Ian Shand, Richard Leech, Katy Wild
Directed by Richmond Harding Designed by Terry Green

38. ***The Big Thinker*** Dec 15, 1962

Teleplay by Martin Woodhouse

Cast included Honor Blackman, Walter Hudd, David Garth, Marina Martin, Anthony Booth, Allan McClelland, Penelope Lee, Tenniel Evans

Directed by Kim Mills Designed by James Goddard

39. ***Death Despatch*** Dec 22, 1962

Teleplay by Leonard Fincham

Cast included Honor Blackman, Gerald Harper, Maria Andipa, Valerie Sarruf

Directed by Jonathan Alwyn Designed by Anne Spavin

40. ***Dead on Course*** Dec 29, 1962

Teleplay by Eric Paice

Cast included Jon Rollason, Bruce Boa, Margo Jenkins, Elizabeth Murray, Janet Hargreaves, Peggy Marshall, Donal Donnelly, Edward Kelsey, Liam Gaffney, John McLaren

Directed by Richmond Harding Designed by Robert Fuest

At this time – half way through the second season – Leonard White took over as Producer in charge of *Armchair Theatre*.

APPENDIX III

—*Armchair Mystery Theatre*—

—*Out of This World*—

—*Armchair Theatre*—

Single Teleplays – 1960-69
Produced by Leonard White
(Unless otherwise stated)

Title	Writer	Screened
———*Armchair Mystery Theatre* – 1960———		
Eye Witness	Leslie Sands	Jun 5, 1960
The Cupboard	Ray Rigby (Transferred to *Armchair Theatre* – screened December 11, 1960)	
The Big Wheel	John Glennon	Jun 12, 1960
The Case of Paul Danek	Morten Wishengrad & Virginia Mazer	Jun 19, 1960
Flag Fall	Royston Morley	Jun 26, 1960
Toff and Fingers	Robert Kemp	Jul 3, 1960
Flight from Treason	James Mitchell	Jul 10, 1960
Madeleine	Alan Caillou	Jul 17, 1960
Web of Deceit	J.D. Barton	Jul 24, 1960
False Witness	Philip Levene	Aug 7, 1960
Machinal	Sophie Treadwell	Aug 14, 1960
The Man with a Feather in his Hat	Peter Barnes	Aug 21, 1960
Cul de Sac	Sebastian Shaw	Aug 28, 1960
The Dummy	Ray Rigby	Sep 4, 1960

Title	Writer	Screened

Out of this World – 1962

Title	Writer	Screened
The Yellow Pill	Leon Griffiths (Original story by Rog Phillips)	Jun 30, 1962
Little Lost Robot	Leo Lehman (Original story by Isaac Asimov)	Jul 7, 1962
Cold Equations	Clive Exton (Original story by Tom Goodwin)	Jul 14, 1962
Impostor	Terry Nation (Original story by Philip Dick)	Jul 21, 1962
Botany Bay	Terry Nation	Jul 28, 1962
Medicine Show	Julian Bond (Original story by Robert Moore Williams)	Aug 4, 1962
Pictures Don't Lie	Bruce Stewart (Original story by Katherine Maclean)	Aug 11, 1962
Vanishing Act	Richard Waring	Aug 18, 1962
Divided We Fall	Leon Griffiths (Story by Raymond F. Jones)	Aug 25, 1962
The Dark Star	Denis Butler (Novel by Frank Crisp)	Sep 1, 1962
Immigrant	Terry Nation (Story by Clifford Simak)	Sep 8, 1962
Target Generation	Clive Exton (Story by Clifford Simak)	Sep 15, 1962
The Tycoons	Bruce Stewart (Story by Arthur Sellings)	Sep 22, 1962

Armchair Theatre – 1963 – 7th Season

Title	Writer	Screened
Blue and White (Produced by Sydney Newman)	Kenneth Jupp	Jan 6, 1963
The Hot Potato Boys (No producer credit given)	Alun Richards	Jan 20, 1963
Into The Dark (No producer credit given)	Ken Taylor	Feb 3, 1963

Title	Writer	Screened
The Paradise Suite	Robert Muller	Feb 17, 1963
The Cruel Kind	Norman King	Mar 17, 1963
The Invasion	Angus Wilson	Mar 31, 1963
Power and Glory	Karel Capek	Apr 14, 1963
Wagger	Stephen Lewis	Apr 28, 1963
Jungle Juice	Bruce Stewart	May 12, 1963
The Wednesday Caller	Lynne Reid Banks	May 26, 1963
The Monkey and the Mohawk	Donal Giltinan	Jun 9 1963
The Push-Over	Gwen Cherrell	Jun 23, 1963
Late Summer	Alexander Baron	Jul 7, 1963
A Little Night Music	Ronald Mavor	Jul 22, 1963
The Snag	Donal Giltinan	Aug 4, 1963
Living Image	James Broom Lynne	Aug 18, 1963
A Kind of Kingdom	Hugh Leonard	Sep 2, 1963
The Front Room	Robert Storey	Sep 15, 1963

———*Armchair Theatre* – 1963-64 – 8th Season———

Mr Big	Ken Taylor (Original story, *The Dwarf*, by Ray Bradbury)	Sep 29, 1963
Little Doris	David Perry	Oct 13, 1963
The Chocolate Tree	Andrew Sinclair	Oct 27, 1963
Long Past Glory	Len Deighton	Oct 17, 1963
The Higher They Fly	Christopher Hodder-Williams	Dec 1, 1963
The Swindler	John Hall	Dec 15, 1963
A Way of Living	David Mercer	Dec 29, 1963
Sharp at Four	Donald Churchill	Jan 12, 1964
Last Word On Julie	Lynne Reid Banks	Jan 26, 1964
The Pretty English Girls	John Hopkins	Feb 16, 1964
Realm of Error	Hugh Leonard	Mar 1, 1964

Title	Writer	Screened
Always Ask For The Best	Stephen Lewis	Mar 15, 1964
Mug's Game	Robert Storey	Mar 29, 1964
Prisoner and Escort	Charles Wood	Apr 5, 1964
Cradle Song	Hugo Charteris	Apr 12, 1964
A Nice Little Business	Marc Brandel	Apr 26, 1964
Pleasure Where She Finds It	Robert Muller	May 3, 1964
A Jug of Bread	Jack Malton	May 17, 1964
St Ernie Leatherbound	Alan Gosling	May 24, 1964
That's Where The Town's Going!	Tad Mosel	Jun 7, 1964
Exit Joe—Running	John Hall	Jun 14, 1964
A Certain Kind of Silence	Hugo Charteris	Jun 28,1964

——*Armchair Mystery Theatre*——

Title	Writer	Screened
Time Out Of Mind	John Hopkins	Jul 19, 1964
The Blackmailing of Mr S.	Michael Gilbert	Jul 26, 1964
The Lonely Crime	James Mitchell	Aug 9, 1964
The Last Coach	Paul Erickson	Aug 16, 1964
Admirer at Number Eight	Virginia Hewett	Aug 30, 1964
You Must Be Virginia	Richard Harris	Sep 6, 1964
The Trial of Dr Fancy (Produced by Sydney Newman in 1962)	Clive Exton	(unscheduled) Sep 13, 1964

————*Armchair Theatre* – 1964-65 – 9th Season————

Title	Writer	Screened
The Cherry on the Top	Donald Churchill	Sep 27, 1964
Something to Declare	William Marchant	Oct 4, 1964
Old Soldiers	Andrew Sinclair	Oct 18, 1964
They Throw It At You	Allan Prior	Oct 25, 1964
The Importance of Being Earnest	Oscar Wilde	Nov 15, 1964
The Girl in the Picture	Allan Prior	Nov 29, 1964

Title	Writer	Screened
Sally	William Wood	Dec 6, 1964
The Hothouse	Donald Churchill	Dec 13, 1964
I've Got a System	Allan Prior	Jan 3, 1965
The Gaming Book	Simon Raven	10 Jan 1965
The Lady With The Albatross	Robert Storey	Feb 14, 1965
Putty Medal	Robert Storey	Feb 21, 1965
The Keys of the Café	Edna O'Brien	Mar 7, 1965
I Took My Little World Away	John Hopkins	Mar 14, 1965
A Voice in the Sky	Christopher Hodder-Williams	Mar 21, 1965
I Loved You Last Summer	Hugh Leonard	Apr 4, 1965
The Man Who Came To Die	Reginald Marsh	Apr 11, 1965
The Incident	Alan Plater	Apr 25, 1965

——*Armchair Mystery Theatre*——

Title	Writer	Screened
The Last Reunion	Kenneth Hyde	May 9, 1965
Licence to Murder	Elaine Morgan	May 16, 1965
The Hunter	N.J. Crisp	Jun 6, 1965
Man and Mirror	Robert Muller	Jun 13, 1965
Time and Mr Madingley	Richard Harris	Jun 27, 1965
The Welcome	Allan Prior	Jul 4, 1965
The Finishing Touch	Julian Symons	Jul 18, 1965
The Lodger	Anthony Skene (From a novel by Mrs Belloc Lowndes)	Jul 25, 1965
The Madam	Gwen Cherrell	Aug 8, 1965
The Challenge	William Marchant	Aug 15, 1965
Wake a Stranger	Donald and Derek Ford	Aug 29, 1965
Charlie Never Warned Us	Douglas Livingstone	Sep 5, 1965
Ask Any Neighbour	Tony Williamson	Sep 19, 1965
The Stairway	John Whiting	Sep 26, 1965
Ambrose	Mary Hocking	Sep 26, 1965

Title	Writer	Screened

Armchair Theatre – 1965-66 – 10th Season

Title	Writer	Screened
The Paraffin Season	Donald Churchill	Dec 4, 1965
The Gong Game	Michael Harald	Dec 11, 1965
A Cold Peace	Robert Muller	Dec 18, 1965
The Sweet War Man	Barry England	Jan 1, 1966
Ready for the Glory	Alun Richards	Jan 8, 1966
Neighbours	Arkady Leokum	Jan 15, 1966
The Pity of it All	Stan Barstow	Jan 22, 1966
Man Without a Mortgage	Donald Churchill	Mar 19, 1966
The Battersea Miracle	Wolf Mankowitz	Mar 26, 1966
The Night Before the Morning After	Jack Rosenthal	Apr 2, 1966
Don't Utter A Note	Anton Delmar	Apr 9, 1966
Daughter of the House	Guy Clark	Apr 16, 1966
The Walls Came Tumbling Down	Nicholas Salaman	Apr 23, 1966
The Match	Norman Bogner	Apr 30, 1966

Armchair Theatre – 1966-67 – 11th Season

Title	Writer	Screened
Pretty Polly	William Marchant (From a story by Noel Coward)	Jul 23, 1966
The Wager	Hugo Charteris	Jul 30, 1966
The One-Eyed Monster	Allan Prior	Aug 11, 1966
Great Big Blonde	Hugh Leonard	Aug 13,1966
A Fair Swap	Jeremy Paul	Aug 20, 1966
The Signal Box of Grandpa Hudson	David Nobbs & Peter Tinniswood	Aug 27, 1966
The Noise Stopped	John Hale	Sep 3, 1966
Dead Silence	Monty Doyle	Sep 10, 1966
Barrett Keller—His Mark	Gerald Vaughan-Hughes	Sep 17, 1966
Light the Blue Touch Paper	John Hale	Sep 24, 1966
The Tilted Screen	Noel Robinson	Oct 1, 1966

Title	Writer	Screened
The Three Barrelled Shotgun	Donald and Derek Ford	Oct 8, 1966
The Long Nightmare	Michael Harald	Oct 15, 1966
The Floating Population	Donald Churchill	Jan 28, 1967
A Magnum for Schneider	James Mitchell	Feb 4, 1967
What's Wrong With Humpty Dumpty?	Hugh Whitemore	Feb 11, 1967
Never Mind the Quality, Feel the Width	Vince Powell & Harry Driver	Feb 18, 1967
Easier in the Dark	Robert Muller	Feb 25, 1967
Reason for Sale	Donald and Derek Ford	Mar 4, 1967
The Happy Sacking	Donald Churchill	Mar 11, 1967
The Exploding Azalea (Produced by Lloyd Shirley)	John Mortimer	Mar 18, 1967
Any Number Can Play	John Harrison	Mar 25, 1967
A World of Time	Robert Muller	Apr 1, 1967
Call Me Daddy	Ernie Gebler	Apr 8, 1967 / Apr 25 & 27 1968
I am Osango	Giles Cooper	Apr 15, 1967
Compensation Alice	Jack Rosenthal	Jul 1, 1967
Slight Formality	Richard Harris	Jul 8, 1967
Quite an Ordinary Knife	Jordan Lawrence	Jul 15, 1967
Another Branch of the Family	Emanuel Litvinoff	Jul 22, 1967
Love Life	Hugh Leonard	Jul 29, 1967
The Education of Corporal Halliday	Robert Holles	Aug 5 1967
Nursery Tale	Derek Monsey	Aug 12, 1967
Marriage and Henry Sunday	Emanuel Litvinoff	Aug 19, 1967
The Girl	William Trevor	Aug 26, 1967
Split Level	Stewart Farrar	Sep 2, 1967
Poor Cherry	Fay Weldon	Sep 9, 1967
Don't Forget the Basics	Terence Frisby	Sep 16, 1967
The Heroism of Thomas Chadwick	Peter Terson (Based on 2 original stories by Arnold Bennett)	*(The Story Teller)* Sep 23, 1967

Title	Writer	Screened
	***Armchair Theatre* – 1968 – 12th Season**	
Mrs Capper's Birthday	William Marchant (Story by Noel Coward)	Jan 31 & Feb 3, 1968
The Wind in a Tall Paper Chimney	Robert Holles	Feb 7 & 10, 1968
The Scallop Shell	William Corlett	Feb 14 & 17, 1968
A Second Look	Donald Churchill	Feb 21 & 24, 1968
The Contact	Roger Woddis	Feb 28 & Mar 2, 1968
A Very Fine Line	C. Scott Forbes	Mar 8 & 9, 1968
Unscheduled Stop	Derek Bond	Mar 15 & 16, 1968
Recount	Kenneth Burley	Apr 18, 1968
No Easy Walk	Guy Slater	May 2 & 4, 1968
The Escape Club	James Gibbons	May 9 & 11, 1968
Home Movies	Peter Lewis	May 16 & 18, 1968
You and Me	Robert Muller	May 23 & 25, 1968
The Glove Puppet	Frank Marcus	May 30 & Jun 1, 1968
The Three Wives of Felix Hull	Fay Weldon	Jun 6 & 8, 1968
One Night I Danced With Mr Dalton	Ken Campbell	Jun 13 & 15, 1968
The Ballad of the Artificial Mash	Peter Terson Peter Cheeseman (Adapt.)	Jul 25 & 27, 1968
	Playhouse	
Star Quality	William Marchant (Story by Noel Coward)	Aug 5, 1968
Bon Voyage	William Marchant (Story by Noel Coward)	Aug 12, 1968
The Kindness of Mrs Radcliffe	William Marchant (Story by Noel Coward)	Sep 23, 1968

Title	Writer	Screened
	***Premiere* (live)**	
Flower Dew	Roy Clarke	Oct 2, 1968
The Night of Talavera	Robert Holles	Oct 9, 1968
My Country 'Tis of Thee	Don Cornelius	Oct 16, 1968
Foxhole in Bayswater	Emanuel Litvinoff	Oct 23, 1968
No Reflection on You	C. Scott Forbes	Oct 30, 1968

Armchair Theatre – 1969 – 13th Season

Title	Writer	Screened
The Frobisher Game	David Perry	Jan 6, 1969
A Foot in the Door	Emanuel Litvinoff	Jan 13, 1969
What's a Mother For?	Charles Laurence	Jan 20, 1969
The Mandarins	E.Y. Bannard	Jan 27, 1969
Go On – It'll Do You Good	Michael Chapman	Feb 3, 1969
The Good Son	Ted Allan	Feb 10, 1969
The Brophy Story	Guy Slater	Feb 17, 1969
Edward the Confessor	Leigh Vance	Feb 24, 1969
The Story-Teller	William Corlett	Mar 3, 1969
On Vacation	Gert Hofman	Mar 10, 1969

Playhouse

Title	Writer	Screened
Romans and Friends	William Marchant (Original story by Leonore Coffee)	Sep 29, 1969
Like Puppies in a Basket	Kenneth Burley	Oct 20, 1969
The Swan Won't Go In The Fridge	Charles Laurence	Oct 27, 1969
The Beauty Operators	Janet Burroway	Nov 3, 1969

The Writers

Writer (alphabetically)	Title	Screened
Ted Allan	*The Good Son*	Feb 10, 1969
Lynne Reid Banks	*The Wednesday Caller*	May 26, 1963
	Last Word On Julie	Jan 26, 1964
E.Y. Bannard	*The Mandarins*	Jan 27, 1969
Peter Barnes	*The Man with a Feather in his Hat*	Aug 21, 1960
Alexander Baron	*Late Summer*	Jul 7, 1963
Stan Barstow	*The Pity of it All*	Jan 22, 1966
J.D. Barton	*Web of Deceit*	(*AMT*) Jul 24, 1960
Norman Bogner	*The Match*	Apr 30, 1966
Derek Bond	*Unscheduled Stop*	Mar 15 & 16, 1968
Marc Brandel	*A Nice Little Business*	Apr 26, 1964
Kenneth Burley	*Recount*	Apr 18, 1968
	Like Puppies in a Basket	(*Playhouse*) Oct 20, 1969
Janet Burroway	*The Beauty Operators*	(*Playhouse*) Nov 3, 1969
Alan Caillou	*Madeleine*	(*AMT*) Jul 17, 1960
Ken Campbell	*One Night I Danced With Mr Dalton*	Jun 13 & 15, 1968
Karel Capek	*Power and Glory*	Apr 14, 1963
Michael Chapman	*Go On – It'll Do You Good*	Feb 3, 1969
Hugo Charteris	*Cradle Song*	Apr 12, 1964
	A Certain Kind of Silence	Jun 28, 1964
	The Wager	Jul 30, 1966
Gwen Cherrell	*The Push-Over*	Jun 23, 1963
	The Madam	(*AMT*) Aug 8, 1965
Donald Churchill	*Sharp at Four*	Jan 12, 1964
	The Cherry on the Top	Sep 27, 1964
	The Hothouse	Dec 13, 1964
	The Paraffin Season	Dec 4, 1965
	The Floating Population	Jan 28, 1967
	The Happy Sacking	Mar 11, 1967
	A Second Look	Feb 21 & 24, 1968
	Man Without a Mortgage	Mar 19, 1966

Writer (alphabetically)	Title	Screened
Guy Clark	*Daughter of the House*	Apr 16, 1966
Roy Clarke	*Flower Dew*	(*Premiere*/live) Oct 2, 1968
Giles Cooper	*I am Osango*	Apr 15, 1967
William Corlett	*The Scallop Shell*	Feb 14 & 17, 1968
	The Story-Teller	Mar 3, 1969
Don Cornelius	*My Country 'Tis of Thee*	(*Premiere*/live) Oct 16, 1968
N.J. Crisp	*The Hunter*	(*AMT*) Jun 6, 1965
Len Deighton	*Long Past Glory*	Oct 17, 1963
Anton Delmar	*Don't Utter A Note*	Apr 9, 1966
Monte Doyle	*Dead Silence*	Sep 10, 1966
Harry Driver & Vince Powell	*Never Mind the Quality, Feel the Width*	Feb 18, 1967
Barry England	*The Sweet War Man*	Jan 1, 1966
Paul Erickson	*The Last Coach*	(*AMT*) Aug 16, 1964
Clive Exton	*The Trial of Dr Fancy*	Sep 13, 1964
Stewart Farrar	*Split Level*	Sep 2, 1967
C. Scott Forbes	*A Very Fine Line*	Mar 8 & 9, 1968
	No Reflection on You	(*Premiere*/live) Oct 30, 1968
Donald and Derek Ford	*Wake a Stranger*	(*AMT*) Aug 29, 1965
	The Three Barrelled Shotgun	Oct 8, 1966
	Reason for Sale	Mar 4, 1967
Terence Frisby	*Don't Forget the Basics*	Sep 16, 1967
Ernie Gebler	*Call Me Daddy*	Apr 8, 1967
James Gibbons	*The Escape Club*	May 9 & 11, 1968
Michael Gilbert	*The Blackmailing of Mr S.*	(*AMT*) Jul 26, 1964
Donal Giltinan	*The Monkey and the Mohawk*	Jun 9 1963
	The Snag	Aug 4, 1963
John Glennon	*The Big Wheel*	(*AMT*) Jun 12, 1960
Alan Gosling	*St Ernie Leatherbound*	May 24, 1964
John Hale	*The Noise Stopped*	Sep 3, 1966
	Light the Blue Touch Paper	Sep 24, 1966

Writer (alphabetically)	Title	Screened
John Hall	*The Swindler*	Dec 15, 1963
	Exit Joe—Running	Jun 14, 1964
Michael Harald	*The Gong Game*	Dec11, 1965
	The Long Nightmare	Oct 15, 1966
Richard Harris	*You Must Be Virginia*	(*AMT*) Sep 6, 1964
	Time and Mr Madingley	(*AMT*) Jun 27, 1965
	Slight Formality	Jul 8, 1967
John Harrison	*Any Number Can Play*	Mar 25, 1967
Virginia Hewett	*Admirer at Number Eight*	(*AMT*) Aug 30, 1964
Mary Hocking	*Ambrose*	(*AMT*) Sep 26, 1965
Christopher Hodder-Williams	*The Higher They Fly*	Dec 1, 1963
	A Voice in the Sky	Mar 21, 1965
Gert Hofman	*On Vacation*	Mar 10, 1969
Robert Holles	*The Education of Corporal Halliday*	Aug 5 1967
	The Wind in a Tall Paper Chimney	Feb 7 & 10, 1968
	The Night of Talavera	(*Premiere*/live) Oct 9, 1968
John Hopkins	*The Pretty English Girls*	Feb 16, 1964
	Time Out Of Mind	(*AMT*) Jul 19, 1964
	I Took My Little World Away	Mar 14, 1965
Kenneth Hyde	*The Last Reunion*	(*AMT*) May 9, 1965
Kenneth Jupp	*Blue and White*	Jan 6, 1963
Robert Kemp	*Toff and Fingers*	(*AMT*) Jul 3, 1960
Norman King	*The Cruel Kind*	Mar 17, 1963
Jordan Lawrence	*Quite an Ordinary Knife*	Jul 15, 1967
Charles Laurence	*What's a Mother For?*	Jan 20, 1969
	The Swan Won't Go in the Fridge	(*Playhouse*) Oct 27, 1969
Arkady Leokum	*Neighbours*	Jan 15, 1966
Hugh Leonard	*A Kind of Kingdom*	Sep 2, 1963
	Realm of Error	Mar 1, 1964
	I Loved You Last Summer	Apr 4, 1965
	Great Big Blonde	Aug 13,1966
	Love Life	Jul 29, 1967
Philip Levene	*False Witness*	(*AMT*) Aug 7, 1960

Writer (alphabetically)	Title	Screened
Peter Lewis	*Home Movies*	May 16 & 18, 1968
Stephen Lewis	*Wagger*	Apr 28, 1963
	Always Ask For The Best	Mar 15, 1964
Emanuel Litvinoff	*Another Branch of the Family*	Jul 22, 1967
	Marriage and Henry Sunday	Aug 19, 1967
	Foxhole in Bayswater	(Premiere/live) Oct 23, 1968
	A Foot in the Door	Jan 13, 1969
Douglas Livingstone	*Charlie Never Warned Us*	(*AMT*) Sep 5, 1965
James Broom Lynne	*Living Image*	Aug 18, 1963
Jack Malton	*A Jug of Bread*	May 17, 1964
Wolf Mankowitz	*The Battersea Miracle*	Mar 26, 1966
William Marchant	*Something to Declare*	Oct 4, 1964
	The Challenge	(*AMT*) Aug 15, 1965
	Pretty Polly (From a story by Noel Coward)	Jul 23, 1966
	Mrs Capper's Birthday (From a story by Noel Coward)	Jan 31 & Feb 3, 1968
	Star Quality (From a story by Noel Coward)	(*Playhouse*) Aug 5, 1968
	Bon Voyage (From a story by Noel Coward)	(*Playhouse*) Aug 12, 1968
	The Kindness of Mrs Radcliffe (From a story by Noel Coward)	(*Playhouse*) Sep 23, 1968
	Romans and Friends (Original story by Leonore Coffee)	(*Playhouse*) Sep 29, 1969
Frank Marcus	*The Glove Puppet*	May 30 & Jun 1, 1968
Reginald Marsh	*The Man Who Came To Die*	Apr 11, 1965
Ronald Mavor	*A Little Night Music*	Jul 22, 1963
David Mercer	*A Way of Living*	Dec 29, 1963
James Mitchell	*Flight from Treason*	(*AMT*) Jul 10, 1960
	The Lonely Crime	(*AMT*) Aug 9, 1964
	A Magnum for Schneider	Feb 4, 1967
Derek Monsey	*Nursery Tale*	Aug 12, 1967
Elaine Morgan	*Licence to Murder*	(*AMT*) May 16, 1965
Royston Morley	*Flag Fall*	(*AMT*) Jun 26, 1960

Writer (alphabetically)	Title	Screened
John Mortimer	*The Exploding Azalea*	Mar 18, 1967
Tad Mosel	*That's Where The Town's Going!*	Jun 7, 1964
Robert Muller	*The Paradise Suite*	Feb 17, 1963
	Pleasure Where She Finds It	May 3, 1964
	Man and Mirror	(*AMT*) Jun 13, 1965
	A Cold Peace	Dec18, 1965
	Easier in the Dark	Feb 25, 1967
	A World of Time	Apr 1, 1967
	You and Me	May 23 & 25, 1968
David Nobbs & Peter Tinniswood	*The Signal Box of Grandpa Hudson*	Aug 27, 1966
Edna O'Brien	*The Keys of the Café*	Mar 7, 1965
Jeremy Paul	*A Fair Swap*	Aug 20, 1966
David Perry	*Little Doris*	Oct 13, 1963
	The Frobisher Game	Jan 6, 1969
Alan Plater	*The Incident*	Apr 25, 1965
Vince Powell & Harry Driver	*Never Mind the Quality, Feel the Width*	Feb 18, 1967
Allan Prior	*They Throw It At You*	Oct 25, 1964
	The Girl in the Picture	Nov 29, 1964
	I've Got a System	Jan 3, 1965
	The Welcome	(*AMT*) Jul 4, 1965
	The One-Eyed Monster	Aug 11, 1966
Simon Raven	*The Gaming Book*	10 Jan 1965
Alun Richards	*The Hot Potato Boys*	Jan 20, 1963
	Ready for the Glory	Jan 8, 1966
Ray Rigby	*The Dummy*	(*AMT*) Sep 4, 1960
	The Cupboard	Dec 11, 1960
Noel Robinson	*The Tilted Screen*	Oct 1, 1966
Jack Rosenthal	*The Night Before the Morning After*	Apr 2, 1966
	Compensation Alice	Jul 1, 1967
Nicholas Salaman	*The Walls Came Tumbling Down*	Apr 23, 1966
Leslie Sands	*Eye Witness*	(*AMT*) Jun 5, 1960
Sebastian Shaw	*Cul de Sac*	(*AMT*) Aug 28, 1960
Andrew Sinclair	*The Chocolate Tree*	Oct 27, 1963
	Old Soldiers	Oct 18, 1964

Writer (alphabetically)	Title	Screened
Anthony Skene	*The Lodger* (From a novel by Mrs Belloc Lowndes)	(*AMT*) Jul 25, 1965
Guy Slater	*No Easy Walk*	May 2 & 4, 1968
	The Brophy Story	Feb 17, 1969
Bruce Stewart	*Jungle Juice*	May 12, 1963
Robert Storey	*The Front Room*	Sep 15, 1963
	Mug's Game	Mar 29, 1964
	The Lady With The Albatross	Feb 14, 1965
	Putty Medal	Feb 21, 1965
Julian Symons	*The Finishing Touch*	(*AMT*) Jul 18, 1965
Ken Taylor	*Into The Dark*	Feb 3, 1963
Ken Taylor	*Mr Big* (Original story, *The Dwarf*, by Ray Bradbury)	Sep 29, 1963
Peter Terson	*The Heroism of Thomas Chadwick* (*The Story Teller*)	Sep 23, 1967
	The Ballad of the Artificial Mash	Jul 25 & 27, 1968
Peter Tinniswood & David Nobbs	*The Signal Box of Grandpa Hudson*	Aug 27, 1966
Sophie Treadwell	*Machinal*	Aug 14, 1960
William Trevor	*The Girl*	Aug 26, 1967
Leigh Vance	*Edward the Confessor*	Feb 24, 1969
Gerald Vaughan-Hughes	*Barrett Keller—His Mark*	Sep 17, 1966
Fay Weldon	*Poor Cherry*	Sep 9, 1967
	The Three Wives of Felix Hull	Jun 6 & 8, 1968
Hugh Whitemore	*What's Wrong With Humpty Dumpty?*	Feb 11, 1967
John Whiting	*The Stairway*	(*AMT*) Sep 26, 1965
Oscar Wilde	*The Importance of Being Earnest*	Nov 15, 1964
Tony Williamson	*Ask Any Neighbour*	Sep 19, 1965
Angus Wilson	*The Invasion*	Mar 31, 1963
Morten Wishengrad & Virginia Mazer	*The Case of Paul Danek*	Jun 19, 1960
Roger Woddis	*The Contact*	Feb 28 & Mar 2, 1968
Charles Wood	*Prisoner and Escort*	Apr 5, 1964
William Wood	*Sally*	Dec 6, 1964

Index of People and Productions
See also Appendices II and III

D

E

F

M

N

T

Y

Z

Leonard White was an actor for some twenty years in all media, with highlights at Stratford-upon-Avon, London's West End, New York and Toronto.

Directing *Shadow of the Stone* for STV – 1986

He then became a director in theatre, starting at the Playhouse in Oxford and working in the Civic theatres in the UK and Canada.

He was trained in television directing and producing at the CBC in Toronto. From there he went on to work with ITV companies in the UK: TWW-TV, Tyne Tees Television, Southern Television, HTV, Scottish Television, BBC Television, and ten years at Teddington Studios (ABC Television and Thames Television).

Among many other credits, he was the original producer of *The Avengers* series, being responsible for the first forty episodes, which included the introduction of Honor Blackman as Cathy Gale.

He produced some 165 single teleplays – mostly commissioned new writing – for ABC-Television's *Armchair Theatre*. Overall, he has produced (and in some cases directed) over 350 drama teleplays (single and series) for the UK Television Networks.

He says, "If I am to be remembered at all (and I doubt that I will be in this ephemeral show-biz) I would like it to be for my work in launching new talent."

Leonard White is a member of Alexandra Palace Television Society, British Academy of Film and Television Arts, Royal Television Society, Director's Guild of Great Britain, and Guild of Drama Adjudicators.